EDUCATION
IN TRANSITION

INTERNATIONAL LIBRARY OF SOCIOLOGY
AND SOCIAL RECONSTRUCTION

Editor : Dr. Karl Mannheim

EDUCATION IN TRANSITION

A SOCIOLOGICAL STUDY OF THE IMPACT OF WAR ON ENGLISH EDUCATION
1939-1944

by

H. C. DENT
author of A New Order in English Education

GREENWOOD PRESS, PUBLISHERS
WESTPORT, CONNECTICUT

Library of Congress Cataloging in Publication Data

Dent, Harold Collett, 1894–
    Education in transition.

    Reprint of the 1948 ed. published by Routledge
& K. Paul, London, issued in series: International
library of sociology and social reconstruction.
    Includes bibliographical references.
    1. Education--Great Britain--History. 2. World
War, 1939-1945--Education and the war. I. Title.
LA631.8.D42 1973   301.5'6'0942   73-8255
ISBN 0-8371-6976-3

BCL-2

This edition originally published in 1948 by Routledge
& Kegan Paul Ltd., London

Reprinted with the permission of Harold Collett Dent

Reprinted in 1973 by Greenwood Press,
a division of Williamhouse-Regency Inc.

Library of Congress Catalogue Card Number 73-8255

ISBN 0-8371-6976-3

Printed in the United States of America

CONTENTS

PREFACE

It is broadly true to say that up to the outbreak of the present war the average English man or woman was not interested in education. Today the reverse is the case ; there is throughout the country the keenest interest. It would be idle to pretend that this is yet universal ; but it is undeniably widespread, it is found among all sorts and conditions of people, and it grows daily in extent and intensity.

With the growth of interest there is emerging a broader and deeper conception of the meaning, the purpose and the scope of education. The intimate relationship between the educational system and the social order is being increasingly realized. It is becoming widely recognized that education is one of the main instruments for promoting the development of society, and that consequently if we desire a new order of society one of the inescapable conditions is a new order in education.

Much planning is being done by educationists, and others, of such a new order. The proposals some have in mind would revolutionize English education. Their aim is to deepen and clarify its purpose, to unify its administration, increase its diversity of provision, extend its period, bring its content up to date, and relate the entire educational process to the social context in a manner and to a degree hitherto unknown in this country or any other.

Such plans are not impossible of achievement. They are in no sense utopian ; on the contrary, they are but logical, and practicable, developments of already existing trends. They are revolutionary only in the boldness of their conception and the far-reaching nature of their vision. *And they are the only safe plans.* " In dealing with this question of education," W. E. Forster told the Cabinet in 1870, " boldness is the only safe policy. Any measure which does not profess to be complete will be a certain failure." If those words were true seventy years ago, they are far more so today. For, whether we like it or no, education in England is in transition. The old order is dead ; the new is being shaped before our eyes, in part deliberately, but more, as yet, by circumstance. Time and ourselves alone will decide whether intention or circumstance shall prevail.

vii

Little as there has been of structural change in the educational set-up during the war (though there has been more than most people realize) the educational order of 1939 has passed beyond recall. It died on September 1 of that year, the day on which evacuation began. It can never be reborn ; there has already been too much of change. How much, this book attempts to show. In a narrative mainly factual, and chronological save that the episodic method has been used to analyse out the main elements of change, I try here to show how impressive has been the impact of the war on English education and how far we have already travelled away from 1939.

It is a story of surpassing interest, which I trust I have not too much dulled : the story of a period of dynamic change, which has witnessed the all but disintegration of a great national institution ; its recuperation from what might well have been a mortal blow, and its restoration to something resembling (yet how different from !) the previous state of affairs ; its continuous adaptation—at times spectacular, at others almost imperceptible, yet never ceasing—to war-time conditions and exigencies. And arising out of all this, a mighty ferment of ideas, a great surging impulse to reform, to plan a new and better order in education and society, an order rid for ever of the inequalities, injustices and inadequacies of the order of 1939.

These four processes—of disintegration, recuperation, adaptation, and ferment—have been going on coincidentally, acting and reacting upon each other in most intimate and intricate fashion. I have in this book attempted to separate them out, and have dealt with each in a chapter by itself. The method is not ideal ; it tends to over-simplification and inevitably involves overlapping. But I felt it to be preferable to the alternative of a wholly chronological account, which would of necessity have had perpetually to leap from one aspect of change to another, and would, I feared, have almost certainly obscured what I want above all else to make clear—that during, and because of, these four years of war English education has literally " suffered a sea change ". It is, by the force of circumstance rather than by conscious endeavour, being transformed into " something new and strange ", the shape of which we have not known before.

This transformation is still in full tide. Its total significance is as yet impossible to assess. This book pretends to be no more than a crude first contribution towards that assessment—which must be made, and with as little delay as possible. For man must be master of circumstance, or chaos and perversion will ensue. Much that has happened in the field of English education during the past four years can hardly fail to exert a beneficent influence on the future ; but of not all that has happened can this be said. There are trends which may prove sinister or retrograde. Emergency measures have been taken which are doubtless necessary in war-time, but which must not be allowed to receive the stamp of permanency.

They may do so unless we are on our guard. It is imperative that we be constantly on the alert to distinguish the good strands from the bad in this war-time pattern that is being woven, so that when peace returns and we begin to weave what we hope may be a more permanent pattern in education all the strands that are good may be preserved and used, all that are not good discarded and done away with. This war period is essentially an abnormal period ; and every element of change it introduces must be scrutinized with that in mind.

The warning applies, of course, not only in the field of education. It applies to every aspect of the life of society. But it has, I feel, a special application in respect of education. One of the most encouraging features of present-day thought is its increasing recognition of the interrelation and interdependence of all aspects of social life, but I have an uneasy suspicion that this recognition is perhaps hardly so full and clear among educationists as it should be. Our minds seem still to tend to cling to ideas belonging to the days when education was regarded as a thing apart, as an activity divorced from and independent of the other activities of society. It is imperative that we purge our minds of all such ideas.

Education is the basic activity of society. It conditions, and is conditioned by, all the other activities—political, economic, industrial, social, religious, personal. The educational system is not only an integral part of the social system ; it is a main source of its strength or of its weakness. The development of a society cannot but be fundamentally affected—for good or for ill—by the education its members receive ; on the other hand, the nature, and consequently the value, of that education is determined—at least in a democratic society—by the state of society and by the attitude which society as a whole takes towards the whole problem of education. This point is of vital importance to us in England at the present moment ; and any planning of educational reform which fails to take full account of it is bound to be highly dangerous.

In this book I have tried at every point to relate educational trends and changes to the social context. Where I have failed, the fault has been one of technique, not intention. The difficulty of writing any book in war-time, with a full-time job absorbing the bulk of one's time and energy, needs no emphasis. It may serve perhaps as some excuse for the inadequacies, errors and omissions of this study. Normal sources of information are inaccessible or hard to come by. The friends whose wisdom one would wish to consult are remote or overpressed with affairs— or both. Such thought as can be put into a book, being of necessity limited to the rare and fleeting moments of one's spare time, is bound to be hurried, disconnected, and regrettably superficial.

I am deeply grateful to the Management of The Times Publishing Company for permission to make extensive use of the files of *The Times Educational Supplement* for the purpose of the factual record, and for much illustrative material.

I am grateful to the Ministry of Health and the Board of Education for helping me out with copies of circulars and memoranda (I trust they will pardon me for having handled the contents of some of these in critical fashion) ; to the Ministry of Information and the Management of the *Christian Science Monitor* for permission to incorporate in the book the substance of articles written for them ; to the National Federation of Women's Institutes for permission to quote freely from their report on evacuation conditions ; to Dr. J. H. Oldham, editor of the *Christian News-Letter*, and Mr. Geoffrey Vickers, for permission to summarize and quote largely from the latter's Supplement to the *Christian News-Letter* entitled " Educating for a Free Society " ; and to Mr. F. le Gros Clark for permission to use material from reports compiled by him on the war-time progress of school feeding. The extracts taken verbatim from the White Paper, " Educational Reconstruction " (Cmd. 6458), are by permission of the Controller, H.M. Stationery Office, to whom also I wish to express my gratitude.

My indebtedness to Dr. Karl Mannheim, the general editor of the International Library of Sociology and Social Reconstruction, and to Dr. Julia Mannheim, cannot well be compressed into a few words ; their encouragement, advice and criticism have been invaluable to me. I am deeply indebted to my wife and to my colleagues Miss Sarita Bushell and Mr. David Browning, who read the book in typescript and made many valuable suggestions and criticisms, and to another colleague, Miss Joyce Burrell, who with imperturbable cheerfulness and complete efficiency coped with my execrable manuscript. Without the help of these my friends this book could never have been completed. But they are not therefore to be held responsible for any of its defects ; for those I am alone to blame.

H. C. DENT.

BOVINGDON, HERTS.
August 1943.

PREFACE TO FIFTH EDITION

The first edition of this book carried the story only as far as the publication of the Coalition Government's White Paper, *Educational Reconstruction*. That is to say, the story was broken off just before the climax was reached. In this edition that defect has been remedied, though most inadequately; a brief description of the Education Act, 1944, has been added. To make room for this the Epilogue to the original edition has been omitted.

The story is not, of course, ended ; it has in fact only just begun. Education in Britain will be in transition for many years to come. But the passing of the Education Act, 1944, by recording the noble intentions of a great people greatly moved, brought one epoch to an end and opened another. Let us hope that that second epoch will live up to the aspirations of those who brought it to birth.

CHAPTER I

DISINTEGRATION

Mass Migration

Friday, September 1, 1939, was to have marked an advance in English education. Not a very substantial one, nor one about which the educationist could feel particularly happy ; but, nevertheless, an advance. From that date, under the terms of the Education Act of 1936, no child was to be permitted to leave school at the age of 14 unless he could obtain from the local education authority a certificate sanctioning his entry into "beneficial employment". Otherwise, he was to remain at school until 15.

That advance never took place. Instead, there began on that fateful Friday—the day on which Nazi Germany invaded Poland —the greatest educational retreat that Britain has ever known ; a retreat which for a while threatened to deteriorate into a rout ; even, conceivably, to end in the complete disintegration of the educational services. •

On Thursday, August 31, the public was warned that—" as a precautionary measure "—" it has been decided to start evacuation of schoolchildren and other priority classes . . . tomorrow ". At an early hour on the following morning, from London and more than forty other heavily populated areas in England and Scotland, there began an exodus unprecedented in history.

The plans for assembling evacuees and getting them out of the potentially dangerous areas had been skilfully laid and well rehearsed. With clockwork precision innumerable parties, large and small, of schoolchildren in the charge of their teachers, of mothers with children below school age, and of expectant mothers, converged from every point of the compass upon the railway stations, marched in endless but ordered streams up the platforms, were swiftly loaded on to waiting trains, and as swiftly borne away to unknown destinations. It was every-where done coolly, quietly, and with notable efficiency on the part of all concerned—the staffs of the railways, the local authori-ties, the Food Department (which supplied emergency rations), the teachers, the thousands of voluntary helpers, and, not least, the children themselves. Nowhere was there any sign of panic, and rarely any of confusion.

In many places the rate of despatch was phenomenal. At one London junction, for example, 8,000 persons an hour were entrained. Leeds evacuated 40,000 in seven hours. Other places achieved comparable feats. Yet the whole vast operation, which lasted altogether for eleven days, and was at its height for four, was carried out virtually without mishap of any kind. The London Passenger Transport Board, which must have handled more than a million people, had not a single accident to report. The railways had but an infinitesimal number, and none of major consequence.

By the Friday afternoon the safe arrival of parties at their new homes was already being announced. By the evening messages were pouring in from all parts of the country to ease the minds of anxiously waiting parents and relatives. Day succeeded day without untoward incident. An immense sigh of relief went up from all the evacuating areas. The children were safe. Now—let Hitler do his worst.

But even before the first raptures of relief had died away there began to be heard the angry mutterings of a thunderous storm that was to lower darkly over the country for many months; and the echoes of which have not yet ceased entirely to rumble.

URBS RURI—AS ANTICIPATED

To transport efficiently, at short notice and in the space of a few days, nearly a million and a half people from a limited number of points of departure to a very large number of destination points was no inconsiderable feat. It must have involved a mass of complicated and carefully co-ordinated administrative arrangements, and it called in addition for a high degree of executive skill. But it raised no absolutely new problems, nor did it include any imponderable factors. The railways, which bore the main brunt of the great dispersal, had been tackling with marked success similar, and more difficult, problems year after year during the holiday seasons. So had the road transport services and the steamship companies. Even the incidence of enemy air attack or widespread panic—neither of which, mercifully, occurred—would not have presented the railway and other services concerned with an entirely novel situation, nor one with which they would have been at a loss to grapple.

But abruptly to uproot so huge a number of people—the majority of them young children—from the security of their homes and the familiarity of their home environment, and to attempt to replant them suddenly in an utterly strange environment, and in the homes of strangers ; that is an altogether different matter. If it has never been done before, it constitutes a social experiment of the first importance. If (as was the case) such an experiment is planned and initiated by people having apparently no inkling of its implications; and without anything worth speaking of in the way of psychological or sociological preparation of those who are to play the major parts in it—the receiving households and their guests—it becomes an exceptionally hazardous, not to say dangerously rash, experiment.

This would have been so even if the social and physical conditions in which hosts and guests-to-be had previously lived had been approximately comparable ; because whatever other complications might have been avoided, evacuation would still of necessity have disrupted the oldest, most closely knit, and most intimate of all the social units—the family ; and that cannot be done without the gravest repercussions. But in a country so socially stratified and so parochially minded as was the England of 1939 (and until evacuation took place nobody quite realized how caste-like and how numerous were our social stratifications, nor how localized our knowledge of life) ; in a country in which the physical conditions of living varied so enormously (and that too was never before so clearly revealed), the sociological and psychological complications of such a mass migration as that which took place in September were certain to be as grave and far-reaching as they were multitudinous. Yet, save on the most superficial level, this appears to have been anticipated by hardly anyone ; and least of all by the Ministry of Health, the Government department in charge of evacuation.

The full implications could not, of course, have been foreseen with any completeness. The experiment was without precedent, and much of the planning in anticipation of it had necessarily to be tentative. But it must be admitted that the mere possibility of many of the situations which arose seems to have been utterly unsuspected, and that in general the seriousness of the implications of evacuation was tragically underestimated.

In a memorandum (Memo. Ev.4) setting out the "broad outlines of a complete scheme both for an evacuating and for a receiving area" which was issued by the Ministry of Health in April 1939, considerable space was given to consideration of a number of eventualities which it was anticipated might occur, and fairly detailed suggestions were made as to how these might be met. The Ministry pointed out (what was obvious) that householders who undertook the care of evacuated children would do so at considerable inconvenience to themselves, and suggested that it was very important that the local authority and the voluntary organizations of the district should do everything practicable to minimize this inconvenience. In particular, receiving householders would be greatly assisted by arrangements for the care and supervision of children during part of the day. Which, of course, was very true.

The most important single service, said the Ministry, would be the making of arrangements for carrying on the education of the children. These arrangements were, very properly, to be the subject of a memorandum from the Board of Education (of which more later), but meanwhile the Ministry assumed that children brought into a reception area by evacuation would go to school in much the same way as the children native to the area. This was a comforting, but, as the event proved, a somewhat imprecise, assumption.

About other matters the Ministry were more precise. The advisability of providing communal midday meals and of organizing communal recreations, especially at week-ends, for the children was urged, and special attention was paid to medical and sanitary arrangements to prevent and cope with illness and infections. Receiving authorities were warned that the Government stores of bedding and blankets were inadequate to meet fully the anticipated demand, and advised to make local collections of these. They were told also that some of the parents sending away children would doubtless find it beyond their resources to provide the full list of clothing required. They were even told that the enlistment of voluntary help for the washing and mending of clothes would be of very great assistance.

All this was very wise and practical advice ; the pity is that in so many localities so much of it was ignored. It was when the Ministry embarked upon consideration of " General Welfare and Settlement of Disputes " that they demonstrated in almost every line how completely unwitting they were of the nature and gravity of the problems which awaited the authorities and the inhabitants of the receiving areas. It is evidently difficult in Whitehall to realize how Camberwell lives (though the two places are only a 2d. bus ride apart).

" Householders ", they wrote, " should ordinarily have no great difficulty in controlling the children and preserving reasonable discipline." Yet, " it is inevitable that an influx of strangers on the scale contemplated will give rise to a certain number of difficulties and *minor* (my italics) disputes, particularly at the outset ". To deal with these a local tribunal was considered the appropriate instrument (can anyone see Stepney accepting the verdict of Little Dumpington ?).

Perhaps, occasionally, something more than minor disputes might arise ; but of course not very often.

For the rare cases of difficult characters, both among children and among mothers or other adults accompanying them, special arrangements and supervision will be necessary which will relieve the individual of what experience may have proved to be an unreasonable burden. The local authority should consider whether these individuals could not be accommodated in buildings, e.g. empty houses equipped for the purpose, where the accommodation would be of an institutional character and where the occupiers would be under some definite supervision.

How ironical those two sentences must later have seemed to many receiving authorities ! (Or even to the civil servant who wrote them, if he had a sense of humour.) Hardly less so is the following :

Cases will no doubt also come to light where houses to which children have been sent are subsequently found for one reason or another to be unsuitable, and *the local authority may find it necessary to arrange for a certain amount of interchange after the children have been allotted.* (My italics.)

The " local authority " certainly did—in how many scores of thousands of cases, one wonders ? But perhaps the most naïve conjecture in the whole memorandum is to be found in a section in which authorities are advised to set up small local committees to exercise a general supervision over the welfare of the evacuees and to deal with the difficulties of householders.

" The greater part of the work of such a committee ", assumed the ministry, " would lie among the unaccompanied school-children."

Shades of the 90 per cent of evacuated mothers who departed, mainly unregretted, from the reception areas during the early months of evacuation !

The Board of Education issued, before evacuation took place, two circulars (Nos. 1469 and 1474) on the education of children sent to the receiving areas. The first appeared in May, the second on August 29. Circular 1469 dealt largely with the work of the evacuated teacher, on whom it was realized extra burdens would be imposed. Improvisation, said the Board cheerfully, would often be necessary, and they made various bright suggestions about dramatic work, lantern lectures, singing and dancing, the making of local surveys, and so on. (But they did not tell the urban teachers how few rural schools had assembly halls or how difficult it is to sing and dance when desks occupy the entire floor-space, and the next class is separated from yours only by a curtain.) They did, however, feel it prudent to warn them that in some districts there might be the danger of overcrowding (what a masterpiece of understatement !), and consequently they advised consideration of the " double-shift " system which was adopted in 1914-18. By this system two schools would use the same building, either alternately morning and afternoon, or as separate units. " No doubt," the circular added as though by way of afterthought, " some outside accommodation could be secured as well."

When one remembers the frantic efforts some receiving authorities had to make, to secure sufficient " outside accommodation " to get a roof over the heads of the evacuees who came, one wonders precisely what would have happened had all the children expected to be evacuated actually travelled to the receiving areas.

Circular 1474 had a foreword written by the President of the Board of Education. This contained the astonishing statement that " the extensive preparations for evacuation being well forward,

it is time to consider what is to happen to children after evacuation ".
(My italics.) On August 29 ! Apparently, according to the
circular, what was to happen to them was that they were going
to have a prolonged and altogether delightful summer holiday ;
a large part of the text was taken up with a glowing description
of the educational possibilities which the new conditions would
present. Evidently the author of the circular knew and loved
the countryside (though perhaps chiefly in its week-end
aspect) ; but he certainly did not know urban children—or
teachers.

There was virtually no hint of any realization of the graver
educational problems which were so soon to arise. Of course,
it was acknowledged, there would be difficulties. The " double-
shift " system was paraded again as a panacea for these, and the
authorities and teachers were told (presumably for their encouragement) that where this system had to be operated in the 1914–18
war it was " commonly felt " that " children who experienced it
over a period of four years or more showed a falling off in attain-
ments which was equivalent to no more than about six months'
retardation ". It seems incredible, but there is no suggestion
that the Board regarded other than with equanimity the possibility of very large numbers of children suffering a comparable
retardation during this war.

And there are still, in 1943, thousands of English schoolchildren working on the " double-shift " system.

But Whitehall was in no way exceptional in failing to anticipate the graver consequences of evacuation. The following
quotation from a leading article in *The Times Educational Supplement* of September 9 is typical of the almost universal lack of
comprehension of the kind of sociological and psychological
problems which evacuation was to throw up, and of the light-
hearted, even frivolous, attitude of the country at large towards
this unprecedented migration.

Nor is there any reason to anticipate that the children will prove
difficult to manage. It must be remembered that school journeys
and organized country holidays have existed for many years, and
that therefore a large number of boys and girls realize that good
manners and avoidance of mischief are expected of them.

Everything in the garden was undoubtedly going to be, with
very minor exceptions, extremely lovely.

URBS RURI —WHAT HAPPENED

As the event proved, a large proportion of the children who were evacuated satisfied all reasonable standards of behaviour. But there were others who did not ; and for very valid reasons. There existed—unknown to the vast majority of respectable English citizens—in the slums and near-slums of our cities and congested industrial areas living conditions, and consequent ways of life, of a squalor and sordidness almost beyond the belief of anyone who had not had personal experience of them. The results of decanting the inhabitants of these areas into the prim and decent villages and small towns of rural England were such as to send a spasm of horror shuddering the length and breadth of the country. Different indeed was the note struck in *The Times Educational Supplement* the following week (September 16) :

. . . some householders found themselves charged with the care of youngsters who knew little or nothing of the amenities of a middle-class home. A retired medical man was surprised to find that his young guests had never slept between sheets or worn night clothes or washed before going to bed. Brushing their teeth and saying their prayers were exercises of which they knew nothing. Another householder found that her party would not eat green vegetables or home-cooked food, explaining that what they liked best of all was tinned salmon or fish and chips.

But the experiences of these two householders were mild compared with those of many others, as the following quotations taken at random from reports made to the National Federation of Women's Institutes will show :

The state of the children was such that the school had to be fumigated after the reception.

Except for a small number the children were filthy, and in this district we have never seen so many verminous children, lacking any knowledge of clean and hygienic habits. Furthermore, it appeared that they were unbathed for months. One child was suffering from scabies, and the majority had it in their hair, and the others had dirty septic sores all over their bodies.

Bed-wetting was very general among the children.

The habits of the children were disgusting. The play meadow by the end of the first week was worse than any stockyard.

They all used bad language, had no idea of telling the truth, and were quite undisciplined.

On arrival, almost equalled wild animals.

Few children would eat food that demanded the use of teeth—in almost every case could eat only with a teaspoon.

Very few of the children were used to any green or cooked vegetables, and would not eat them at first. They liked highly spiced and seasoned food. A large number, even from apparently well-off homes, were quite unused to sitting down to table . . . were used to having their food handed to them to take out, or eat anywhere.

Billettors had difficulty in making them go to bed at reasonable hours.

. . . did not undress to go to bed, but put night clothes over day clothes.

Their clothing was in a deplorable condition, some of the children being literally sewn into their ragged little garments.

Condition of their boots and shoes—there was hardly a child with a whole pair, and most of the children were walking on the ground—no soles and just uppers hanging together.

These quotations could be paralleled by hundreds of others from the most varied sources. No wonder the innately decent countryfolk were shocked. But before passing judgment (a restraint which, regrettably, was only too rarely exercised at the time) it is imperative to reflect upon the conditions in which these children had been born and had spent their entire lives —the dank, lousy basements of London, the foul slums of Liverpool, Southampton, and other ports, the gloomy and depressing back streets of Birmingham, Manchester, Sheffield, and a hundred other cities and towns, and the appalling overcrowding and the complete lack of facilities for the preservation of even the rudiments of decency which were (and are) widespread in almost all our industrial areas.

What could one expect of children who had had to endure such conditions year in year out, without break or remission : who indeed knew no others except vicariously by way of the cinema ? What sort of parents were such conditions likely to produce ? The following quotations, also taken from **reports** sent in to the National Federation of Women's Institutes, are illuminating : but are they really surprising ?

Many of the mothers and children were bed-wetters, and were not in the habit of doing anything else.

Some were simply crawling with lice, etc., and actually never used a lavatory. The children simply sat down in the house anywhere to relieve themselves. One woman who was given the guest-room always sat the baby in the bed for this purpose.

Approximately one-third did not wash the children or their clothes, or teach them to be clean.

The babies were never changed, but allowed to remain with wet napkins and knickers.

The majority were opposed to all the generally accepted rules of decent living, and some returned home as soon as a hot bath was suggested.

One mother out of the 26 was clean and industrious, four others took some pride in their appearance, but were otherwise unconcerned. The remaining 21 mothers . . . were dirty, lazy, and insanitary, and observed no decency, even when it was easy to do so.

The young mothers were the worst. . . . Their children were not trained to be clean. They did not seem able to cope with them.

The children were only accustomed to obey when cuffed or shouted at. This was true of at least 50 per cent. In quite a few cases the mothers had no control over their children at all.

Some mothers arrived smoking cigarettes over their babies' heads, and had to be fetched from the pub by their hostesses to put their children to bed, or else took them with them till 10 p.m. They used worse language than had ever been heard in the village.

. . . these mothers were only able to cook with a tin opener . . . (they) cannot even cook a rice-pudding. I saw a baby given a raw sausage to eat, because the mother was too idle and dirty to cook it, though offered all facilities. There was no proper time set aside for meals . . . the children in several instances just grabbed what they fancied and ran about eating it.

Children had never seen their mothers cook anything, and had no hot meals at home.

Only two out of the twelve mothers ever did any darning or needlework.

The appalling apathy of the mothers was terrible to see. " Pictures " and cheap novelettes were their one desire. They had no wish to knit, sew or cook.

A volume could be written in commentary on these quotations ; but its argument can be summed up in three sentences written by a Derbyshire correspondent of a Women's Institute :

I had no conception such awful people existed, but we are to blame that we allow the Government to have such housing conditions. These children should have a chance to be brought up to be decent citizens. Under present conditions they cannot.

It must be emphasized that observations such as the above applied to only a minority of the evacuated mothers and children. " There are no exact statistics as to the number of children showing various faults and physical defects," state the authors of an exhaustive study of the state of affairs revealed by evacuation,[1] " but the evidence suggests that those with insanitary habits due to lack of training represented from 5 to 10 per cent." Dr. Kenneth Mellanby, who has made careful inquiry into the question, suggests that as many as 50 per cent may have been verminous. But all things considered it can be safely said that by far the greater number of the young evacuees were as clean, decent, well-behaved, and well-mannered as were the members of the families which received them.

"An extremely nice collection of children, well-behaved and clean," was typical of many reports from rural areas. Nor were all the evacuated mothers undesirable. Some won golden opinions from those among whom they came to live. Of those from Jarrow, for example, it was recorded that they " were a very nice set of women, anxious to help wherever possible in the work of their new home, taking an interest in what went on in the village generally ".

But the adverse reports came from every part of the country, and thus made it abundantly clear that conditions calculated to produce apathetic and ignorant parents and dirty, unhealthy and uncivilized children obtained in almost all the large towns and industrial areas. Evacuation had, in fact, lifted the lid to reveal a seething stew of social degradation hitherto unsuspected —or if suspected, ignored—by increasingly comfortable and comfort-loving middle- and upper working-classes which had for years been enjoying rising standards of domestic luxury and social amenity, and which had more and more tended to overlook their obligation to care for the interests of their less fortunate brothers and sisters.

It would, of course, be quite wrong to suggest that bad living conditions in Britain are confined to the towns or that, in September 1939, a " stainless countryside " was " called upon to bear with a universally degraded town population ". The authors of *Our Towns* are rightly emphatic upon this point.

In justice to the townspeople, they say, it ought to be said that the complaints were by no means all on one side, and that in some instances the shortcomings of the billets and billettors themselves produced the faults of conduct, especially in children, which were

[1] *Our Towns. A Close Up.* A study made in 1939–42 with certain recommendations by the Hygiene Committee of The Women's Group on Public Welfare, in association with the National Council of Social Service. Oxford University Press, 1943.

the source of complaint. Not all the billets were clean and whole-some, and many hostesses failed in common kindness and hospitality towards families on whom no slur could be cast.[1]

Yet after examination of the results of recent authoritative research, they are forced to the conclusion that dirt, degradation and disease are particularly associated with the industrialized areas, and that—

The rural countryside is entitled to look askance at the social conditions of the industrial town. The outcry against the evacuees, therefore, represented no mere ill will or hostility to strangers ; it had a very serious background of facts . . .[2]

But that, unhappily, is by no means the last word which must be said about this outcry. There were, it has to be admitted, very widespread manifestations of ill will and hostility on the part of the inhabitants of the reception areas ; and these had very grave results. These manifestations demand analysis.

It may be agreed that, in the first instance, " People in the reception areas approached the invasion of their dwellings with, on the whole, a praiseworthy measure of good will." [3] What exactly happened when the realities of the invasion had sunk in ? As a general statement, it is true to say that the working classes on the whole reacted commendably to the situation, but that the shock was too severe for the middle classes. Their reaction was in many instances deplorable. Repulsion ousted pity and any sense of duty. The agonized shriek of " lousy children " which for weeks went echoing through the correspondence columns of the press was hardly a creditable reflection on the Christian charity of those who gave vent to it. Nor were the innumerable " indignation meetings " held in village streets and shops and country parlours, when in exaggerated accents of self-pity were endlessly retailed heart-breaking stories of the unspeakable vile-ness of the disgusting evacuees who were foully desecrating the immaculate homes of their faultless and irreproachable hosts. Most shameful of all were the instant and inflexible decision of many receiving householders—notably among the moderately well-to-do—to rid themselves at once of such undesirable guests, and the ruthless methods to which they resorted to achieve this end.

---

[1] *Our Towns. A Close Up.*   [2] Ibid.   [3] Ibid.

The fact that Britain was at war weighed little with these selfish and self-centred beings. The fact that their attitude and their actions condemned women and children to return to homes which might at any moment be blown to pieces by bombs was callously ignored. All that mattered to them was their own personal comfort and the preservation of their self-indulgent way of life. In defence of these there were no lengths to which they were not prepared to go.

That the inhabitants of the receiving areas had often grievous cause for complaint is not to be denied. The burden laid upon some of them was in truth intolerable. But in too many instances much was made out of very little. An unhappy result of the quite disproportionate outcry which was raised concerning a relatively small number of neglected or ill-mannered children, and of lazy or sluttish mothers, was that almost everywhere the physical condition and the behaviour of evacuees came to be the object of the most suspicious scrutiny. The slightest falling below or deviation from local standards was made excuse for loud and prolonged criticism. Trifling peccadilloes on the part of children were magnified into evidence of innate depravity and deplorable upbringing. Petty inconveniences and irritations resulting (inevitably) from the bringing under one roof of people from totally different environments and accustomed to totally different ways of life were magnified into major disruptions and resented as fiercely as if they had been calamities deliberately caused. Most regrettable of all, there was a widespread failure to comprehend—and so to allow for and sympathize with—that terrible sense of loneliness, of uprootedness, which must so sorely have afflicted so many of the evacuated, young and old, and doubtless materially affected their behaviour during the earlier days of their exile.

I believe firmly that the root causes of the greater part of the friction and unhappiness which ensued from evacuation, and which brought about its partial failure, were social ignorance and lack of imagination. The English are not by nature either an unkind or an uncharitable people ; on the contrary they are kindly, sympathetic, charitable and generous to the point of sentimentality. But socially they are appallingly ignorant, and normally they are only too content to remain so, particularly if by so doing they can evade awkward facts and avoid disturbing situations. Viewed objectively, this is not perhaps so surprising. In most cases their limited period of formal education ends before they are of an age to appreciate social problems ; and these are never later brought home to them. Their natural tendency to mental sluggishness, when encouraged by material well-being, makes them strongly egocentric and limits their vision to their immediate social grouping. While all goes well with this they have neither desire nor imagination to peer beyond it. Only a shock such as evacuation gave suffices to shake them out of what is no less than a stupor of self-complacency. Even evacuation proved insufficient to awake more than a minority, stark though were its revelations. This *was* surprising ; and it is an indication of how profoundly moral standards had declined in England between the two wars.

Never before had it been so clear that the one half of England had no idea how the other half lived. Town and country were discovered to be utter strangers to each other. Social strata were shown to be far more numerous than had ever been imagined, and to be separated from each other by yawning and abysmal gulfs. The condition of the submerged was revealed to be appalling beyond conception. Yet there was no general demand that these wrongs be put right. The social conscience of most of the comfortable remained unmoved. It remains unmoved still.

One of the main tasks of applied sociology in the future must be to teach the art of living together. This is not merely a matter of providing better buildings and superior amenities for the poor : it is a matter of inculcating a spiritual affinity, of inducing an attitude towards living which genuinely acknowledges the brotherhood of man.

It was not to be expected that the heterogeneous and often antipathetic elements which were thrown together by evacuation could without long, careful and sympathetic preparation undertake harmoniously this most difficult of all arts. Habits, behaviour, customs, traditions, ethos—the entire attitude towards life and the whole practice of living—all were different. Yet scarcely anyone seems to have anticipated this and prepared against it. Few contacts had been made between the evacuating and receiving areas. In the case of London it was impossible to make any, for the transport authorities had flatly refused to guarantee that any party would be sent to any given destination. In other areas teachers were actually discouraged from visiting in advance the districts to which their schools were allotted.

A very great deal of the trouble—of all kinds—which occurred would have been avoided had the reception and billeting of the evacuees been organized on any sort of scientific basis. But almost everywhere the arrangements had been made with a literally sublime disregard of psychological and sociological considerations. It had apparently been assumed that if a prospective hostess had said she was prepared to receive into her home, say, three children or two adults, all that would be necessary would be to number off three children or two adults in the party which arrived, and send them along. It is true that hostesses were asked to state their preferences with regard to their guests-to-be, but they rarely seem to have got much beyond saying girls rather than boys, or children rather than adults ; and few authorities seem to have pressed them beyond this point. When the day came some householders went to the detraining point and selected evacuees they liked the look of ; others merely took whatever was left on their doorsteps. Many wretched children were hawked from house to house like peddlers' goods.

It was a catastrophic over-simplication of the problem. It was made worse by the fact that, as no clearing centres with sleeping accommodation had been set up at the detraining points, it was necessary to hurry all the evacuees into billets on the day of arrival. Consequently, as most of the parties arrived in the afternoon or evening, no attempt at scientific selection, or even common-sense sorting out, was possible. The sole consideration was to get everyone under a roof without delay. So slum-bred children were bustled off to lordly mansions and opulent country houses, delicately nurtured youngsters bundled into labourers' cottages, boisterous young " toughs " thrust upon elderly folk of retiring habit, sensitive and introverted adolescents dumped into the midst of loud and hearty families of the " Good Companions " type, pregnant women landed with confirmed spinsters or presented as an additional burden to already overburdened working housewives. Every possible kind of sociological and psychological misfit was made in abundance.

Inevitably, there ensued immediately an enormous amount

of avoidable friction, dissatisfaction, discontent and unhappiness. Re-billeting on a vast scale became obligatory ; and even this did not prevent innumerable hasty returns to the evacuating areas. " Better to be bombed than put up with this," said many a lonely and unhappy exile—and back they went, in thousands, to the perilous security of the towns. Nearly 90 per cent of the mothers had returned before Christmas, and a large proportion of the children.

CHAOS IN THE COUNTRYSIDE

The sociological complications which arose out of this mismanagement of evacuation had, as can be imagined, grave and far-reaching repercussions upon the educational situation. The strictly educational complications which developed were as numerous and, in their way, equally serious.

In theory, the educational situation after evacuation was to have been quite simple. The country had been divided into three types of areas : evacuating, neutral, and receiving. It had been taken for granted that, as there would no longer be any schoolchildren in the evacuating areas, there would be no further need for schools in these areas. Accordingly, it was arranged that the schools were to be closed down for the duration of the war. Their premises would therefore be available for other purposes, and they had been allotted in large numbers to the fire services, the civil defence organizations, the hospitals, and the military, which on the outbreak of war immediately occupied most of them. As neutral areas were neither to evacuate nor receive children, it was assumed that the position there would be the same as in peace-time. All schools were to be closed while evacuees were being moved to the reception areas, but schools in neutral areas were to reopen and resume normal work as soon as the buildings were equipped with adequate air-raid shelters. The receiving areas would certainly be somewhat uncomfortably full of children, but it was considered that with good will on the part of all concerned, the use of the " double shift " system and of some extra accommodation, everyone would soon be fitted in. As soon as the necessary adjustments had been made the schools were to reopen. Shortage of space and equipment would call for initiative and a certain amount of improvisation on the part of the teachers, and the normal curriculum would doubtless hardly be possible everywhere ; but the essentials of a general education were to be preserved, and as little administrative dislocation as possible to be permitted. To assist in the latter aim, evacuated and native schools were to retain their separate identity and, no matter what sharing of premises there had to be, to function as independent units. The Board had been quite firm about that.

Such the theory ; the practice proved quite otherwise. Why did this exquisitely simple and tidy plan break down ? The causes of failure were many and complex. To begin with, evacuation necessarily broke up the oldest, most fundamental, and most jealously cherished of all social groups—the family. Only the wisest and most skilled propaganda could have made the idea of evacuation really popular or indeed generally acceptable ; but the propaganda put out was lamentably superficial, and was quite unrelated to the action taken. The preparatory arrangements for evacuation (except those for transport) were naïve, unimaginative and muddled. The refusal to guarantee a known destination for London children was a colossal error. It was probably a mistake for what was essentially a single job to be divided between two government departments. It was almost certainly a mistake for the Ministry of Health to be put in charge.

It is essentially the task of the local education authority to have to deal with people as *people*, and particularly with children. (How efficiently they could do it they were later to prove.) To have to deal with people is not essentially the task of the local health authority, which in attempting it had to step outside its experience. Grievous delay in making preparatory educational arrangements was caused because the Board of Education and the local education authorities could not move until they had learned from the Ministry of Health the billeting arrangements made by the local health authorities. The delay was in some instances so gross as to prevent any educational arrangements at all being made. For example, the secretary for education in West Suffolk reported in October 1939 that :

It was impossible to make any educational arrangements beforehand for the evacuated children, even of the most tentative nature . . . because no one had any accurate information as to the area from which the children would come, the numbers in which they would arrive, the type of school which they had been attending, and to what village or town they were to go.

The fact that the areas of the local health and local education authorities are frequently not co-terminous made co-operation difficult even where full information was available in time and the utmost good will was shown on both sides—and the latter was unhappily not always the case.

Such arrangements as could be made in advance for the education of the evacuated children were therefore in many places both tentative and incomplete. They were almost everywhere completely upset when evacuation actually took place. Large numbers of parents backed out of their engagement at the last moment, and therefore far fewer children travelled than had been anticipated. Often the number which arrived was less than a quarter of what had been expected. This might appear on the surface to have been an advantage ; in fact, it caused the most acute dislocation of any plans for the education of the children that had been made. In particular, it played havoc with the carefully fostered idea of preserving the corporate identity of the evacuated schools. Instead of whole schools, or even large fractions of schools, at many places there arrived relatively small groups which could not by themselves constitute educational units.

Chaos was worse confounded by the way in which billeting was handled at the detraining points. There had, of course, to be hurried re-arrangements of the previously arranged schemes. These were made by the billeting officers, who thought solely in terms of billets. Despite the protests of education officers on the spot, scant if any consideration was paid to the educational welfare of the children. Whether school accommodation would be available surely did not matter all that much ? Get the children into homes ; that was the important thing. All the other little troubles could be sorted out afterwards. So education officers, and even the teachers who had brought the children, were allowed no say in the distribution of the young evacuees. In many instances they were not even told where they were being sent.

Consequently, the amazing situation developed that, so far as the education authorities and the teachers were concerned, a considerable proportion of the evacuated schoolchildren were literally lost. Hundreds of urban teachers began their stay in the reception areas by tramping an unknown countryside day after day throughout the hours of daylight (and often far into the night) searching for the children they had so carefully and so efficiently shepherded from the cities.

But large as was the number of mislaid evacuees, it was far from constituting the total of lost schoolchildren in Britain at that time. This was colossal; because (i) vast numbers of children expected to evacuate had remained at home, (ii) considerable numbers of children had been evacuated, not under the Government scheme, but privately by their parents—in not a few cases into or from neutral areas, and (iii) as evacuation began on the last day of the elementary school holidays, many children, especially secondary school pupils, were away from home on holiday, and no one in authority knew whether they had (a) remained where they were, (b) gone home, (c) travelled to their allotted reception area, or (d) been privately evacuated elsewhere.

When the evacuated teachers had at last tracked down the pupils they had brought with them (it took some of them up to a fortnight to do so), they found themselves confronted with the most baffling problems of accommodation. Many a school party was discovered to be dispersed in half a dozen to a dozen villages scattered over many miles of countryside. " One headmaster ", wrote a correspondent to *The Times Educational Supplement*, " has about 100 children billeted in six small villages in the south of the county, while 70 more are in a country town 20 miles to the north." One half of a girls' senior school was spread over thirteen villages. Such cases were frequent—one had almost said typical. Instances were even brought to light of two halves of a school party being found at opposite ends of the country, simply because it had not been possible at the point of departure to load them all on to the same train.

This indiscriminate scattering of the children, which broke up into fragments the fractions of schools that had travelled, in many instances made any attempt to preserve the identity of a school both futile and silly. Yet almost everywhere some evacuated teachers strove to achieve the impossible; some (probably most) because of an honourable pride in their schools; some because they feared that " merging " with the native school would mean the reduction of their salaries to the level of that of the rural teachers in the area ; some because they dreaded the administrative inquiries that would follow upon merging ; and some, no doubt, simply because their instructions were that separate identities were to be preserved. " Theirs not to reason why . . ."

Individual teachers went to fantastic lengths to get and keep their schools (or what was left of them) together. They wore themselves (and the billeting officers) out in their endeavours to regroup and rebillet their pupils so as to have them all together. Cases are on record of teachers in charge of the merest handful of pupils insisting upon having half a classroom curtained off for their exclusive use, and persisting for months in such dignified if pathetic isolation. It was all very noble, but it didn't really help ; especially as it early became obvious to discriminating observers that the evacuated children benefited far more by being taught along with the native children than by being kept apart from them.

Though it became a major issue of professional policy which was disputed for months, the question of identity versus merging was not the cause of the more serious problems of school accommodation in the receiving areas. In a sense this was an artificial problem ; and there were plenty of others that were only too real. In many places there was no school accommodation at all for the evacuated ; one London secondary school, for instance, found itself billeted eight miles from a school building. In other places the accommodation was grossly inadequate or quite unsuitable, or, as frequently happened, both.

The difference in the quality and type of school accommodation and equipment as between urban and rural areas caused infinite trouble. Broadly speaking, premises, amenities and equipment in the towns were much superior to, and more up-to-date than, those in the country. This was especially the case in respect of the provision for children over 11. Most of the older elementary schoolchildren evacuated had been in schools reorganized under the " Hadow " Scheme as separate and specially equipped units for seniors, but a large majority of the rural schools were still " all-age " units containing children of every age from 5 to 14, and in no way equipped for specialized senior work.

The following is a sample situation :

On the appointed day there arrived groups of children from three different central schools, some elementary schools, a convent school, and a secondary school for girls.   In the district there are two elementary schools, and an endowed school for boys with one for girls on the same foundation.   There is no central or senior school, and the two elementary schools are ill-adapted for even their usual work. The small town has a few small rooms used for meetings, dances, or bridge drives, and there is a tiny evening school conducted in quarters over a grocer's shop.   No accommodation for carrying on the work of central school pupils is available.—*The Times Educational Supplement*, September 16, 1939.

" Experiences of this kind ", commented the *Supplement*, " may be rare, but they are frequent enough to suggest a lack of forethought in high places, and a failure to picture the inevitable results of a rapid, wholesale migration of children." Unhappily, they were soon found not to be rare, but distressingly common, and much worse in the villages than in the small towns. The situation described above may, in fact, be considered a relatively easy one.   For example, not many miles away from this particular town 150 boys and girls of all ages from 3 to 14 were unloaded on a village containing one small and extremely primitive school—already full to capacity—which had accommodation for less than 50 children.   It was indeed fortunate, as the leader writer of *The Times Educational Supplement* ironically observed, that " the first few days of their stay were warm and sunny ".

But a temporary spell of fine weather was no solution of the accommodation problem ; in a sense it served to aggravate it, for it tended in places to delay the quest for a genuine solution. " Removed from their familiar surroundings and deprived of many of their familiar aids," the Board of Education had chanted in circular 1474 (issued, be it recalled, only three days before evacuation started), " the schools and the teachers will have to rely on their own initiative and the resources of the countryside." How bravely the urban teachers (encouraged no doubt by the sunny weather) strove to observe this instruction !   But many of them, through no fault of their own, quickly found themselves at the end of an initiative severely limited by the fact that they were completely ignorant of the resources of the countryside, and that no other resources were available.   They and the

children alike found " little satisfaction in an endless round of
country rambles "—especially when conducted in unsuitable
or inadequate footgear, and for no discernible purpose save to
pass the time away. The delights of the emphasis on " speech
and the power to understand and use it " advised by the Board
soon palled when there was little else to do but talk and walk
all day ; and in the absence of any kind of material equipment
the opportunities for " music and dramatic expression " did
not appear to them to be either overwhelmingly abundant or
satisfying. In short, formal education for the evacuated came in
many places to a full stop, because neither teachers nor children
understood it in any terms other than those of buildings and
books.

At the time the almost unbelievable ignorance of even the
commonplaces of country life which was exhibited by so many
evacuated children (and teachers) was considered by the general
public to be exquisitely comic. Countless anecdotes, true and
apocryphal, were gleefully related in the press, or passed round
by word of mouth. Few people seemed to realize how in-
expressibly tragic, and what a shameful reflection upon our
social and educational systems it was, that, for example, a little
girl, seeing sheep in a field, should cry out " They move ! "—
and innocently explain that " I thought they were only in
pictures ". Or that an adolescent schoolboy should exclaim in
astonishment, " Look, Bill, plums *on a tree* ! " Fewer people
still realized how socially disastrous it was that many urban
teachers were, to all intents and purposes, as unaware as their
pupils of the beauty, the interest, and the rich variety of the
English countryside. The " endless round of country rambles ",
which should have been a never-ending source of delight, inspiration, and instruction, was in fact in all too many cases no more
than an ever more wearying procession of the blind leading the
blind.

How could these things come to be among a people calling
itself civilized ?

Saddest of all, and to my mind most detrimental to the
cause of education in these early days of evacuation, was the
fact that so many of the urban teachers, though obviously mental
paupers in a land of plenty, nevertheless affected an air of lofty
superiority over their country colleagues. Why, I have never

been able to determine.   It is true that the buildings and equipment to which they had been accustomed were (in general though
not always) better than those to which they came, that their
salaries were larger, their academic and professional qualifications
often higher, their teaching methods more up-to-date, their
knowledge of theatres, cinemas, and (sometimes) current literature
more extensive.   But all that did not necessarily make them
better men and women, or even better teachers.   In fact, on their
own ground, and in their own way, the rural teachers were on
the whole as good as the urban ones—if not better—as some
of the latter had later the grace to acknowledge and admit.

It would be of the utmost value if a psychological investigation
could be made into the fundamental causes of this ignorant and
pervert attitude on the part of so many evacuated teachers.
To what extent was it induced by fear—fear of the unknown, the
complex, the terrifyingly strange environment in which they
found themselves, and which, try as they might, they could not
understand ?   To what extent was it due to a feeling of frustration, to a sudden unconscious sense that something of priceless
value, to which by heritage they were surely entitled but of
which they had all their lives been deprived, lay tantalizingly
displayed before them—but that they could now never hope
to enter into full possession of it ?   To what extent was the
attitude adopted as a defence mechanism against an all too
likely loss of prestige in the eyes of their pupils due to their
obvious ignorance of their new surroundings ?   To what extent
because of a deep-down feeling of inferiority to the rural teachers,
to the humblest rural inhabitant even ?

And, most relevant to a study such as this, to what extent
did this unhappy attitude adversely affect the education given
to the children in the receiving areas ?   I believe, to a far greater
extent than has yet been generally realized, than has even been
suspected.   It undoubtedly sent many children back to the
evacuating areas who would otherwise have remained in the
country.   And it bred an antagonism, a suspicion and distrust
as between town and countryside which persisted for months
(it is not dead yet in some areas), which led to a thousand opportunities of co-operation being missed, and to many a positively
unco-operative act pregnant with maleficent results.

Of course, the fault was not all on one side ; rural teachers

showed themselves possessive, resentful of intrusion, unwilling
to enter into partnership with the newcomers : in some cases
really stupid, ignorant, malevolent, and obstructive. But in
my opinion there is no doubt where the balance of blame lies.

This lack of willingness to co-operate with those whose
attitude to and ways of life are somewhat different from our own
is one of our greatest obstacles to real democracy. The war is
doing much to break down the spirit of unco-operativeness, but
it is doubtful if it will do enough. Education for co-operative
attitudes must rank high among the tasks of the future, and
there must be literally a crusade against false ideas of prestige.

CALAMITY IN THE TOWNS

If conditions in the receiving areas were immediately rendered
chaotic by evacuation, it was not long before they bordered on
the calamitous in the evacuation areas. At least a million
schoolchildren—one-fifth of the total school population—did
not evacuate. In some evacuating areas more children remained
than left. From London—which sent away a relatively high
proportion—only 49 per cent were evacuated. (Of these 7 per
cent were back within a few weeks.) From Derby only one
child in five went away, from Leeds only two out of every seven.
30,000 schoolchildren remained in Liverpool, an equal number
in Manchester.

For none of these million or more " left behind " children
were there any schools or teachers. Should that have mattered
so very much ? One can understand a certain amount of disquiet in the public mind that the formal education of such large
numbers of children should be temporarily suspended ; but even
so, should what was, in effect, no more than an unexpected
prolongation of the summer holidays have brought results which
quickly caused profound alarm ? If, as was (and still is) so regularly and confidently asserted in this country, the family is the
basic unit of our civilization, and family life the source and
inspiration of its virtues, why did the cessation of schooling in the
evacuating areas prove so catastrophic ?

For catastrophic is the only word to describe what happened.
Within a month there were reports from all sides that the children
in the towns were " running wild ", creating disturbances everywhere, and in many places resorting to hooliganism and crime.

Doubtless these reports were frequently exaggerated, and certainly the children responsible for them constituted only a small minority of the child population ; nevertheless, the trouble was undoubtedly serious and widespread enough to justify genuine alarm. It is a depressing commentary on the state of society in 1939 that the temporary breakdown of the public system of education in the evacuating areas should have resulted in so brief a period of time in such a shocking state of affairs.

Why did the home prove so ineffective as a controlling influence upon the children ? It is not a satisfying answer to suggest that the absence of parents was the main cause. At that time relatively few fathers had been called up or had moved away from home for other reasons, and mothers had hardly begun to be absorbed into the war industries. Nor does it help particularly to say that in some instances both parents were at work all day ; that has always been the case. And there is no evidence, so far as I know, that the troublesome children came in the main from homes from which one or other of the parents was absent. The brutal fact is that, put to a crucial test, many a home failed completely to rise to its responsibilities.

The reasons are not far to seek. The struggle for existence had been so exhaustive of their vitality and energy, the narrowness of circumstances so restrictive of their outlook, and their education so pitifully inadequate, that the vast majority of parents in this country had never been able even to realize their responsibilities, much less carry them out. Nor will they be able to do so until the social, economic, industrial, and educational systems of this country undergo radical reconstruction. The effect of these systems upon the individual should be stimulating and exhilarating ; at present it is largely inhibiting and repressive.

There is a great deal of loose talk in England about the sanctity of the home and the responsibility of the parents. It is much of it uttered by people who oppose the extension of State-provided facilities for education. These people never seem to realize two points. First, that, however good the home, it cannot by itself meet more than the nucleus of the child's educational needs. He has progressively to become acquainted with an ever wider variety of social groupings and circumstances if he is to learn the art of living and co-operating with his fellows ; and this can only be done by his becoming a member of other social units. Secondly, the home is a healthy influence only if the parents are sufficiently educated to make it so ; otherwise it is a stronghold of superstition and the most potent maker of bad and anti-social habits. One of the benefits which should emerge from this war—largely as a result of evacuation—is a better realization of the function of the home in society, and of its dependence upon publicly provided educational and welfare services for carrying out that function.

The disorderly outburst of juvenile ebullience in the evacuating areas was at one and the same time a notable tribute to the disciplinary efficiency of the public elementary school and a shame-provoking reflection upon the educational policy of the nation. It revealed—and this was literally a revelation to many people—that the elementary school, which had had during the second half of the nineteenth century the hard task of civilizing the children of Britain (brutalized by the poverty and degradation to which they had been condemned by the industrial revolution), was still not only the most powerful and effective instrument for the preservation of law and order among the youthful section of the population, but an absolutely necessary one. What should have been ensured by education was in fact being secured by the educational system.

The Government's Dilemma

The presence in the evacuating areas of very large numbers of children of school age—numbers daily being swelled by returns from the receiving areas—placed the Government in a fearful dilemma. On the one hand, as the Board of Education said in circular 1479, sent out on September 29 :

It would clearly be intolerable that a substantial proportion of the school population should continue indefinitely to be deprived of education and its allied services, and should suffer the demoralization which must inevitably follow the removal of school discipline and control.

On the other, to reopen the schools in the evacuating areas would be in effect to reverse the policy on which the evacuation scheme was based, that of dispersal, and virtually to invite the parents of evacuated children to bring them back home. Quite properly the Government stood by its evacuation policy, but as it resolutely set its face against any suggestion of compulsory evacuation, or indeed against doing anything really positive, it was forced by events—notably by the continued non-occurrence of bombing and the return in ever larger numbers of children to the evacuating areas—into a weak and hesitant attitude, at very grave cost to the education and welfare of the children concerned.

The depressing effects of lack of direction at the centre were heightened by certain restrictive measures taken by the Government during the early weeks of the war. At the outset, all the schools were closed. Strictly speaking, this for a time applied to the elementary schools only, since the secondary schools, the institutions for technical, commercial, and art education, and evening schools of all types were not due in any case to reopen after the summer vacation until between mid-September and early October. But secondary, junior technical, art, commercial, and trade schools were evacuated, so that in fact they may be reckoned along with the elementary schools. This left the technical and other comparable institutions for higher education, the evening schools, the universities, and the varied provision of semi-educational, semi-recreational facilities for adolescents and adults made by voluntary organizations for the moment unaffected by evacuation.

But not by other aspects of the war situation. Technical and other institutions for vocational training were ordered to remain closed. When the date approached for the reopening of the evening schools, this was postponed. The universities, being independent bodies, made their own dispositions, and except in one case—London—decided to carry on as near normal as possible. (Evacuation was clearly the only rational course for London.) The voluntary organizations, also independent bodies, desired to do the same, but were prevented by three desperate wounds inflicted simultaneously. Large numbers of their most virile leaders, being Territorials or reservists, were called to the fighting Forces, the Government commandeered a considerable number of their buildings, and the flow of private subscriptions upon which they so largely depended suddenly diminished to the merest trickle. Some of the organizations were better organized and equipped to meet such blows, but boys' and girls' club work, in particular, for a time almost ceased to exist. Had not the newly formed National Youth Committee come to the aid of the organizations promoting it, it is doubtful whether this form of voluntary social activity would, save in isolated instances, have survived the winter. As it was, clubs closed down by the hundred, and thousands of adolescent boys and girls were deprived of what was probably the most steadying and inspiring influence in their lives—at the very time when they stood most in need of it.

In September the Government postponed the operation of the 1936 Education Act until after the war, and announced that any consideration of the report of the Consultative Committee of the Board of Education on Secondary Education (the " Spens " Report) would similarly be deferred. The Consultative Committee itself was disbanded, and a very considerable proportion of the Board's administrative and inspectorial staffs were transferred to other government departments. The building and reconditioning of schools (which had been active) were abruptly brought to an end—premises almost approaching completion alone being excepted. All of which clearly indicated where the Government ranked education—well outside the war effort, and not particularly important even then.

As will be related in the next chapter, sporadic attempts were made to check the obvious disintegration of the publicly provided educational service. A number of local education authorities in evacuating areas quickly set in motion various gallant if woefully inadequate makeshift measures to ensure that some children at least received a modicum of instruction and medical care. The Board, in circular 1479, bestowed their blessing on the Sheffield " home tuition " scheme, which was quickly taken up in many areas, and at the same time gave permission for the reopening of a limited number of schools for purposes of medical inspection and treatment. The President went to the microphone and implored parents to send their children to the receiving areas, or if they had already done so, to keep them there—an appeal which, so far as can be judged, had no effect whatsoever. His officials suggested to the local education authorities in the evacuating areas that they took steps to find out how many children there were in their areas—a virtually impossible task, because nothing less than a simultaneous house-to-house visitation could have ensured accurate statistics.

Meanwhile, in the country the children rambled in the lanes and fields while the authorities searched desperately for any sort of accommodation in which to house them ; in the towns the children played in the streets—innocently or mischievously according to bent—or stayed in bed till noon and toured the dance-halls, cinemas, and pin tables by night. The children in the rural areas improved immensely in health and considerably in morals ; the children in the towns regressed in both.

As the situation deteriorated, public anxiety mounted. So did public dissatisfaction with the Government's lack of grip of the problem. Questions in Parliament multiplied : letters to the press increased daily. It was clear something had to be done. On November 1 the Board of Education at last made a substantial propitiatory move ; the President announced in Parliament that " such schools in evacuation areas as can be made available for educational purposes shall be reopened for the education of the children of parents who desire them to attend ".

This sounded better than in fact it was. To begin with, as the President had to admit, a great many schools were not immediately available, and could not be made so before Christmas at least. They were being used as A.R.P. posts, auxiliary fire stations, casualty clearing stations, soldiers' billets ; and their occupants were by no means anxious to give them up. Or they were, in the words of the Board of Education circular 1483, issued as supplement to the President's announcement of November 1 (but unaccountably not sent out till November 11), " unsuitable for reasons either of location or construction "—in plain English, because they were in districts potentially too dangerous for the risk of putting children into them to be faced, or because they had nothing adequate in the way of air-raid shelters. The latter was much the more frequent cause of unsuitability. It was to prove for months a grave hindrance to the full resumption of the education service, not only in the evacuating but in the neutral areas.

Moreover, the wording of the announcement made it perfectly clear—though the fact was not mentioned in Parliament—that the law enforcing compulsory attendance at school, if it had not been formally abrogated, was certainly considered as in abeyance for the time being. Attendance at school was till further notice voluntary. It was a dangerous precedent, which was to be responsible later for a considerable amount of deliberate absenteeism.

Retrieving school premises which had been commandeered for military or civil defence purposes proved a slow and difficult task. Education was still regarded as the least important of the social services, which as a whole were looked upon as of quite secondary significance in war-time. The implications of total war had as yet barely begun to be realized. The status of the Board of Education among the government departments was low, and its bargaining power almost negligible. Without strong backing from the centre, the local education authorities were grievously impeded in their truly heroic attempts to rebuild the shattered educational services. They received their strongest support from public opinion, which in this matter showed itself well ahead of the Government.

Looking back, it is easy to see why. The breakdown of the educational system personally and intimately affected hundreds of thousands of parents, who felt the effects in their own homes, and were alarmed and exasperated by them. In numerous instances it was the only problem of any magnitude which really penetrated into their consciousness during these early months of the war, when everyone was waiting for something to happen in our part of the battle front and when nothing did. Consequently, for the first time in their lives, people found themselves talking and thinking really seriously about education.

It was a striking illustration of the sociological rule that the significance of an institution of society only becomes really appreciated in a marginal situation. Previously, save in comparable situations—e.g. during 1917–18—most of us tended to regard education rather as one of the more embarrassing conventions imposed upon us by civilization. We felt we had to subject our children to it, so that their rough-hewn timbers might be suitably planed and veneered, but otherwise we were quite vague as to why it was necessary. Now, it began to dawn upon us that perhaps, after all, this business called education really did matter. It became increasingly clear that, in a variety of ways we did not as yet understand, it somehow exercised a positive influence on the life of society.

To the Government, preoccupied with many other problems, realization of this did not come till much later. The breakdown of the State educational system doubtless seemed to them an annoying but not terribly important temporary dislocation of one of the lesser social services, which they probably anticipated would right itself in time, and which meanwhile was all rather remote from the graver realities of war. It will be remembered incidentally (but perhaps the fact is significant) that Conservative cabinet ministers and higher grade civil servants do not usually send their children to public elementary and secondary schools ; they prefer the more exclusive independent schools. These certainly had their troubles at this time—many of them had their buildings somewhat discourteously commandeered—but they had, generally speaking, managed to secure reasonably comfortable war-time quarters in castles, country mansions, luxury hotels, or accommodation loaned to them by schools in the same category. And the parents of their pupils had not, as a rule, the domestic difficulties to meet which confronted poorer homes.

But public opinion remained perturbed and persistently aggressive ; and in January 1940, the Government thought it wise to make a special statistical survey of the position. This was the result (Hansard, 6 February, 1940, Vol. 357, col. 34/44) :

EDUCATION OF CHILDREN IN EVACUATION AREAS

Type of Education.	Attending School.		Home Service Classes.		Receiving no Education.		Total.
	No.	% of Total.	No.	% of Total.	No.	% of Total.	
Elementary .	708,637	47·5	367,819	24·6	417,511	27·9	1,493,967
Secondary .	79,051	85·5	887	0·9	12,481	14·5	92,419
Total .	787,688	50·5	368,706	23·7	429,992	27·6	1,586,386

Note : The figures are approximate, as they include a number of children in neutral parts of county areas containing both neutral and evacuation zones. But substantially they show the true position.

No Government could remain unmoved by such figures. Upwards of half a million children receiving no education at all, five months after the educational system had first been disrupted, and upwards of 400,000 more receiving what was admittedly a totally inadequate form of education, was sufficient to deflate any amount of complacency. On the following day, February 7, 1940, the President of the Board of Education announced that compulsory attendance at school was again to be enforced, on a full-time or half-time basis, as soon as sufficient accommodation was available. This, he hinted to local authorities, should be not later than April 1, the beginning of the summer term for the elementary schools.

Easier said than done. There were still stern battles to be fought over commandeered schools ; there were still air-raid shelters to be built, with materials in short supply to which everyone seemed to have a prior claim over the schools. But the President's declaration, and the accompanying instructions to local education authorities to prepare to resume operation of the law making school attendance compulsory, certainly initiated a new and much firmer policy. There were still to be moments of hesitation and agonizing delays ; but February 7, 1940, may be taken as definitely marking the turn of the tide. The physical disintegration of the educational system was on that day definitely arrested.

I say *physical* disintegration advisedly, because I wish to stress that another type of disintegration began also on September 1, 1939, and has continued ever since. This is the breaking down of old habits of thought, of the traditional conception of education, in the minds of teachers and administrators and, though more slowly, in the minds of the general public. This is bringing with it a corresponding, and consequent, disintegration of the old forms and techniques of education. With this process I have not been here concerned ; it will be dealt with in later chapters. All I have tried to show so far is how the State educational system, as a piece of working machinery, was disrupted by evacuation (and non-evacuation), the closing of the schools and other educational institutions, the commandeering of their premises for defence purposes, and other measures taken on the outbreak of war.

CHAPTER II

RECUPERATION

Heroes of the Reception Areas

It has ever been the habit of the English to find through defeat the way to victory. It would seem, indeed, that nothing short of catastrophe can call forth their finest qualities or induce them to put out the maximum effort of which they are capable. The weeks following Dunkirk were a supreme example of this. Such a disaster would have sapped fatally the spirit of many a people : its effect upon the people of Britain was wholly tonic. Under the inspiring leadership of Winston Churchill—in whom was and is to be found the quintessence of the pugnacious qualities of the British—the nation rose as one man (though in quite unspectacular fashion) to the height of the crisis, and with a complete absence of emotionalism, yet with a determination and an intensity of purpose rarely equalled in the history of mankind, set itself doggedly to the task not merely of repairing what seemed irreparable damage but of laying the foundations of ultimate victory.

The story of Dunkirk has been blazed across the world. The educational disaster of 1939 has received no publicity in any way comparable. Yet the situation which resulted from the evacuation of our schoolchildren was, on a long-term view, every whit as serious as that which resulted from the evacuation of our soldiers from the Continent. It constituted as grave a threat —though not, of course, so obvious or immediate a one—to the future of the nation.

As a people, our reaction to the situation was neither united nor impressive : education had not yet begun to matter to most of us. We were exasperated rather than stimulated by the debacle. Yet something more than exasperation was born out of it. It is no exaggeration to say that, as Dunkirk administered a shock sufficiently staggering to shake the entire British people completely out of their habitual and ingrained complacency concerning the conduct of their military affairs, so evacuation administered a shock sufficiently staggering to shake some of them out of something of their complacency concerning the conduct of their social affairs.

Meanwhile, true to the English tradition, many concerned with the service of education, and a host of others whom evacuation drew temporarily into the spheres of education and welfare, instantly saw their path of duty clear before them, and without a moment's hesitation set out upon it with unsparing resolution. They began at once to work, as did the factory workers after Dunkirk, to repair what seemed at first irreparable damage. In so doing, though they knew it not, they were laying the foundations of ultimate victory in the field of education.

Though it was not until February 7, 1940, that fully effective measures were taken at the centre to arrest the disintegration of the English educational system, it would be utterly wrong to assume that the process of recuperation did not begin until that date. In fact, it began on September 1, 1939. Many education officers, teachers, billeting officials, and voluntary workers had, while making preparations for evacuation, come to realize some of the problems which awaited them. Directly evacuation started and they saw their worst forebodings pale into insignificance before the awfulness of the reality, they flung themselves into the struggle with a self-sacrifice and a devotion beyond praise. It proved far grimmer than anything they had imagined, but they never faltered, though they often came near despair. For weeks on end many education offices in the reception areas were never closed. Education officers and billeting officers worked day and night. Teachers performed superhuman feats. Voluntary helpers toiled as though their lives depended on it.

There was so much to be done ; and all at once. Children by the thousand to be regrouped and rebilleted. New foster-parents to be found for them, original foster-parents persuaded to keep them. Real parents, anxious, angry, silly, stupid, come post-haste from home, to be soothed and sent back happy—if possible without their children. Irate farmers, raging at crops endamaged, to be pacified. Bridling natives, furious at urban insults, to be mollified. Family feuds, fanned into flames by strangers' presence, to be damped down ; inter-family quarrels to be checked ; town and country conflicts to be prevented. . . . And the inquiries ! Inquiries by the million, official and unofficial, important and unimportant, serious and silly, to be patiently listened to and, when possible, answered ; inquiries about feeding, clothing, washing, bathing, mending ; about children's allowances, adults' allowances, husbands' allowances, teachers' allowances, helpers' allowances ; about buses, trains, cinemas, shops ; about schools, schooling, supervision in school, supervision out of school, week-end supervision ; about lost children, strayed children, sick children, sad children, difficult children, naughty children, delinquent children.   There was no end to the inquiries ; they drove strong-minded men and women to the verge of madness.   And in between the inquiries and the interviewings, conferences, committees and consultations, planning, replanning, and planning again, adjusting, improvising, compromising . . . whirl without end.

Gradually, bit by bit, chaos was reduced to some sort of order.   An imperfect order, a patchy and piecemeal order ; but definitely order and not chaos.   Children continued to pour out of reception areas back to their homes (the adults had nearly all gone in the first few weeks), but gradually it became clear that a large nucleus was going to stay put ; they were in billets where they felt at home and they had settled down at school. The lousy children had been deloused, the scabby children unscabbed, the ragged children clothed, the undernourished children filled with good food, and the naughty children placed under observation.   Something of an air of peace began to settle on the countryside ; and those who had brought it about felt free at least to breathe again.

There has been far too little recognition of the superlatively magnificent sustained work done in the reception areas during the autumn of 1939 by literally thousands of unknown heroes. They were no less.   Due credit has been paid to the foster-mothers who took the evacuated children into their homes ; and quite rightly.   But much less than due credit has been accorded to those who got them to these homes, who transferred them to other homes, and then retransferred them, again and again, to still other homes ; to those who found the children schools, or at least places in which they might learn and be taught—those who begged the use of churches, chapels, Sunday-schools, parish halls, public rooms, private houses, warehouses, barns, stables, garages, for the children's education ; to those who kept the children profitably occupied and reasonably happy, in school and out, whether they had a roof over their heads or not —who went and fetched furniture and equipment, with their own hands, and at their own expense, from the evacuating areas, who bought furniture and equipment, begged it, borrowed it, made it—even, if report speaks truly, stole it when all other means failed ; who devised lessons without books, games without kit, entertainment without entertainers ; who found clothes for ragged children, saw that under-nourished children were properly fed, cared for sick and sorry children, were sympathetic with lousy and scabby children, kept an eye on naughty children, and by their superb example were an inspiration to all children.

What miracles of improvisation were wrought in the receiving areas in those early days of evacuation ! The leaders of one group of five schools, sizing up the situation immediately on arrival, divided their area into eight districts, allotted teaching staff and helpers to these, begged the use of a disused school and made of it a play centre, information bureau, first-aid post, communal laundry, and area headquarters. The staff of a London girls' secondary school which arrived at a Midland town to find five other schools already there and all billets occupied, packed their pupils into buses, took them to another town, billeted them, and set out to find school accommodation for them. By September 21 the school was at work on a full time-table. They were sharing rooms with the local High School, using the laboratories of the technical institute, studying in the reference room of the public library, and holding classes in the billiards-room and skittle alley of the Y.M.C.A. A boys' school, having insufficient classroom space, dismantled an Army hut— 60 feet by 18 feet—and re-erected it in the village school play-ground. Using boy labour, they put down concrete pier founda-tions, laid on water, and wired the hut for electric light.

These instances are merely by way of illustration ; they could be paralleled by scores, probably hundreds, of others. In many places an efficient school service was functioning within a few days. Take the district mentioned in Chapter I,[1] for instance, where several elementary schools, a central school, a secondary school and a convent school were deposited in a small town having no central school, poor elementary school accommodation, and little in the way of available halls or public rooms. Despite the fact that the school population of this district had been increased by over 50 per cent, by September 18 92 per cent

[1] P. 21.

of the elementary schools had been reopened, most of them on a full-time basis, the central school had been found comfortable quarters in a local grammar school, and both secondary schools provided with appropriate accommodation—though in one case only at the cost of replanting the school in another district.

The head teacher who found 100 of his children billeted in six villages, and another 70 in a county town 20 miles away, had within a week of his arrival made contact with the local heads and worked out with them a satisfactory scheme for the education of all his pupils. Another head teacher—a " native " one—in a similar period of time devised, in collaboration with his " evacuee " head, a scheme whereby his school became a complete boys' school in the morning and a complete girls' school in the afternoon.

In one southern district all the schools were formally opened on September 18. Before this date members of the staff of a girls' senior school evacuated there had been to London to collect urgently needed books and equipment and had transformed a room in the local senior school into a commercial and art room, complete with typewriters and easels, and a room in the junior school into a housewifery and first-aid centre. Local help did the rest. The domestic science centre at the senior school was placed at the disposal of the evacuees, a sixteenth-century inn turned into a secondary school offered laboratory facilities, the Methodist hall a place for physical training and singing lessons, and its vestries shelters for tutorial groups. Even so more room was needed, so some of the staff billets were borrowed for French and shorthand classes, while some of the French was done on outdoor expeditions. Despite all this ingenuity and goodwill, the school had to work on the " double-shift " system, its loaned accommodation being available only in the afternoons, so the mornings were spent on the local playing fields, in the neighbouring meadows, and on the heathland near by, the time being divided between organized games and biological, geological and historical surveys.

Because of the specialized nature of their curriculum and equipment, secondary schools found themselves particularly at a disadvantage when moved from town to countryside. The story of how one London secondary school overcame its difficulties well illustrates the resolute spirit displayed by many.

By some error of transport the school was dumped in an entirely rural district which had prepared for the arrival of mothers with babies. Boys and staff were distributed among six villages, none of which had educational facilities in any way suitable ; and to complicate matters, shortly afterwards the army commandeered many of the village halls and rooms. On its own initiative and by its own efforts the school moved to a neighbouring town, and arranged for the transport thereto of books, desks and other equipment from its London premises. It made an agreement with the local secondary school, which had just moved into new buildings, for the use of the " temporary " huts the latter had occupied for 18 years and for sharing the gymnasium, laboratories and workshop in the new buildings.

The school was able to settle down to a comparatively normal time-table only a week or two later than would have been the case had evacuation not taken place. But the school authorities were not satisfied with that. Believing that if the boys were really to enjoy and profit from their new life the school must become a dynamic social centre and enter fully into the activities of the neighbourhood, they organized a general club and extended the scope of their dramatic work, in addition to keeping going all their usual school societies—musical, geographical, scientific, and world affairs.

The town reacted most happily to the initiative and enterprise of its self-invited guests. Offers of help of various kinds came from the Co-operative Society, the Rotary Club, the Churches and other bodies, and from many private individuals, and the most cordial relations and effective liaison were established between the school and the foster-parents. The result was that each side began immediately to benefit from the presence of the other, and town and country quickly learned an understanding of each other's problems and attitudes to life.

Nature takes a Hand

This was evacuation at its best ; here the social experiment was amply justified. So it was to be in many places, and in the case of many thousands of children. Though it caused chaos, evacuation brought also blessings which compensated even for chaos. Over and above all human endeavour (though often largely aided by it) the English countryside played a great and

healing part in the process of recuperation. Something of the
story is admirably told in the illustrated brochure entitled *The
Schools in Wartime*, issued by the Board of Education in 1941,
from which the following excerpts are taken :

It is true to say that practically all the children have improved
in physique, general health, poise and bearing . . . increases in
weight and height, rosier cheeks, greater physical strength, have not
been mere fiction but sober fact.
. . . the advantages are by no means all simply physical. The
experience of living for the first time away from home has given to
many children a new poise and self-reliance, and more thoughtfulness
for others. Contact with a different way of life and rubbing shoulders
with country children—and for that matter with children from
different kinds of homes from other evacuation areas—have done
much to broaden the outlook of those whose lives had been confined
to a few streets.

These excerpts do not in any way exaggerate ; they may
rather be described as a sober underestimate.

A correspondent to *The Times Educational Supplement* wrote
on October 28 :

Fresh air, good food, and sleep are working wonders already
among many little boys and girls. Infants between five and six
years old showed in 10 days an increase of from one to two pounds
in weight. Some children from a poor area have become almost
unrecognizable within a few weeks. One small girl was so chubby
that she needed a larger size gas-mask. . . .
Life on farms has brought a wealth of new experiences. . . . To
the smaller children berries in the hedges were a source of excitement.
An unfailing interest has been watching animals . . . one small
group of people waited 40 minutes in order to see a young pig wake
up. . . .
. . . the children especially have absorbed so much of country
ways and country lore that teachers say they learn as much from
the children on their walks as the children learn from them.

" All this," commented the writer, " is of much educational
value." How true—and how much less than the whole truth !
It was the first real education—save in degradation—some of
these children had ever had. People living in the reception
areas (and I can speak as one of them) were amazed at the transformation, bodily and mental, which was seen to come over these
town children within the space of a few weeks, often within
a few days. Pale, thin, repressed, and seemingly unintelligent

when they arrived, they blossomed, brightened and browned in an incredibly short time. And, " I shall always remember ", wrote one hostess, " as the most arresting single change in the children's bearing the change in the eyes of the shifty-eyed ones. They became able to look you squarely in the face."

It was a startling vindication of the theory some of us have always held tenaciously, that the English are still among the finest human material in the world, despite the appalling treatment to which so many of them were subjected throughout the nineteenth century, and to which some of them were still being subjected as late as 1939. If anything could give renewed and added vigour to the determination that they shall no longer after this war have to endure the depressive and deteriorative effects of poverty, squalor, insecurity, and ignorance, this experience could—and did.

Evacuation was an education, too, for others than the children. Urban teachers—those who remained—also benefited ; for many of them the great migration proved the beginning of a new and infinitely fuller and more inspiring life. And for many residents in the reception areas evacuation marked the beginning of a sociological education. Not a few of them have taken it seriously, and are still persisting with it.

One particularly interesting feature of the mingling of town and country children, noticed by observers all over the country, was that—

> . . . it has been the country children who have called the tune and the town children who have followed it. Rarely has the country child adopted the manners, customs or speech of the town visitor. On the contrary, the town child has been most eager to imitate those of the country, with the result that after a time, the evacuees are scarcely distinguishable from the natives. . . .

It might be argued, of course, that this was only natural, seeing that the country child was on his own ground, and therefore confident and secure, while the town child was a stranger in a strange land. But those who studied this phenomenon became convinced that there was more to it than that. The town child seemed to realize that the country child's life was somehow fuller and better than his own, while the country child felt no corresponding attractiveness in the life of the town child. Rather he seemed to judge that it was but a thin, *ersatz* kind of existence,

an experience not worth even discussing. It was noticeable that
he avoided this. The town child who boasted of the attractions
of the city street could rarely command an attentive audience
of country children ; he was much more likely to be met with
pitying contempt or a crushing snub. Man may be, as Aristotle
said, the animal who lives in cities ; but it was clear that the
country child had no inclination to become the animal who
lives in city slums.

Fundamentally there is little doubt that it was the creative
character of the country child's life which appealed. The leisure
life of the child born in the poorer part of the modern town is,
save for its privations, almost entirely one of make-believe. The
country child is always doing real things : digging a garden,
feeding poultry, tending cattle, gathering crops : and he is in
daily and intimate contact with adults while they too are doing
real things. The town child has to spend his time on invented
pastimes, and often has little close contact with adults during
their hours of their employment. He may live for years without
ever seeing his father at his work, or even having been in his
place of employment. When he has close contact it is often in
most undesirable conditions.

The educational value of this broadening of outlook and
opportunity for creativeness has been invaluable to hundreds of
thousands of town children. It is not so much that they have
learned to garden, to milk, to ride and drive horses, to tend
cattle, look after poultry, know trees and flowers and wild
animals ; it is the birth of a new attitude to life that has mattered.
That new attitude is to-day having a profound effect in schools
throughout the country, in evacuating areas as well as in receiving.
It has had, I am convinced, most important repercussions upon
the curriculum, which is in many places becoming more and
more genuinely practical and realist.

It is true that long before the war practical work was being
increasingly introduced into schools, notably the reorganized
senior schools. But while much of it represented absolutely
genuine progress, a great deal of it had an artificial flavour ; it
was done because it was fashionable, it had no discernible
purpose, the various activities practised were unrelated to each
other and to the more academic work of the school, and above
all, they had no obvious relevance to the life of the larger society

outside the school. Today both purpose and cohesion are plainly to be seen in the practical work which is being done, and its relationship to the life of society becomes more obvious every day. I believe that if the causes of this could be analysed out, the release of the creative impulse due to the evacuation of so many children to the countryside would be found to be the fundamental one.

Concerning the many benefits which evacuation has brought to children who have been allowed by their parents to remain in the receiving areas a very large volume could be written. Here they can merely be glanced at, and borne in mind as a continuing factor aiding—indirectly perhaps rather than directly—the process of educational recuperation. It is necessary to return now to the direct steps taken to re-establish the State educational system.

CENTRAL AND LOCAL EFFORT

The efforts of the administrators, teachers, and voluntary workers in the receiving areas were alternately aided and impeded by advice and instruction from the centre. On the credit side must be mentioned the issue by the Board of Education in September of a helpful circular (No. 1475) dealing with fees and maintenance grants, the school leaving age, the provision of meals and milk in schools, courses in child welfare, and school use of first-aid posts ; and the publication in the same month of the first of their admirable series of pamphlets entitled *The Schools in Wartime*. This dealt with food production by schools and undoubtedly did much to promote the school garden movement which has since become so extensive and valuable.

A week or two later the Ministry of Health, in circular 1882, urged evacuating authorities to do everything possible in the way of releasing medical officers, school dentists, nurses, and health visitors, so as to enable the public health services in the receiving areas to cover the needs of the evacuated children. They also suggested special arrangements of a residential nature for difficult and " problem " children, and short-stay nurseries for young children temporarily separated from their mothers by reason of the latter's illness or confinement—suggestions which, enlarged and expanded, were later to mature into two very important developments, the residential hostels for difficult children and the war-time nurseries.

Meanwhile, various bodies not integral parts of the educational system but more or less closely in touch with it in pre-war days gave valuable assistance. The B.B.C., which had during the summer worked out plans for war-time school broadcasting, began an emergency programme, which included talks aimed at helping town children to understand and appreciate the countryside, as early as September 6. On September 25 this was superseded by a schools programme containing all the main elements of the peace-time programme except modern languages —all things considered, a remarkable achievement. The British Film Institute announced that they had lists of available films on geography, history, biology, nature study, physical and domestic science, craft work, music, foreign languages and physical training, and films were sent to the receiving areas by the London County Council, the G.P.O., the Empire Film Library, and other organizations. The London and Home Counties Branch of the Library Association, at the request of the Metropolitan Boroughs Joint Standing Committee, prepared a scheme for the transfer of children's books from evacuating to receiving areas. The Museums Association circularized its members to suggest that where the " double-shift " system was in operation children not at school might be taken to museums and art galleries, where facilities would be given for study of specimens, for lectures, and wherever possible, for reception of school broadcasts. In November the English School Theatre Society began to tour the reception areas, and in the same month the two companies of the Pilgrim Players—so rightly named— started on a career which has brought joy to innumerable villages and small towns.

In the Towns

The work of restoring some form of educational service for children of school age could not, as has been seen, begin so soon in the evacuating as in the receiving areas. But measures designed to repair other forms of educational damage were taken with commendable promptitude. On September 16, the Board of Education authorized the reopening of technical schools, evening institutes, and boys' and girls' clubs, though they attached to the permission conditions which for a while at least rendered it largely invalid : adequate air-raid protection had to be handy, and the number of students in the building had not to be " so great as to impede their rapid and orderly evacuation to a place of safety ".

The story of the reopening of the London evening institutes is one of the minor epics of the earlier days of the war. London had during the summer made preparations for the greatest session ever during the winter of 1939–40, and had indulged in a lavish publicity campaign which included a series of brilliantly amusing posters by Grimes, the famous cartoonist. Public attention had been arrested, and the response had been almost overwhelming. When on the outbreak of war it was announced that the opening of the evening institutes was to be postponed, the disappointment was acute, especially among young people. As soon as it was known that permission had been given for reopening, would-be students by the thousand lined up outside the institutes, clamouring to be admitted. When they learned that, owing to lack of black-out or shelter protection—or both— the premises were not yet available and classes could not begin, their exasperation knew no bounds.

They quickly found a way round the difficulties. Staff and students organized themselves into working parties and covered acres of windows with black-out material—often at their own expense. They filled sandbags by the thousand and improvised air-raid protection in every available corner. Where they could not make shelter they invented it. Then they opened the institutes, and devised a system of mathematics whereby, however many students there might be in the building, the registration figures never showed more than the prescribed safety number. (It is only fair to the authority to add that this was done without the cognizance of the London County Council or the official cognizance of the responsible heads of the institutes.) By such means 86 of London's 200 evening institutes were open by November 9, and 114 by December 1.

On September 29 the Board of Education, in circular 1479, after expressing serious apprehension at the possibility of any general return of children to evacuating areas, and recognizing nevertheless that the children in these areas should not be deprived of education and its allied services, made reference to the fact that certain authorities had already begun " in a tentative way to organize a system of visits by teachers to the homes of the children ", commented that this method had " the advantage of allowing the contact between teacher and child to be continued without involving the assembly of more than small groups ", and indicated that they had " no objection to the use by pupils of the school premises to collect books and receive their tasks ". Schools and school clinics might also be opened " for the purpose of providing medical inspection and treatment for small groups of children ". Thus, though " no suggestion put forward by the Board is to be taken as authorizing the opening of schools for ordinary instruction ", the door of the school was once again open. Not very wide ; but definitely ajar. A few days later the Parliamentary Secretary to the Board of Education announced that it had been decided to relax the rule which required secondary schools in evacuating areas to be closed, to the extent of allowing schools on the fringe of such areas, or in sparsely populated districts, to reopen, subject to there being adequate air-raid protection, and on the understanding that attendance was entirely at the parents' discretion.

Meanwhile some local authorities were already opening schools or planning to open them. Some areas, such as Coventry or Middlesbrough, had under the Government scheme been divided into evacuating and neutral areas ; many of these devised schemes whereby the children in the evacuable part of the area were fitted into schools in the neutral part. Attendance was normally on a voluntary basis, and this being the case, Birmingham at least opened its " neutral " schools without air-raid protection. Liverpool and other areas opened schools in the evacuable districts on condition that the children attending them could be dispersed within three minutes. Barnsley arranged that older children should attend a school within ten minutes' walk of their homes, infants within four minutes.

Other local authorities, in the words of a director of education, " accepted the position, and endeavoured to frame a substitute system of home education to save as much as possible out of the wreckage of the educational machine ". This system was most fully worked out in Sheffield, where rooms were taken, usually in the homes of parents, for groups of children—up to 12 for school work, to 25 for organized games—which were visited by peripatetic teachers. In this way it was found that children could get about 1½ hours' instruction daily, and further education through assigned tasks.

One instance of how a home teaching scheme was built up and operated will illustrate the initiative and industry put into the system. Following a conference of head teachers and administrative staff, a circular letter was sent to the parents of the pupils on roll, and personal visits were made to them by members of the school staffs. As a result, one head teacher found upwards of 60 homes placed at his disposal, from which he selected the 22 most suitable. For all these aid-raid shelter was available, and in 14 instances he was given the use of the home radio. Each class of 40 in his school of 316 boys was divided into four groups, and the groups were allocated to " home schools ". The class teacher took three of the groups on three separate occasions, while a specialist teacher was responsible for the fourth. A fortnightly time-table was drawn up, and each pupil received 12½ hours' instruction a fortnight between the hours of 9.30 and 4 p.m. In addition, homework estimated to occupy an equal number of hours was set. Although the scheme was voluntary, attendances were marked, and the parents co-operated heartily in seeing that these were regular and punctual. All work set and done was entered in full in the official class record book. It was a splendid example of co-operation between parents, teachers, and children.

The importance of the home teaching system may be judged from the fact that as late as January 1940 nearly 370,000 schoolchildren, or close on a quarter of the total number in the evacuating areas, were enrolled in home service classes.

Four days after sanctioning the first limited reopening of schools the Government made an educational move of fundamental importance ; it announced the appointment of a committee to advise it on problems of juvenile welfare in war-time, and the establishment of a special branch in the Board of Education to deal with the administrative aspects of welfare provision for boys and girls between the ages of 14 and 20. No attempt will be made at this juncture to tell of the progress of the " Service of Youth ", which, being a new departure, does not fall properly under the heading of " Recuperation ". The story will be found in Chapter III. Yet its initiation must be recorded at this

point, for it is an essential and highly important strand in the
transitional pattern of education that is being woven in England
as a result of the war.   Though for the purposes of this study recuperation and adaptation are being treated in separate chapters,
in fact they interlocked very intimately in 1939 and 1940, and
much more than the germs of reform are clearly to be distinguished in measures taken with purely recuperative aims.

On November 1, the President of the Board of Education
announced in Parliament that some schools would be reopened in
evacuating areas for the children " of parents who desired them
to attend ".   *The Times Educational Supplement* commented :

Only the future can show whether the President of the Board
of Education has made a wise or a disastrous decision by announcing
the reopening of schools in areas which are supposed to be empty
of children of school age.   In making it he has met the insistent
demand that thousands of children in those areas should not run
wild without discipline, medical care, or schooling.   But the decision
does not mean that all running wild will cease forthwith ; far from
it.   As Mr. Kenneth Lindsay pointed out in the Commons, military
and A.R.P. authorities are in occupation of many schools ; the
remainder are probably without proper air-raid shelters.   With luck,
running wild may have stopped in time for everyone to turn over a
new leaf at the New Year.   Meanwhile—and this was not pointed
out in either House—it will be impossible to enforce school attendance.

That comment fairly sums up the situation as it was seen at
the time by thoughtful people.   The event proved that the
President had made a wise decision.   He was pressed from many
quarters to order compulsory attendance.   But it would have
made little difference in fact ; attendance cannot be enforced if
accommodation is not available, and large numbers of schools
were very firmly in the grip of other authorities who were
exceedingly reluctant to hand them over.

That the President's step was right there can be no doubt ;
that it gave a powerful stimulus to the process of recuperation
is equally certain.   The local education authorities, in spite
of having to wait till November 11 for their official instructions
(in circular 1483), took the President at his word, and set
energetically about the task of getting schools released and in
fit order for their proper tasks.   They were not all ready to
" turn over a new leaf " at the New Year, but as the table in
Chapter I shows, they had at least got rather more than half

the children in the evacuating areas back into school—or rather, back on to the school rolls ; for not all those 787,688 children were in school every day. Even when allowance is made for this fact, it was no mean achievement.

Between November 1, 1939, and February 7, 1940, when the Government came to the decision to enforce attendance at school, a number of minor moves were made to help on the process of recuperation. Early in November the Board of Education, in circular 1480, suggested that where an evacuated school was so badly located that its efficiency was being seriously impaired steps should be taken to rebillet it, either in the same area or an adjoining district. At the same time it was announced in Parliament that the Ministry of Home Security was making a survey of school premises in evacuating areas to decide which were the most suitable for reopening and what was the most appropriate form of air-raid protection. Later in the month circular 1487 from the Board of Education announced that by a new Defence regulation education authorities could provide air-raid shelters involving the alteration or improvement of the buildings of voluntary elementary schools (which previously, under the Education Act, 1921, would not have been allowed). Restrictions affecting the purchase of land for shelters for non-provided schools were also waived.

CHRISTMAS FESTIVITIES

It was in the same month that a circular (1482) from the Board of Education suggested that special arrangements might be made in reception areas to keep the children there happy and occupied over the Christmas holidays.

The prodigious efforts which were made on behalf of the evacuated children during this first war-time Christmas did not prevent a large number of children returning home—some only temporarily, more, probably, permanently—but they deserve record, not only because they certainly retained very considerable numbers who would otherwise have left, but also because they helped to build up that new sense of community which was developing in English life as a result of the war.

Civic authorities, teaching staffs, voluntary societies, and public-spirited private individuals linked up and worked together in a manner never known before to provide parties, concerts, outings, and presents for the children in their areas. As a result that Christmas was undoubtedly the jolliest known in rural England for many a year—perhaps the jolliest ever. The festivities, and the preparation for them, probably did more than most of us have ever guessed to bring together people of varying social grades and differing interests, and so to strengthen that desire for a more egalitarian social order which has grown so strong and so widespread during these years of war.

The following is typical of what was done in hundreds of districts. A town with some 3,500 evacuated children made arrangements for ten Christmas parties. Local firms provided Christmas trees, toys and sweets, and local inhabitants made stacks of Christmas puddings. One of the cinemas was thrown open on Christmas Day as a club for the evacuated mothers, the café being turned into a canteen run by the W.V.S. During the daytime rambles, treasure hunts, salvage parties, and football matches were arranged for the children, the town playing fields being placed at their disposal and the schools kept open for indoor amusements. For the evenings competitions that could be done at home were arranged, and the W.V.S. organized a convoy and transport service to take children to and from concerts, parties and pantomimes.

An evacuated head teacher whose pupils were billeted in eight villages wrote in her diary for Christmas week :

Monday. Morning at B. . . . we had a practice for our carol party on Friday, made card books for our visitors, wrote invitations to foster parents and friends . . . printed woodcuts for covers of books and Christmas cards. Afternoon to D. to take presents and decorations sent by children's parents, and on to C. for children's party . . . found tables heaped with food, a loaded Christmas tree, and all the village people busy . . . . So many children that games had to be played in relays.

Tuesday. A letter from a friend with a cheque for the parties, so parties now all right, with teachers' gifts, parents' gifts, and this money.

Wednesday. The party at G. had been provided mainly by an evacuated firm . . . many people in the village had given the evacuees party dresses.

Thursday. Got home to find our home Education Committee had sent Christmas cards to every evacuated child. I rang up the village post-office, and they rang up neighbouring offices, and we thought of a plan for delivery. I should sort them and tie them up ; the girls should frank them the next day, and some billeting officers in the bigger villages offered to help.

Friday. After a busy day a lovely peaceful evening of carols, with a speech of thanks to the village by a group of girls.

Saturday. Shopping . . . planning presents . . . 60 parcels, all of which had to be " surprises ".

Sunday. . . . a visit to thank for a very nice extra money gift for the party, which will buy a big orange for every child. A lot of London parents about.

Christmas Day. After breakfast, a day off.

Boxing Day. At 3 o'clock went to the hall. The tables looked pretty, with crackers and lots of food, thanks to a big extra box sent us at the last moment . . . the girls had arranged everything. They waited on themselves, and cleared up—quite miraculously . . . then the fun began . . . uproarious noise . . . they all went home happy. (Abridged from *The Times Educational Supplement*, January 6, 1940.)

It would be difficult to overestimate the value of such magnificently co-operative efforts carried out in such a spirit of good will. One of the speakers in the Commons debate on education on November 16 had prophesied that Christmas would be the zero hour for evacuation. I believe on the contrary that the care lavished on the children in the reception areas did more to establish evacuation on a permanent basis than almost any other single cause.

One of the happiest features of the Christmas period was the cheap travel made available to parents in order that they might visit their evacuated children. Special trains and motor coaches were run throughout December at excursion rates, and proved highly popular. The experiment resulted, no doubt, in a few children being surreptitiously smuggled home, but it certainly gave great joy to many thousands of parents and children. The irruption of entire families, with friends, into the homes of foster-parents sometimes put a heavy strain on the resources and the patience of hostesses, but nevertheless the meeting of blood-parents and foster-parents initiated many friendships that have proved both true and deep.

COMPULSORY ATTENDANCE

Though the Government did not decide until the spring of 1940 to re-enforce compulsory attendance at school, some local authorities anticipated the decision. In December the Middlesex

Education Committee announced that they had reopened a considerable number of schools, and had arranged to reopen all of them as soon as possible. On some of the reopened schools, they said, protective measures against air-raids had not yet been begun ; in such cases they felt that the decision whether they would take the risk of sending their children ought to be left to the parents. But, they added, when the schools had been protected the school attendance by-laws would be enforced.

Much of the Middlesex area was scheduled as neutral. London, being wholly an evacuating area, not unnaturally proceeded more cautiously. In its " emergency schools ", the first of which were opened in December, attendance was voluntary, with the consent and knowledge of the parents, and at the parents' risk. The difficulties to be overcome in the L.C.C. area were appalling. There were estimated to be in it, in December 1939, about 192,000 children of school age, and about 71,000 children, mainly under 5, who were not on the school rolls. Most of this vast host were living in the more congested and dangerous districts in the county ; no authority would have been justified in opening schools unprovided with adequate air-raid shelters in such districts. Large numbers of the school buildings were occupied in whole or in part by civil defence or military personnel ; a survey made towards the end of the year showed that it was then possible to provide school accommodation for children of 11 years old and upwards, and that only on a double-shift basis. In view of the strong criticism made both at the time and later of the position in London, it is only fair that these facts be recorded. Nor did they constitute the only problems ; it must be admitted that in many districts parents were singularly unhelpful.

In the north of England a much higher proportion of children had remained in or returned to the evacuating areas than was the case in the south. The authorities in the northern areas tackled their heavier task with courage and vigour. The Sheffield home service has already been described. Manchester began by opening schools daily for children to receive tutorial guidance from teachers, and clinics for their medical attention and treatment. But these measures, it was quickly apparent, were inadequate ; the city proceeded, therefore, to arrange for full-time reopening of schools. By January 1940, six of the 8 secondary schools and 38 elementary schools were at work ; a further 22 elementary schools began work shortly afterwards.   Leeds had provided by early January 40,000 school places for the children in the city ; Liverpool had opened 20 schools, all provided with shelter accommodation.

These instances indicate the general spirit in which the problem of recuperation was attacked.   In the circumstances it seemed like adding insult to injury for the President of the Board of Education on January 4, 1940, at the annual meeting of the Incorporated Association of Assistant Masters in Secondary Schools, to appeal to local authorities to realize that it was up to them to follow the Government's lead and see that adequate buildings were provided for the education of children in evacuating areas.   Public and professional opinion saw it the other way round ;   it was the local authorities who were leading. There was no evidence of a clear lead from the centre.

This view was stated without any mincing of words in a pamphlet issued by the Workers' Educational Association in January 1940.   " The time has now come," it stated bluntly, " when full educational facilities must be restored."   The whole business of evacuation, it said, should be taken over by the Board of Education and the local education authorities, and the Board should

state publicly that compulsory education, which is still the law of the land, will be enforced as from April 1, 1940, and that by February 1 parents must choose whether they wish their children educated in a reception or in an evacuation area.

The W.E.A. in this pamphlet expressed the opinion of many informed and thoughtful people, especially those in the forefront of the educational battle.   A correspondent to *The Times Educational Supplement* wrote about the same time :

Among the most pressing problems facing educational administrators just now is how to resolve into a coherent whole the odds and ends of schools and staffs that are scattered about the country.   The present state of chaos cannot, obviously, be allowed to continue much longer.   Buildings, accommodation, accessibility, supervision, equipment, curriculum, recruitment, teaching hours, organization—all will have to be reviewed, not on the basis of a temporary makeshift but on the assumption that war conditions may last for years. (*January 20, 1940.*)

Such a review could obviously be made only by the central authority. As has been noted in Chapter I, the Government had in fact a review of the situation in hand at the time, though not nearly so complete and exhaustive a one as this correspondent suggested. In January the Ministry of Health published the results of a statistical survey of the evacuation position. This showed that 59 per cent of the mothers and children evacuated on the outbreak of war had gone home. Of the 260,276 accompanied children (i.e. children below school age) 85 per cent had returned ; of the 166,306 mothers 87 per cent. Of 734,883 schoolchildren evacuated under the Government scheme 43 per cent were back in the evacuating areas. The receiving areas contained only one-sixth of the number of children for whom evacuation had been intended.

On January 31 a strong deputation from the Workers' Educational Association waited on the President of the Board of Education to present the case for the restoration of compulsory attendance at school by Easter. The deputation urged that special measures be taken to recover requisitioned schools from military and civil defence authorities ; that as a matter of urgency a small committee be set up to survey evacuation problems ; and that camps be used to take evacuated persons for short periods from their billets in order to give householders some respite.

Professor R. H. Tawney appealed to the Board to give a lead to the local education authorities by fixing a date after which attendance at school would be compulsory, and thus to put an end to the " partial paralysis " which had overcome the educational system. Mr. W. O. Lester Smith, director of education for Manchester, declared that the proper working of the social services depended on the resumption of normal education, and cited in evidence the fact that in his area, although the school clinics were open, only a quarter of the children who should be attending were in fact doing so. Dr. J. J. Mallon, Warden of Toynbee Hall, described the serious deterioration of discipline among East End children ; some, he said, were going to bed at midnight and getting up at noon.

Meanwhile the Archbishop of Canterbury had put down a motion for a debate on education in the House of Lords. The debate took place on February 7. The Primate in his speech agreed that at the outbreak of war dislocation of the educational system was inevitable, but insisted that this must not continue. Between 400,000 and 500,000 children had had no schooling for five months. They had been running wild in the streets, losing the benefit of the school medical service, of free meals and cheap milk. It was of vital importance that schools be opened in the evacuating areas.

How far, he asked, had the Board of Education been able to persuade the civil defence and military authorities, who had been needlessly grasping, to release commandeered schools ? As regards the safety of children in the towns, if shelters were available on the school premises or near by the children were no more exposed to danger than when they were in the cinema or the streets ; in fact, they were probably safer, because they were under the control of their teachers. The Archbishop hesitated to suggest that evacuation be made compulsory—that was against our tradition and probably impracticable—but he insisted that there must be a greater measure of stability in both the evacuating and the reception areas.

Replying to the debate, the President of the Board of Education, Earl de la Warr, said that it had become quite clear that a further lead from the Government was needed if the children in the towns were to be saved from growing demoralization. He had felt hitherto that it would be dishonest to speak of enforcing attendance when the facilities were not there ; but from now on we must see that every child went to school somewhere. The moment the children could be accommodated in the schools attendance must be enforced. There was no reason to wait for schooling to be full-time, or for every age-group, though full-time schooling should and must be the objective. As a purely interim goal, for those authorities which could do no better, he would regard half-time provision for all children by, say, the beginning of April as an acceptable minimum.

He recognized that even this limited objective would be difficult for some authorities to attain, and that they would need assistance. The Government was prepared to allow authorities to admit children into a school if a start had been made upon the provision of air-raid protection for the building, and if this was likely to be completed within, say, three or four weeks. A circular was being sent to local authorities by the Ministry of

Home Security urging early release for their proper use of school premises at present occupied by civil defence units.

This firm statement was hailed with relief and gratification by local authorities, administrators, teachers, and the general public alike. " Not a moment too soon " and " Now we can really get on with the job " were the normal reactions, though there were not wanting those who pointed out that a Government statement of policy, however resolute, would not by itself necessarily ensure the release of commandeered premises, and would certainly not build air-raid shelters. But it was generally felt that the period of indecision and hesitancy was at last over, and that the complete restoration of the educational system was now only a matter of time.

Circular 1489, issued by the Board of Education the following day, confirmed the impression that the Government were really in earnest. It reiterated that full-time education for all children, including infants—who had been very generally excluded from the reopened schools—was to be the objective. It expressed disapproval of the complete cessation of infant education in many neutral areas, and advised authorities to reopen all schools for which shelter was being provided as quickly as possible, provided the Regional Commissioner did not advise against it. It informed authorities that the Home Office were sending out a circular concerning the employment of children who ought to be at school, offered them every assistance in recovering buildings, and concluded—

It is the Government's policy that no obstacle should be allowed to stand in the way of the restoration of educational conditions to normality, and in no case should authorities acquiesce in a situation in which they cannot fulfil their educational obligations without laying their difficulties before the Board.

A few days later the Minister of Health, Mr. Walter Elliot, announced in the House of Commons a new plan for evacuation differing substantially from, and generally agreed to be much better than, the original one. The Government had come to the conclusion that neither evacuation nor billeting were likely to be entirely successful except when air attack had made both inevitable. Plans were therefore being drawn up by which any congested area could be evacuated immediately it was bombed or in imminent danger of being bombed. Evacuation was still to be voluntary, but parents who desired their children to be sent away in an emergency must register them now for evacuation, and also sign an undertaking to keep them in the reception area until their school party returned. Not less than 36 hours' notice of evacuation would be given, and every effort would be made to inform in advance both evacuating and receiving areas of the destinations to which the children were bound.

The memorandum (Ev.8, accompanying M.O.H. circular 1965) in which the details of this plan were given contained other important emendations of the original scheme. No child was to be sent away suffering from any disease or uncleanliness which ordinarily would require exclusion from school. If medical examination was impossible before evacuation, the sending authority was asked to allow doctors and nurses to accompany the children, to organize examination on arrival. The local authorities were told that steps should be taken to prevent children who were from any cause unsuitable from being lodged in a private house ; those who suffered from any disability or who were specially difficult should be cared for in a hostel. Different types of difficult children should not be placed in the same hostel. More sick bays should be set up. The value of communal meals was again emphasized, and authorities were told that coupons would not be required for rationed foods. Finally, the billeting allowance to householders, which previously had been 8s. 6d., except for a single child or children of 16 and over, in which cases it was 10s. 6d., was advanced to 10s. 6d. for all children of 14 and over—a welcome if inadequate concession.

At the same time the Ministry of Health announced the formation of an Advisory Committee on Evacuation representative of all types of local authorities and of the teachers.

These measures considerably clarified and eased the general situation. The local authorities went to work with a will. The London County Council had by March 1 275 schools open, with accommodation for 85,000 pupils, had made attendance compulsory for all children of 11 and upwards, and fixed Easter as the date at which attendance would become compulsory for children between 8 and 11. By the middle of the month over 300 schools were open, with 60,000 on roll, including some children as young as 5. Manchester had by then 58 schools open, and another 68 rapidly approaching readiness to open. Before the middle of the month all the secondary, technical, and day continuation schools in this city were, with one exception, in operation. By the beginning of April Liverpool had 112 schools working normally, and Birkenhead had announced that full-time education was available for all non-evacuated children in the borough.

In the first week of March the President of the Board of Education was able to say in a broadcast that of nearly 5,000,000 children of school age well over 3,500,000 were receiving full-time education, nearly 700,000 half-time, and many of the rest home service teaching. In the reception areas, where there were 2,000,000 local children, and over 400,000 evacuees, 95 per cent were receiving full-time education. In the evacuating areas the numbers not in school had been reduced during the past few weeks by 70,000 ; in two cases—Smethwick and part of Lancashire—full-time education for all children had been achieved, and 16 other local authorities expected to reach this goal by the end of March.

Among the 400,000 evacuated children receiving full-time education in reception areas were the occupants of the first of the 30 camp boarding schools which have been established during the war. On February 19 the boys of the Beal Central School, Ilford, moved into Kennylands Camp near Reading, and other camps were shortly afterwards occupied. The story of this highly important and most successful educational experiment will be told in Chapter III ; suffice to say here that the camp boarding school has amply justified itself on both educational and sociological grounds.

About the same time the first of the nursery centres for the young children of evacuated mothers were opened. This marked the start of another war-time development which must find a place in Chapter III. Almost all the 20 or more of the earliest centres were established by voluntary bodies, but proposals sponsored by local authorities at Dorking and St. Albans were approved by the Ministry of Health in the early spring of 1940. Another most valuable enterprise—which unhappily has not been so widely developed as it might have been—was that for providing play-centres for schoolchildren under 11. In London, thanks to the initiative of Mrs. G. M. Trevelyan, over 20 centres were in operation in London by the spring of 1940, and were caring for some 8,000–9,000 children a week. The L.C.C.—which eventually was to take over the centres—was at this stage making a grant of £2 a centre for the purchase of equipment. All the rest of the funds were contributed from private sources.

On April 6, Earl de la Warr was succeeded as President of the Board of Education by Mr. Herwald Ramsbotham, who had had previously (1931–5) a lengthy experience (as such experiences go) as Parliamentary Secretary to the Board. His term of office was to prove momentous, for during it the Board prepared and circulated for discussion proposals for post-war reconstruction of the educational system which set everybody in the educational world, and many only indirectly connected with it, also formulating proposals for the education of the future and the machinery necessary to make it effective.

One of Mr. Ramsbotham's first acts as President was to announce that the Chancellor of the Exchequer had agreed to supplement the sum of money made available by the Pilgrim Trust (£25,000) for the encouragement of music and the arts, and any sums similarly forthcoming from other voluntary sources, by an equal contribution from the Exchequer up to a maximum of £50,000 ; and that he was setting up a small council, under the chairmanship of Lord Macmillan, to supervise the administration of the fund. Thus there came into being the Council for the Encouragement of Music and the Arts (C.E.M.A.), which was very shortly to bring comfort and consolation to thousands of blitz-wracked people in air-raid shelters and emergency rest centres, and has since taken good music, good drama, and good pictures all over the country to rejoice hundreds of thousands who hitherto had had little if any opportunity to enjoy them. Something of the story of C.E.M.A., which I believe to be the harbinger of a new form of adult education, is told in Chapter III.

In April the London County Council made a significant move ; they decided that their schools should remain open throughout the normal summer holidays. The teachers' holidays were to be spread over July and August so as to permit half-time education to be given continuously in all the schools. This step was taken so that ground lost, through evacuation, in the routine medical examination might be made up, and that the Government's evacuation scheme, if it had to be put into operation during the normal holiday period, might work as smoothly as possible.   In taking it the L.C.C. set a precedent which has been put to a variety of uses, and which it seems likely will have a permanent influence on school administration.   For one reason or another, school holidays, for the elementary schools at least, have never been quite " normal " since.   At the time it had an important effect in that it kept teachers and children in close and daily contact—an effect that was to prove invaluable later on in the year, when the raids began.

At the same time the Council announced that they were aiming at the provision of full-time education for all London children of school age before the autumn, and made known the details of a report submitted to their Education Committee on the work of London schoolchildren in the reception areas.   This report, the first of a number of such to be made to the committee, shows not only that the London children still remaining in the reception areas (a very large number) had by now settled down to steady work, generally side by side and in co-operation with their " country cousins ", but that the schools were developing a wide variety of new activities and doing much enterprising experimental work.

Farming and gardening are occupying both boys and girls.   One boys' school runs a small chicken farm, another is keeping poultry and pigs.   Other schools are sharing in raising vegetables, poultry, and pigs, and even geese, guinea fowl, and mink.   Gardening classes and lectures for teachers have been organized.   Good use is being made of educational visits.   The pupils of a school in Oxford obtained permission to riddle dredgings from the Thames.   Their finds brought them into touch with the Keeper of the Ashmolean Museum, who was so interested that lectures for children on the " Progress of Man " have been given at the museum by university professors on the museum staff.—*The Times Educational Supplement*, April 20, 1940.

One mixed central school, said the report, had adapted completely for school use a very dilapidated house, modernizing the sanitary arrangements.   A school on the Norfolk Broads was learning to handle a wherry.   In Bedford local and evacuated teachers had drawn up together programmes for the study of local geography and history.   Many schools had expanded their dramatic work, and were making all the necessary scenery and properties.   Films were in great demand ; over 3,500 altogether had been sent out, and the weekly number shown exceeded 300.

Concerts, often with ambitious programmes, were common. Many school magazines were being published.

It was an encouraging picture ; and I can testify from personal visits that it was in no way overdrawn. There were still plenty of bad patches in the reception areas ; there were still far too many children out of school in neutral and in evacuating areas, and too many on " double shift "—owing largely to the prolonged and bitter struggle between the central Government and the local authorities as to who should pay for school air-raid protection—but it may fairly be said that by the early summer of 1940 the State educational system had got pretty well back into its stride.

That is not to say that it was functioning with anything like the smooth efficiency of 1939. Far from it. The picture is rather that of a convalescent from a terrible street accident which has almost proved fatal, and as a result of which the patient, though he has not actually lost the use of any of his limbs or major organs, is still a mass of scars and injuries, but whose stay in hospital and in the convalescent home has toned up his general health, given him new interests, led him to take up new activities, and generally given him a broader, fresher, and more intelligent attitude towards life.

The position as regards attendance at school in the evacuating areas on April 15 was as follows : In 50 out of the 68 areas attendance was compulsory for all children of school age, in 9 areas for some age groups only, and in 6 for some districts or schools only. In the remaining three areas attendance was not compulsory owing to special difficulties (which were said to be in process of being overcome) in providing sufficient adequately protected school accommodation. In elementary schools 657,345 children, or 50·6 per cent, were receiving full-time instruction, 397,058, or 30·6 per cent, half-time instruction, 8,524, or 0·6 per cent, less than half-time instruction, 120,250, or 9·3 per cent, home service tuition, and 115,044, or 8·9 per cent, no instruction. In secondary schools 52,774, or 86·8 per cent of pupils, were receiving full-time instruction, 4,617, or 7·6 per cent, half-time instruction, 206, or 0·3 per cent, less than half-time, and 3,242, or 5·3 per cent, no instruction.

The figures gave no ground for complacency. Well over 100,000 children—nearly 10 per cent of the total number—still out of school after eight months, was a figure calculated to cause the gravest perturbation to any serious-minded citizen. Considered judgment must be that the Government, on whom rested the ultimate responsibility of decision, were unwarrantably slow in making possible the restoration of school facilities. The local authorities, on the other hand, once they were given a clear lead (and often before), showed for the most part a speedy enterprise. The figure of 115,044 elementary schoolchildren receiving no instruction on April 15 was 65,000 less than the figure for April 1, and over 300,000 less than that of January. And of that 115,044 about half were London children, for all of whom school was promised within the following fortnight.

On one count only can the local authorities be blamed. They felt justly aggrieved that they were allowed only 50 per cent grant on air-raid protection for schools, in view of the fact that other comparable installations were receiving 100 per cent. The burden on the rates was admittedly terrific. Nevertheless, they had no right to hold up their shelter schemes, as many of them did, while their representatives haggled with the central authorities. Children's lives were at stake. They should have gone ahead with the building of the shelters, and left the question of cost to be settled later.

In a democracy, the ultimate responsibility lies always with the people. To what extent, if at all, can the people of England be held to blame for the disintegration of the publicly provided system of education, and for the lengthy delay in restoring it to a reasonable state of efficiency? My opinion is that it would be unfair to blame them all.

Evacuation revealed very clearly major defects and deficiencies in our much vaunted democracy. The people of England, as a whole, were shown to be too ignorant, too uneducated to form a reasoned judgment on the situation which arose, and consequently to take the action which that situation demanded. That was not their fault. They had never had the opportunity to train themselves to form such judgment. There was no genuine democracy in our educational system.

Their opinion on the deplorable state of affairs which resulted was never in doubt, and it was expressed as forcefully and in as many ways as possible. They over-simplified the situation— which, of course, they themselves had largely caused—and they refused to rectify it by the simple and only legitimate form of direct action by which it could have been rectified, that of sending their children into the reception areas. In that they were doubtless gravely in error—but who will dare to be the first to cast a stone at them ?

Evacuation threatened their oldest and most tenaciously cherished habits and traditions. The chaos which prevailed in the reception areas following the first evacuation was certainly no inducement to depart from traditions so rooted as to be instinctive. Nor was the absence of enemy air attack—Hitler's cleverest offensive against the British people. The hesitancies and uncertainties of Government policy further confused minds already bewildered and unclear. But the basic reason for the mess the public made of evacuation was, in Dr. Johnson's famous words : " Ignorance, pure ignorance." We were too uneducated to rise to democratic action.

War in Earnest

The extent to which the state system of education had recovered its equilibrium and its strength was very quickly to be proved. Early in May the war suddenly swung west. Denmark and Holland were overwhelmed, Belgium invaded. In a flash the entire French front, so long dormant, sprang to desperate life. The position was quickly realized to be grave, and among other action preliminary measures were at once taken in preparation for evacuation, if need be on the largest scale.

On Saturday, May 11, the Government—now headed by Mr. Winston Churchill—announced that all children were to be recalled to school on the following Monday (the Whitsuntide holidays were in progress), and that until further notice all schools were to remain open on Saturdays. On the following Monday doctors and nurses of the school medical service in evacuation areas began the medical examination of the children registered for sending away. The following week-end some 8,000 children, evacuees from London and the Medway towns, were moved from the east and south-east coast of England into Wales. The coastal districts of Kent and East Anglia were too near the new battle front to serve longer as reception areas.

It is entirely typical of the relationship which had grown up between foster-parents and the children to whom they had given shelter that when about 400 children were sent away from Canterbury all the women who had " mothered " them came to the station to see them off, and many were in tears.

One of the first results of the sudden intensification of the war was the Government's decision in May to raise the age of reservation for schoolmasters from 25 to 30. This was a very grave blow to teaching efficiency, for it meant not only that the schools lost about 11,000 men, including between 2,000 and 2,500 teachers in secondary schools, but that one of the most vigorous sections of the teaching strength was removed *en bloc*. At the height of their physical and mental vigour, these men had yet had sufficient experience in schools to have become mature and balanced teachers. The schools tightened their belts and carried on.

Graver blows were quickly to fall. The epic of Dunkirk was followed by the bombing of Britain. This was at first on a light scale, but in view of the desperate nature of the general situation the Government decided to restart evacuation. On Tuesday, June 11, all the schools in the Greater London area were closed, on Wednesday the children registered for evacuation were medically examined, and on Thursday 30 trains, each bearing about 800 children, left for the South and West of England.

The evacuation of London children continued for six days. There were about 120,000 children registered to go. About 105,000 actually left. But . . . there were 330,000 who were not registered, and who did not go.

The London County Council, after consulting with the Board of Education, took swift action. Their emergency schools were to remain open. A circular from the Board (No. 1514) had intimated that " after evacuation the schools will, as a rule, be closed for instruction ", though it had suggested that some schools provided with full air-raid protection and situated on the fringes, or in sparsely populated districts in evacuation areas, might remain open. Presumably the L.C.C. told the Board that this was just not good enough.

This bold decision had a most salutary effect. It was the more effective because at that very moment the Government made it perfectly clear that they were inflexible in their determination not to make evacuation compulsory. In explanation to the House of Commons, Mr. Malcolm MacDonald, Minister of

Health, said the fact had to be faced that large numbers of parents, even in evacuating areas, would not be separated from their children. Evidence of this came from every region of the country and was " strong, emphatic, and decisive ". If the Government sought to apply compulsion, they would have two alternatives : to allow parents to break the law with impunity, or to take the children to the reception areas and the parents to prison. Neither alternative could be accepted.

EVACUATION OVERSEAS

A curious episode in the history of evacuation, with interesting sociological implications, was initiated in this month by the Government's adoption of the recommendations of the Inter-Departmental Committee on Evacuation Overseas. This committee, which had been set up in May under the chairmanship of Mr. (now Sir) Geoffrey Shakespeare, Parliamentary Under-Secretary for Dominion Affairs, had reported that offers of safe refuge overseas for children of this country had been received from Canada, Australia, New Zealand, the Union of South Africa, and other parts of the Empire, and from private organizations in the United States of America. The Dominions, it was stated, were anxious to receive children of all classes, who would represent a cross-section of the population. It was not intended that the children should be sent to public institutions, but taken into the homes of persons willing to receive and care for them, and every effort would be made to see that children went to homes socially and economically comparable with those they left. Refugee children from Allied countries were to be included in the scheme.

A Children's Overseas Reception Board was set up, with Mr. Geoffrey Shakespeare as chairman, and applications from parents were invited. The scheme had a most mixed reception. A limited number of parents, chiefly among the middle and upper middle classes, welcomed it enthusiastically—in many cases apparently quite uncritically—and hastened to apply. For some little while the Board was dealing with applications at the rate of 7,000 a day. But the bulk of parents held aloof. Not because they did not appreciate the offer ; on the contrary, the liveliest appreciation and gratitude were everywhere expressed. There were two main reasons. The first was that which had helped to make evacuation within the country so limited a success : parents could not bring themselves to part with their children. The second was a typically English reaction : the fear that, since the children would have to remain overseas for the duration of the war, they would cease to be English. Nurtured and educated during impressionable years in a " foreign " land (it was illuminating to observe how many people thus described the Dominions), among people whose attitude to life, whose traditions, customs, habits and standards were different, they would inevitably grow up Canadians, Australians, New Zealanders, and so on, and the land of their birth and parentage would mean nothing to them. Which, of course, was very possible ; what was, and is, debatable is whether it ought to have seemed to matter so much.

Of the other reasons given by parents for rejecting the scheme, quite the most intriguing was that in times to come children would never forgive their parents for having sent them out of the country at its hour of greatest peril, thus robbing them of what was their birthright, the sharing of the common danger, and putting them in a position of enduring inferiority beside those who had remained in the " island fortress ". As events have turned out, the argument has been justified. Would it have been had Britain been overrun, and treated by the Nazis as they have treated France, Belgium, Holland, Denmark or Norway ? Or, as would have been more probable, if our fate had resembled that of Greece, Czechoslovakia, or Poland ? Only when those unhappy lands have been freed, and the refugees from them who have found shelter in Britain or the United States return, can the answer to that question be given.

The remainder of the story of the overseas evacuation scheme can be briefly told. First it was said to be officially postponed, but a " certain number " of children was allowed to go, and during the summer and autumn of 1940 some 3,000 were safely landed at overseas destinations. In August, a " children's ship " was torpedoed, happily without loss of life. Then, on Tuesday, September 17, the *City of Benares*, which included among its passengers 90 evacuee children in the charge of nine adults, was torpedoed in bad weather in mid-Atlantic, and 294 people, including 83 children and seven escorts, were reported missing. Nine days later a boat containing 46 survivors, among whom were six children, was sighted by aeroplane, and brought to land. Nothing was ever heard of the rest of the passengers and crew.

Evacuation overseas was at once closed down, and has never been resumed.

SCHOOLING IN THE BLITZ

The evacuation of children from London was followed at the end of June by that of children from the Medway towns, and from Southampton, Portsmouth, and Gosport. Reports from the reception areas subsequently showed that, though minor adjustments were necessary here and there, on the whole the absorption of the children was carried out with a complete absence of any of the distressing features which had marred the evacuation of the previous September. In the vast majority of cases the newly arrived children were enjoying full-time education on a single-shift basis within a week or so. In Devonshire, for example, of 28,000 children received, only 2,000 had to be placed on double-shift.

Before the storm, the lull. Despite the desperate situation in which Britain found herself, with invasion of her coasts an hourly possibility—an invasion which, had it happened, she would have had to meet almost literally with sticks and staves—the months of July and August 1940 were in the educational field more settled and peaceful than any which had been known since war broke out.

But the first mutterings of the storm which was presently to burst in all its fury upon England were already being heard. The German aeroplanes were over here almost nightly, if not as yet in great force. Industrial areas, in which children were living and going to school, were being ravaged by bombing, if not seriously at least badly enough to cause some dislocation and not a little apprehension. Shelter life had begun, for children as well as for adults.

On August 31, 1940, *The Times Educational Supplement* published the first of a number of articles entitled " Education under Fire ", in which special correspondents who had visited raided areas told how the local education authorities and the schools were carrying on. The first significant fact they revealed was that, though from most of the " target areas " visited not more than a quarter of the children had been evacuated—

There is virtually no evidence anywhere of desire on the part of parents for further evacuation ; and more than one local authority holds it would be unwise to press it. It is still open to parents to register their children for evacuation, but the response is everywhere slight, and even the fall of bombs in residential areas seems to do little to stimulate it. It may be taken for granted that unless compulsory evacuation is ordered, the bulk of the schoolchildren in the present danger zones will stay put.

The correspondents also reported that " children are still being recalled (by their parents) even to districts where the danger is greatest ".

The fact that reception as well as evacuating areas had been bombed was proving a strong deterrent to further evacuation. Parents had realized that shelter protection was far more liberally provided and more efficacious in the towns than in the countryside. And such schools in evacuating areas as had been hit had nearly always been empty at the time.

Education officers, though they realized that intensified bombing might at any time compel large-scale evacuation, were no longer perturbed at the thought. Provided he could arrange a meeting of the teachers, said one, " evacuation was as easy as falling off a log ; he could fix up details in an hour ". Yet he had a particularly difficult area. Another director of education said he was prepared at any moment to " knock up an evacuation plan in 24 hours ". These very men, and others like them, were amply to prove in the coming months that their words were not mere idle boasts. When the heavy raids came they showed beyond dispute that they could translate them into deeds—and very valiant deeds at that.

Their major preoccupation at the time was shelter protection. This is a long, sad story, but the gist of it is that in the first instance the Board of Education sanctioned forms of shelter for schools which many of the local authorities protested were inadequate. A few went beyond mere protest. Ignoring the Board, they provided protection which satisfied the requirements of the much stricter Civil Defence Code. But most simply got on with the job as advised. Then, after months of labour, and very considerable expenditure, just when many of them had succeeded in providing sufficient protection to permit full-time schooling for all children, they were suddenly informed by the Board that their schools were to be closed unless the shelter protection came up to Civil Defence Code standards.

The consequences of this decision were in some cases staggering. One south coast town, for example, found its school accommodation cut from 17,000 to 6,000. Other authorities were in even worse plight ; their school places were reduced by three-quarters. Not to mention the fresh expenditure with which they were faced—an expenditure in some cases approaching the total annual disbursement of the authority for all purposes in pre-war days.

A second problem was the retention of the original categories of evacuating, neutral, and reception areas. These had in many places become a menace, in others meaningless. The Germans refused to respect them : if they discovered an aerodrome or a factory in a reception area they bombed it. Some evacuating areas remained unscarred while their receiving areas got heavy raids. Further, many small authorities were finding the financial and administrative strain severe almost to breaking-point. Some education offices had had to evacuate, and one authority at least found itself in the anomalous position of being geographically sited among the children for whom it was responsible, yet with no control over them, this having passed to the receiving authority.

The tribulations of officials, however, seldom excite much sympathy. They are mentioned here because the grand work which these education officers and their staffs did in these months, and the physical dangers and mental strain they cheerfully underwent, deserve to be given far greater recognition than has hitherto been accorded them. Without their devoted and brilliant service the English educational system could never have been held together—which means, as I hope has been made clear, that the children of England would have suffered irreparable harm. For education during these first eighteen months of war came to mean infinitely more than the provision of schooling ; in reception and evacuating areas alike it came to mean something approaching the whole care of the child.

Thanks to the efforts lavished on their behalf, the children in the blitzed areas showed no sign of deterioration in health, but rather the reverse. Much credit for this is due to the personnel of the school medical service ; one authority declared they had never done so much or such good work as during the previous six months. To enable children to get sufficient sleep in spite of night alerts schools were opened at 10 or 10.30 a.m., or even later, instead of 9. Bombing and alerts had generally little effect on school attendance ; a few children overslept, that was all. Air-raid drill in schools had been so perfected that parents wrote to say that it was the children who told the adults what to do in a raid. During daytime alerts lessons were conducted in the school shelters, and enterprising teachers devised ingenious techniques for these abnormal conditions. In short, the general report was " business as usual "—or as near usual as possible, with nobody finding any reason why it should not be so.

It must be added, however, that a correspondent wrote in *The Times Educational Supplement* in September 1940 that while most teachers would endorse the general conclusion that schools in raided areas were determined to carry on as normally as possible, not a few would regard it as somewhat optimistic to assume that the approach to normality was such as " makes no difference ". In one town elementary school attendance had dropped by 30 per cent. The raids had aggravated a tendency to absenteeism caused by a general belief that school shelters were inadequate and that attendance at school was optional. Hours of attendance were also affected ; schools began effective work at 10.45 a.m., and closed at 3.40. Even these shortened hours were interrupted by alerts and raids. As a result the balance of the curriculum had been upset, the principle of the three R's become a casualty, and the children's powers of attention impaired.

This correspondent questioned whether in raided areas " normality " should be regarded as the ideal. Should not schooling be orientated to the impact of the war ? Changes in the content and rationale of education were necessary and were bound to come about. In this he was perfectly right ; and his article was in many parts profoundly prophetic of changes that were later to be worked out—often unconsciously—in the schools.

The work of the school medical service during these months deserves at least a chapter to itself. One day I hope someone

will write a book about it.   It was carried on under all sorts
of handicaps and restrictions, and it received much criticism but
little praise.   In August 1940 its operation was made even more
difficult than previously.   Doctors and dentists had been removed
from the list of reserved occupations, and a number had already
been transferred from the school medical service to the fighting
Forces, and more were expected to go.   To meet the situation
the Board of Education suggested that neighbouring authorities
might temporarily pool their staffs.   This, *The Times Educational
Supplement* commented—

looks all right on paper, and will doubtless work well enough in
some areas, but all who have knowledge of the more rural and remote
areas of the country must fear lest the distances to be covered, the
impediments to rapid travelling, and the greatly increased number
of children in these areas may not combine to defeat any such
arrangement.

The Board also suggested a review of the work of school
nurses, to ensure that they were engaged only on such skilled
work as their training merited.   Even with these modifications,
however, they were compelled to admit that the new situation
might necessitate the temporary curtailment, or even in some
areas the cessation, of the service.   Miraculously, it hardly anywhere did.   The school medical service, like the schools, tightened
its belt and carried on.

In September 1940 bombing began in real earnest.   On the
7th the long cruel agony of London started with a savage raid
upon the East End.   On the 14th *The Times Educational Supplement* wrote :   " Upon the teacher, as guide, counsellor, and
instructor of the young, devolves the gravest responsibility in this
hour of Britain's crisis."   No words are adequate to describe
how magnificently the teachers of England upheld that responsibility in 1940 and 1941.   The country owes them a debt of
gratitude which can never be adequately repaid.

In London the educational situation became at once in-
describably fluid.   It varied enormously as between districts,
and from day to day.   In the East End, where the devastation
was tragic and immense, emergency schools, children's play
centres, and nurseries carried on wherever possible :   but attendances were small, and the authorities wisely did not attempt
to enforce compulsory attendance.   They could hardly have

done so. There was a large amount of evacuation, much of it private ; thousands of families, rendered homeless, were living in the emergency centres opened for their benefit : thousands of others were living virtually day and night in air-raid shelters. As the schools emptied, teachers volunteered in hundreds for service in the emergency centres. Here, working anything up to 24 hours a day, they did an invaluable job in a manner worthy of the highest praise. Elsewhere in London there were districts in similar desperate plight ; but others were only moderately ravaged, others again hardly touched or not touched at all. Teachers were given the widest freedom to modify the school curriculum and activities according to the situation : and almost everywhere they used their liberty with wise discretion.

The work of the educational settlements was beyond praise. Overnight they became emergency rest and feeding centres. They organized the collection and distribution of clothes and comforts, kept boys' and girls' clubs, children's play centres, and nurseries going, cared for casualties, comforted the bereaved, arranged evacuation, provided A.R.P. and A.F.S. personnel, constituted themselves inspectors of shelter conditions (which were in some cases deplorable), and day and night combed the streets to seek and succour the destitute. " No wonder ", as one observer wrote, " the people in their districts regard them with a love, almost a reverence, that is touching beyond words in its expression." Mary Ward, Dockland, Bernhard Baron, Toynbee, Oxford House, Clubland—to mention but a few—these are names that will live long in the grateful memories of Londoners.

On September 24 the Board of Education issued circular 1526 urging the maintenance of evening classes in technical schools and evening institutes. There was in this circular a note of determination well in keeping with the spirit prevalent throughout the education service.

One thing is certain . . . that the education service, like other public services, should use every endeavour within the limits imposed by war conditions to keep in being its contribution to the normality and stability of civil life.

The Board recalled the invaluable assistance rendered by all types of evening schools during the previous winter. But, they said, " The situation now confronting us is very different ; the difficulties and hazards are greater." Yet even these, they maintained, could be overcome, though in some areas " any arrangements made must be liable to be interrupted and even to be temporarily suspended ". Earlier hours of opening and closing, shorter meetings, the provision of canteen and lavatory facilities, modification of courses to enable fewer attendances to be made weekly, the spreading of facilities over a larger number of smaller centres, interchange of teachers, supervision of work rather than class teaching—all these were suggested as possible adaptations which might help to defeat the blitz.

Conditions in many areas were to prove too grim to permit evening meetings, however modified, to continue. But the evening schools were not to be beaten. When the evenings proved too dangerous, they met on Saturday, and on Sunday too. Nothing could stop them.

It was in this circular that the Board first referred to the fact that " work is now in progress in most of the major technical institutions directly related to our war effort ". The story of that work, involving in some cases, as the Board said, " a three-shift system covering the whole 24 hours ", cannot yet be told in full ; but some account of it is given in Chapter III.

In October the government facilities for the evacuation of mothers and children were extended to cover the entire Greater London area, and it was announced that from any part of the area mothers with children of school age and under could be evacuated two days after registration. The Government would provide the transport, find the billets, and pay lodging allowances at the rate of 5s. a week for the mother, 5s. for each child over 14, and 3s. each for those under. Boots, clothes and mackintoshes would be supplied to those who could not afford to buy them. Travel vouchers would be given to those who wished to make private arrangements. The Ministry of Health and the Board of Education followed this announcement up on October 18 with circulars (Nos. 2178 and 1528 respectively) giving detailed suggestions as to how evacuation, and life in reception areas, could be made successful. For weeks an intensive campaign for evacuation was carried on in London. Every district was canvassed, street by street and house by house, by voluntary workers, while touring loudspeaker vans daily urged people to go. The authorities were in fact seriously perturbed—

and with good reason—at the large number of children remaining in London. Only 29,000 unaccompanied schoolchildren had left since September 7. There were 125,000 remaining in the L.C.C. area alone, 279,000 in the Greater London area. The position with regard to younger children was equally grave.

Despite all efforts the children stayed, presenting a problem that was always serious and at times profoundly disturbing. Though conditions in the public shelters were improved, no amount of ingenuity could make shelter life healthy for young children ; and the children were in the shelters night after night, week in, week out. Some 40,000 young children were evacuated with their mothers, but the majority of the parents remained obdurate, and the Government would not proceed to extreme measures.

Somehow, the children survived, and, incredible though it may seem, as yet no tests have proved any serious physical or mental deterioration.

The dullest and least understanding of parents in the heavily bombed areas [wrote *The Times Educational Supplement* on November 9] must by now be realizing the magnitude of the physical risks to which they expose their children by retaining them, and something at least of the dangers to health and morals of the life they thus compel them to lead. They—like a correspondent who writes to us on the subject with not unnatural indignation—know that their boys and girls spend their days roaming the streets or mooning idly at home, and that they are growing progressively more dirty, more aimless, and more insubordinate. They daily see them, as our correspondent puts it, " emerge from shelters pale and tired, a dead look on their faces, with apathy and hopelessness in their expression ". They know, because they share it, the dreary blanket-laden trail through the streets to the Tube or the tunnel or the arches or the basement each evening (or afternoon), and the still drearier trail each morning back to a cold and cheerless home—or to a pathetic pile of rubble and rubbish that was recently a home. They know, because they send them, that many of these children " sit for hours on end propped up against the walls of Tube stations ", or railway arches, or dark underground retreats, " keeping the family place for the night ". They know, because they see it, the aimless way in which their children spend the long, empty hours in the shelters, poring over cheap papers, playing endless games of cards, eating odd scraps of meals, talking, larking, or just " mucking about ". They know only too well that in many a shelter it is impossible to sleep before midnight, and that after that time sleep is often but a restless passing from one uneasy doze to another.

Every word of that description is true. I saw it all, every week throughout that winter. Yet the children survived ; and today look none the worse. The English are a tough people.

The growing disquiet felt among teachers at the conditions obtaining in London and other congested areas was expressed in a strongly worded manifesto issued by the National Union of Teachers in November. Education must go on, was the theme of the document, which laid down the minimum conditions rendering this possible. Children must have reasonable safety. Evacuation had abundantly justified itself, but it was clear that nothing short of compulsion would result in the removal of all the children from the danger zones. Adequate shelter must be provided. In no type of area—evacuating, neutral, or receiving —was it at present adequate. Heat and ventilation must be provided, and arrangements for food if necessary. Too much school time was spent in the shelters because there was no distinction made between an " alert " and an " alarm " ; an " imminent danger " warning should be devised. There was no good reason for curtailing the aggregate daily number of school hours. The dispersal of children from school to their homes during an alert was not a satisfactory expedient. Every effort should be made to maintain the education service in heavily bombed areas ; if need be, schools should be set up in rest centres. The manifesto concluded with a fully deserved tribute to the rank and file of the teachers, and added, " The executive have at the present time only one policy, that of service to the nation."

The N.U.T. manifesto was followed by similar expressions of concern. The National Association of Labour Teachers sent a deputation to the Board of Education to point out that thousands of children were without schooling, and thousands more on part-time ; that classes were growing in size, and children losing great stretches of school time through alerts. In December the Workers' Educational Association published a manifesto expressing its serious perturbation at the continued disorganization of the educational system, and asked the President of the Board to receive a deputation.

Certain measures, said the manifesto, were urgently needed. The War Cabinet should review the whole situation. The Board should call for full reports on the position in evacuation, neutral, and reception areas. Attendance should be compulsory. As this depended on adequate shelter protection, the present provision of shelters should be reviewed. Medical and social services should be fully maintained and where necessary strengthened. Many more nursery schools and centres were needed. The Board should consult with L.E.A's and teachers about the best methods of carrying out these measures and consider setting up an Advisory Committee to meet monthly.

The National Union of Women Teachers, in a memorandum sent to the President and the local education authorities, declared that it had become a matter of urgency that the improvisation which appeared to have characterized the war-time educational service should give place to careful planning for the restoration of compulsory education for all children.

On December 3, the London County Council announced that, after consultation with the Board of Education, they had decided to enforce the law of compulsory attendance for all those children not evacuated from their area. On December 7 representatives of the N.U.T. were informed by the President of the Board of Education that the Board had undertaken a survey of the present position in education in order to make a more accurate appraisement than had hitherto been possible of the existing situation and its needs. On December 10, in answer to a Parliamentary question from Mr. C. G. (now Lord) Ammon, the President announced that the Board proposed to pay grants at the rate of 100 per cent of expenditure incurred by local education authorities on the construction and equipment of school shelters under contracts entered into on or after October 19, 1940, on the understanding that shelters so aided should, where required, be made available for the use of the general public after school hours.

These decisions may be said to mark the end of the second period of hesitant policy. It was a period in no way comparable in gravity with the first, that between September 1939 and February 1940, yet there were moments when it appeared as though something approaching the earlier paralysis might again supervene. They were moments only, and they were largely experienced only in London, which presented on account of its size and diffuseness, and the persistence of the air attacks to which it was subjected, a problem as unique in its difficulty as in its range.

When their times of testing came, Coventry, Birmingham, Liverpool, Manchester, Sheffield, Southampton, Portsmouth, and a score of other areas dealt swiftly and effectively with their more compact but not less trying problems. The story of the help given in the organizing and running of emergency services in Sheffield is illustrative of the work done by teachers and members of the administrative staffs of education departments in scores of cities and towns.

On the night of December 12–13, 1940, Sheffield was heavily raided. On the morning of December 15, the City's Emergency Committee asked the education department to organize an emergency service—the pre-arranged service having been badly dislocated through the bombing of essential buildings. The director of education, after making preliminary arrangements, at 3 p.m. the same day broadcast a message asking all teachers and others in the service of the education committee to report for duty. By 6 p.m. 500 had reported and been placed at action stations. Throughout the evening and night hundreds more poured in, despite the fact that the city was again being severely bombed. Between midnight and 6 a.m. the following morning nine new emergency rest and feeding centres had been staffed and opened. By 3 p.m. on December 16, 1,500 people in the service of the education committee were at work, and the education department had become an integral part of the city's civil defence scheme.

It had undertaken as its task the organization and staffing of all the emergency rest and feeding centres and the rebilleting of the homeless. The director of education became controller of the headquarters staff, responsible for the staffing of the service and for dealing with records, reports and communications to and from rest centres, for health and sanitation in the centres, and for any necessary repairs. In each of the six areas into which the city was divided there was an area adviser, responsible for the centres staffed by teachers, a voluntary personnel officer responsible for those staffed by voluntary workers, and a resident supplies officer in charge of the area cooking and equipment depot.

All this had been effected by a simple and logical allocation of functions which ensured that workers undertook in the emergency tasks comparable with those they performed in normal times. The office staff of the department became the head-quarters' staff, the school medical service dealt with all questions affecting health, the buildings branch with repairs, and the teachers with personal needs.

For weeks the education office remained continuously open. A card index system for the registration of people passing through the rest centres was devised which enabled their whereabouts to be known at almost a moment's notice. Immediate information was available to those in the centres about arrangements for more permanent accommodation, for repair of their homes and the care of their furniture, concerning the whereabouts and safety of relatives and friends, and where to go to replace lost documents of value. Rebilleting was effected swiftly and continuously; and meanwhile all the homeless in the centres received every day three good meals—two hot and one cold.

In spite of the almost overwhelming pressure of this work, the educational interests of the children were never for one moment forgotten. On the contrary, the emergency scheme was so devised as to give them a first priority. As the numbers of people in the rest centres diminished, the " first-line " centres, which were staffed by teachers, were closed down, and the homeless concentrated in the " second-line " centres run by voluntary workers. By January 3, 1941—less than three weeks from the establishment of the emergency service—it was possible to arrange that between that date and January 20 all teachers should have a week's leave, while the schools which had been used as centres were cleaned, disinfected, and repaired. On January 20 the schools were reopened, and by February 7, 59,695 pupils were in attendance. Of these 45,800 were receiving full-time instruction.

Space precludes mention of comparable feats in other places. One day the full story will have to be told. It will show that, not only had the physical recuperation of the publicly provided system of education been effectively completed by the end of 1940, but that the education departments of the local authorities were by that time in such complete working order that, in spite of increasing shortage of staff, they were able successfully to undertake a wide variety of tasks outside their own province and without deleterious effect upon their proper work. Not without strain, of course; but certainly without cracking. Though intensive bombing continued until well into 1941, it could no more break the State system of education than it could stop the flow of production from the British factories. Nor—and this is even more significant—could it prevent education from passing to the offensive. From approximately the end of 1940 educational reform, the planning of a new order in English education, was to become a main preoccupation of English educationalists.

CHAPTER III

ADAPTATION

A SEA CHANGE

In the preface to this book I have given it as my belief that the old order in education—the order which existed before the outbreak of the war—" is dead ", and that " the new one is being shaped before our eyes, in part deliberately, but more, as yet, by circumstance ". To some those statements will seem rash ; to others, untrue. In this chapter I offer what appears to me conclusive evidence that both are strictly and literally true. I confine myself in the main to a recital of facts, to descriptions of a dozen major developments in the field of English education which have come about during the war, as the direct result of war conditions, and which are being very largely if not entirely shaped by those conditions. Such deductions as I venture to draw are few and tentative. Let the facts speak for themselves.

These developments are treated under the following headings : War-time Nurseries, School Meals, Camp Boarding Schools, The Service of Youth, Pre-Service Training, School Harvest Camps, The Registration of Young Persons, Technical Education, University Education, Adult Education, and Curricular Trends. They are treated in that order, and not in the chronological order of their coming into prominence, so as to give the reader a survey of the educational field in the normal perspective, that is, from the earliest years of the pupil's life through childhood and adolescence to maturity. The space that can be accorded to each development is slight, and the treatment is therefore of necessity sketchy in the extreme. To do full justice to any one a volume of some size would be required.

Before beginning the survey, I would particularly emphasize one fact which seems to me of the utmost importance. *Not a single one of these developments is wholly new.* Powerful as has been the stimulus which total war has given to educational thought in this country, in the realm of educational practice it has as yet brought into being no absolutely new form or institution. In the realm of theory I believe we have already begun to reach new territory. I believe that in our practice we are on the verge of new inventions, but so far (to the best of my knowledge ; it is impossible to be certain when so much is happening and information is so hard to come by) all we have done is to develop and expand forms of educational provision which were in existence before but which were underdeveloped—in some instances griev-ously so. Up to the present, all we can say in respect of whatever of permanent value has been effected is that war has compelled us to do what in peace we were content to neglect.

But—and the importance of this must neither be overlooked nor underestimated—in this process of enforced development and expansion we are beyond question discovering new ways of approach to old problems, new techniques and new methods of learning and teaching ; and there is good reason to hope that some of these discoveries (with others yet to come) will serve to point the way to the invention of new forms and institu-tions. I believe, for example, that the " school " in which the adolescent of 50 or even 25 years hence (or it may be earlier) will learn will be an utterly different place from the senior or secondary school of today ; and that we may within a decade or so be using forms of adult education which are as yet scarcely advanced beyond the embryonic stage.

The developments I here describe are, I believe, stepping stones to a new order in education. Stepping stones : not necessarily foundation stones. Some of them should prove the latter as well ; but not all. These developments have been forced upon us by circumstance ; and some of them clearly must not be allowed to continue into the new era in their present form. We must pick, and choose, and shape them ; or, however much we plan reform, our new order will be made for us by circumstance. That must not be.

To be able to pick and choose and shape we must first analyse and assess. To have attempted to do that here at any length would have meant overflowing my limits of space very con-siderably. It would have demanded a far fuller factual survey than I have room for, and critical examination of many aspects of change I have been compelled to pass over in silence. All this chapter pretends to do is to present brief factual outlines, with a few suggestions as to points which it seems to me should be carefully watched and closely followed up. Others more competent than I will, I trust, not be lacking to do the necessary research, analysis, and assessment.

WAR-TIME NURSERIES

The Education Act of 1876 laid it down that it was the duty of the parent of every child between the ages of 5 and 14 to cause that child to receive efficient elementary instruction. It has been ever since a main effort of educational reformers to get the upper age limit raised. No attempt to enforce compulsion below the lower age limit has been seriously pressed. It would not be today. But for many years increasing emphasis has been laid by psychologists and educationists alike on the necessity for making adequate provision to meet the educational needs of the child below 5.

To England belongs the honour of having invented a form of education capable of doing this. Margaret Macmillan, one of the very greatest among educational pioneers, began experimenting with the provision of nursery school facilities in Bradford during the closing years of the nineteenth century. In 1911 she opened, at Deptford in Kent, the first fully-fledged nursery school. It was an immediate and overwhelming success ; and so, almost without exception, has been every nursery school since.

The war of 1914–18 underlined the extreme value of the work being done by Miss Macmillan and her collaborators, and in 1918 local authorities were given permissive powers to provide nursery facilities of two distinct kinds and in two different ways. The Fisher Education Act (Section 19(i)) gave to local education authorities for elementary education power to make arrangements for—

(*a*) Supplying or aiding the supply of nursery schools (which expression shall include nursery classes) for children over two and under five years of age, or such later age as may be approved by the Board of Education, whose attendance at such a school is necessary or desirable for their healthy physical and mental development ; and (*b*) attending to the health, nourishment, and physical welfare of children attending nursery schools.

It was further enacted (19(ii)) that, although nursery schools were not ranked as public elementary schools, the Board of Education could pay grants in aid of them provided they were open to inspection by the local education authority, and that the authority were appropriately represented on the body of managers. These sections were re-enacted in the consolidating Education Act of 1921.

In 1918 also the Maternity and Child Welfare Act empowered local health authorities to establish crèches and day nurseries for children from birth to the age of 5, and to claim grants in aid from the Ministry of Health.

The way seemed set for a great advance. The trail had been blazed, the need recognized, and the powers to provide granted. Yet to such a slight extent were these wide and beneficent powers used, and so little pressure was exerted upon local authorities, either by the central Government or public opinion, to use them, that in 1939—twenty-one years after they had been granted—there were in England and Wales only 115 nursery schools (and of these only about half were provided by local authorities), with accommodation for fewer than 10,000 children, and only 104 day nurseries (again, many of them provided by voluntary effort) with accommodation for about 3,700 children. By far the largest provision which had been made was of nursery classes ; there were in these upwards of 170,000 children.

Thus all told there was provision for less than 200,000 children, out of a total number considerably exceeding 2,000,000 ; and nearly nine-tenths of that provision was of an inferior or substitute kind. For the nursery school is the only institution which can offer to the home a co-operation that will enable the latter to meet the whole needs of the young child. The day nursery, by the terms of its reference, does not go beyond meeting physical needs. The nursery class at its rare best approaches nursery school standards : at its not infrequent worst it is little better than a parking place for children. In general it is much behind the nursery school in respect of staffing, amenities, and space. Its sole distinctive virtues are that it is cheap and easy to provide —hence its popularity with local authorities. But these virtues do not necessarily connote educational value.

Evacuation quickly drew public attention, in two different ways, to the fact that welfare and educational facilities for children below school age were grossly inadequate and very ill distributed. The state of some of the children taken to the reception areas provided first-hand, and shocking, evidence of the results of ignorance and neglect. Secondly, evacuated mothers who had been accustomed to make use of welfare clinics, crèches, nursery schools or nursery classes found to their dismay that such provision was non-existent, and often almost unheard of, in the districts to which they had come.

It was not long before sporadic efforts were being made to remedy deficiencies brought literally home in embarrassing fashion. The day nurseries and nursery schools in evacuating areas had on the outbreak of war been for the most part transferred to the reception areas, and converted into residential institutions. Places were found in some of these for children in need of special care and attention. But it quickly became clear to people in many parts of the country that this could meet but the most infinitesimal fraction of the need. Voluntary effort, and one or two local authorities—St. Albans and Dorking were notable examples—set out to make further provision.

The Government saw that something must be done. In January 1940 a joint Circular from the Minister of Health and the President of the Board of Education urged upon local authorities in reception areas the establishment for evacuated children of nursery centres, which it described as " something between a day nursery and a nursery school ". Two alternative methods were suggested : a large group of more than 20 children in a house under qualified or partly qualified supervision, or a quite small group under a warden, supervisor, or teacher, accommodated in a large room. The second alternative was considered the more practicable. The centres should be for children between 2 and 5 only, and open for the same sessions as an infant school. Unless communal meals were provided near at hand the children were to return to their billets for the midday meal.

The scheme hung fire. There were many obstacles to rapid progress. The dual control at the centre proved fruitful of little but delay : the administrative direction suggested for the localities —by a committee representative of the education authority, the welfare authority, the reception authority, and the Women's Voluntary Services—seemed to many cumbrous if not unworkable ; premises and equipment were hard to come by ; the children to be provided for diminished in numbers through the steady return of the evacuated to their homes ; and there was often local dissatisfaction, productive of much delay, at the restriction of the scheme to the children of evacuated mothers. All this in addition to that perennial conservatism which inclines the English to look askance at any new institution, especially one which seems to touch their responsibility for their children.

Even the heavy bombing of London and other congested areas which began in the autumn of 1940, and which revealed with stark clarity the imperative necessity for getting large numbers of young children out of the unsafe and unhealthy conditions in which they were living, failed to stimulate a provision which would have encouraged many more mothers than did to evacuate children below school age. Incredible though it may seem, it was at the time and for long afterwards virtually impossible to evacuate these young children under the government scheme unless they were accompanied by a parent or guardian. Equally incredible, but also true, was the widespread refusal of householders in the reception areas who had spare accommodation to allow this to be used to house nursery centres.

By December 1940, nearly twelve months after the issue of the joint circular, only six nursery centres had been opened in reception areas. Perhaps ten more were in preparation. Such was the response to the Government's appeal that " action should be taken as speedily as possible ".

In 1941 the Ministry of Labour came into the field, and things began to move. Married women were urgently needed in employment, and if they had young children and were without domestic help they obviously could not offer their services. In June a joint circular from the Ministry of Health and the Board of Education swept away many of the difficulties and complications blocking the establishment of nursery facilities for young children. It laid down that nurseries might be established in any area where they were wanted ; that their sole purpose was to meet the needs of all children in war-time, and that no reference was to be made to whether these were local or evacuated children or to the type of employment in which the mothers were engaged. The total cost of establishing and maintaining the nurseries would be met by the Ministry of Health, and one local authority, the Maternity and Child Welfare Authority, was to be made responsible for all special war-time arrangements for the provision of nurseries for children under 5.

In spite of various subsequent addenda to this scheme,

including a 100 per cent grant from the Ministry of Health in aid of special nursery classes reserved for the children of women workers, it cannot be said that the progress which has been made is spectacular. But it has certainly been substantial. By the end of February 1943 there were in operation some 1,200 war-time nurseries, with accommodation for 51,000 children, and a further 446 nurseries, providing for 15,200 children, were being planned. A month previously it had been recorded that there were 570 special nursery classes for the children of women workers, attended by 20,700 children, and that a further 248 classes were being planned. 110,000 children under 5 were attending classes in public elementary schools.

Altogether, including the children in the 70 nursery schools still functioning in England and Wales, and those in the 415 residential nurseries in operation early in 1943, the total number of children below the age of 5 who were at that time enjoying some form of nursery provision possibly exceeded 200,000. There appears little doubt that by the end of the. war the number will be considerably greater.

Even so, numerically this does not represent an outstanding advance on the position in 1939, when at the lowest estimate not far short of 200,000 pre-school children were in attendance at crèches, day nurseries, nursery schools and classes. "The war-time growth of nursery facilities", said *Planning* [1] in March 1943, "has still only scratched the surface of the problem to be solved". That is only too true. Nevertheless, there has been real progress in two respects. The emphasis in the provision for the young child has shifted from the nursery class to the nursery, and, more important, the idea that there should be a nursery stage in education has become widely accepted. It should be more so now that the Government have included the sufficient provision of nursery schools as an item in their post-war policy. If we take full advantage of the best possibilities inherent in this progress, we shall find that they constitute a solid and sound foundation for a very great advance.

Admittedly, many of the war-time nurseries are in the nature of makeshift improvisations. But there are some which in all respect are almost indistinguishable in excellence from nursery

[1] *Planning.* A broadsheet issued by P.E.P. (Political and Economic Planning), No. 203.

schools, and others which approach more or less closely to nursery school standards. These good war-time nurseries are doing much to popularize the idea of a nursery stage in education, and are opening the eyes of numerous parents to the high value of the nursery school.

Admittedly, too, this war-time growth has developed in a way which has already caused administrative complications and may in the future cause more. Broadly speaking, the procedure at present is as follows :

> . . . the initiative in any area is taken by local officers of the Ministry of Labour. In consultation with them, the maternity and child welfare authority, the local education authority, together with the Ministry of Health's regional staff, Board of Education inspectors and local voluntary bodies, all collaborate to work out a local plan. (*Planning*, No. 203, March 16, 1943.)

The dominant partner is the Ministry of Health. Educationists have all along protested against this, regarding the provision of nursery facilities for the young child as essentially an educational matter. There is no space here to tell of the persistent but almost fruitless fight which has been put up by the Nursery School Association, and other bodies, to have the responsibility for the welfare and education of the pre-school child vested in the Board of Education. But the following excerpt from an article contributed to *The Times Educational Supplement* on June 14, 1941, puts the position in a nutshell :

> Those who have watched the gradual development of the Nursery School movement, who have seen the transformation of infant classes and the introduction of nursery classes, may well ask what will be the consequences of this transfer of responsibility from the Education to the Health Department.
> The Ministry of Health has a statutory obligation to care for the physical welfare of children up to the age of 5. . . . The Board of Education has no statutory obligation to provide for children under school age ; its duties are permissive. . . . Since the outbreak of war the Board of Education has tended to withdraw its protection from these children for whom it has no direct responsibility.

Since that date the Board of Education, under the Presidency of Mr. R. A. Butler, has given some evidence of desire to come back into the field of pre-school care. In March 1942 there was set up at the Board a new division to take over administrative responsibility for the work in connexion with war-time nurseries and other facilities for the children of women in employment —work previously dealt with by their elementary and medical branches. This division also deals with the recruitment and training of staff for war-time nurseries and nursery classes. The division does not yet appear to be a very strong one, but its existence does at least mean that should the Board eventually take over—as it should—responsibility for a nursery stage in education, the nucleus of the machinery for administration will be already there. Meanwhile, the Ministry of Health remains in charge of the war-time nurseries.

The general feeling today is that children under the age of 2 should remain the responsibility of the Ministry of Health and the Maternity and Child Welfare authorities, but that the Board and local education authorities should take over full responsibility for all children from the age of 2 onwards. This would appear to be quite the most happy arrangement ; but there will be some stiff battles (not altogether confined to government departments) before it is achieved.

School Meals

Local education authorities were empowered to provide meals for children in attendance at public elementary schools as long ago as 1906. The intention of the original and subsequent Acts was chiefly to secure the better nutrition of necessitous children. For any children " unable by reason of lack of food to take full advantage of the education provided for them ", the authorities, after having " ascertained that funds other than public funds are not available or are insufficient in amount to defray the cost of food furnished in meals under this Act ", were empowered to " spend out of the rates such sum as will meet the cost of the provision of such food ".[1] But from the beginning it was legally permissible for the authorities to supply also meals to children on payment.

In spite of the fact that the principle of meeting necessity was generously interpreted by the Board to include all children who might be held to benefit from a school meal, the total provision of meals, free or on payment, remained small. Mr.

[1] Education Act, 1921, Section 84.

F. Le Gros Clark, Chairman of the Children's Nutrition Council, has stated [1] that

. . . it is probable that in the years before the present war there were few of the school days on which more than 3 per cent of the children were being supplied with a midday meal at their schools, whether free or for payment. At least 70 per cent of these were receiving free meals, as being necessitous ; and 40 per cent were concentrated in 24 large industrial centres.

Three per cent would mean approximately 150,000 children. The average figures, as will be seen later, were lower than this.

The Report of the Committee on Evacuation (the Anderson report) published in July 1938 recognized that in any evacuation scheme " large-scale plans for communal feeding will have to be included ". In May 1939 the Ministry of Health, in Memo. Ev. 4, in making suggestions as to how householders who had taken children as guests might be relieved of some of the burden (" inconvenience ", the Ministry called it) of their care, said :

It will undoubtedly make a great difference to householders in the performance of their own household duties if arrangements can be made in the district which will relieve them of the responsibility of providing a meal for the children in the middle of the day.

The suggestion was seconded by the Board of Education in circular 1469, issued at the same time.

It might have been expected that, as local education authorities had long possessed full powers to provide communal meals for schoolchildren, the responsibility for making such feeding arrangements for evacuated children would have been handed over to them. Not so does officialdom work. In the Ministry of Health Memo. Ev. 5, issued on July 28, 1939, is to be found the following astonishing passage :

It is expected that it will often be desirable to relieve householders by organizing communal meals, and it is suggested that the organization of these meals is a matter which could with advantage be discussed between the local authority, the local education authority, and voluntary organizations such as the Women's Voluntary Services. Where school canteens can be provided, *it may be possible* (my italics) to provide midday meals for the billeted children by the extension of the existing arrangements. Where no school canteens are practic-

[1] *The School Canteen, 1939-40.* Published from 6, East Common, Harpenden, Herts.

able the provision of midday meals *may be made directly by the billeting authority.* (Again, my italics.)

The passage is an illuminating commentary on the regard in which the Ministry of Health then held the Board of Education and its partners the local education authorities. A department with 33 years' practical experience of providing communal meals *might* possibly be able to extend its arrangements ; an improvised and totally untried authority, to be called into being only in the event of an emergency, certainly *would* be able to organize arrangements for a service of which few of its personnel had had any previous experience !

The Ministry blandly informed local authorities in this Memo. that no expenditure need be incurred in advance on equipment and premises, and coyly omitted to mention who would foot the bill if and when expenditure had to be made. Consequently, as might be expected, most of the local authorities just lay low and did nothing.

When evacuation took place there was, of course, a huge drop in the provision of communal meals for children made by the evacuating areas. There was also a decline in neutral areas. Exactly what provision was made in the reception areas during the early days I do not know. Probably very little, but a few authorities at least did some very fine pioneer work on behalf of evacuated children.

In November the Ministry of Health, which had in September trumpeted a fruitless appeal to no one in particular to feed the schoolchildren communally, decided that perhaps after all the Board of Education might be able to do this feeding job better than they could. They handed over responsibility, and in circular 1916, issued on November 21, told the local authorities to pass to the local education authorities any information they might possess, and to assist them to make use of the voluntary agencies.

On the same day the Board of Education issued circular 1484. It went straight to the point.

It is contemplated that the cost of equipment, service, small adaptations to existing buildings and other overhead charges, in so far as they are not met by voluntary bodies, will be regarded as evacuation expenditure and will be met by the Government.

Words such as those warm the hearts of local authorities. But even with all expenses paid the way was far from clear. By February 1940 some 50 of the local education authorities in the reception areas had decided to adopt schemes, but on the other hand 95 authorities sent word to the Board that there was no demand in their areas for midday meals.

The truth behind the headlines was that the Board had *not* said that the *meals* were to be free, and householders accommodating evacuated children were simply not going to part with 1s. 6d. or 2s. out of the 8s. 6d. or 10s. 6d. a week which was all they were paid for bedding, boarding, and generally fathering and mothering their young guests. They would rather cook the midday meals themselves. It will be recalled that by this date most of the householders to whom the billeting money did not matter had got rid of their evacuees, and that the bulk of the evacuated children were in working-class homes which, however kind and generous they were to their young guests (and they were both), still reckoned to make a few pence a week out of them.

In spite of this and other difficulties, however, some progress was made. By the summer of 1940 the reception areas were providing meals for about 13,700 evacuated children, or roughly 3 per cent, and also for about 8,600 more native children than they had previously been feeding. The evacuating areas were resuming provision on a considerable scale, and had reached 43 per cent of pre-war level (31,690 children instead of 74,310), while the neutral areas were up to 78 per cent (17,289 in place of 22,108).

On July 22, 1940, the Board of Education issued circular 1520, dealing, among other matters, with the provision of meals to schoolchildren through the school canteens. Of this circular Mr. Le Gros Clark says : [1]

> Strictly speaking, no novel principle was involved ; but, in effect, school feeding became from that date a recognized part of the war economy. Any study that is subsequently made of this institution will have to take its departure from Circular 1520. The earlier ten months of the war belong to a period of transition and of attempted adjustment to the strange conditions of warfare.

The Board pointed out in this circular that, while valuable provision was being made in many areas for free meals for

[1] *The School Canteen, 1939–40.*

necessitous undernourished children, the total number of children
for whom such meals were provided had fallen since the beginning
of the war from about 120,000 to about 70,000, or 1·5 per cent
only of the number of children attending elementary schools.
The provision before the war, said the Board, was insufficient,
and clearly the present provision was even more so. All authorities were therefore asked to survey the position in their areas and
to consider what increase of provision was required. They were
also asked to press on with the milk-in-schools scheme.

The Board said they regarded it as a matter of great importance
that all schools containing an appreciable number of children
coming from a distance should make provision, either on the
school premises or elsewhere, for the supply of nourishing midday
meals at a moderate cost. It was not necessary anywhere that
definite physical signs of malnutrition should be evident in
children, who might be selected for feeding on the recommenda-
tion of teachers or others in regular daily contact with them.
The income scales for free meals in force in many areas, suggested
the Board, needed revision to ensure that children were not
debarred from receiving extra nourishment for which their
parents were unable to pay.

Local authorities whose areas contained or were near munition
factories were particularly asked to make provision a matter of
urgency, in order to free women for employment. A similar
urgency applied to rural areas, where help on the land was
greatly needed. Elsewhere, even if there was no overt demand
(such was the implication), provision should be made and parents
persuaded to take advantage of it to effect economies in the use
of food and fuel, to reduce distributive costs, and to enable
greater use to be made of foods in ample supply.

The circular had a very considerable effect. There was a
sudden leap in provision towards the end of 1940, that is, about
as soon as authorities could have matured schemes and put
them into operation. In one county, for example, during the
first six months of the war ten new canteens were established,
during the second six months only three, but during the third
(i.e. between September 1940 and February 1941) twenty-one.

The fact that the Ministry of Food sanctioned and approved
this forward policy on the part of the Board of Education gave
circular 1520 more than normal significance ; the move was

instinctively felt to be an integral part of the war strategy. The next big move reinforced this belief, for it was made by the Minister of Food and the President of the Board of Education acting publicly in closest co-operation.

On October 21, 1941, the President of the Board of Education, Mr. R. A. Butler, asked in the House of Commons whether he had any statement to make on the development of the school meals and milk services with a view to ensuring the proper nutrition of children, replied that the active campaign by the Board during the past year had doubled the number of children receiving meals daily, and that he had now in consultation with the Minister of Food decided on further measures which he hoped would secure an immediate and large development of the service.

He had obtained the approval of the Chancellor of the Exchequer to an increase of 10 per cent on local authorities' expenditure on provision of meals, subject to an overriding maximum of 95 per cent. He was raising the minimum rate of grant from 50 to 70 per cent. The Minister of Food was placing at the disposal of local education authorities the chain of cooking depots being set up near large centres of population. With the aim of increasing the proportion of children receiving milk under the Milk-in-Schools Scheme from 60 to as near 100 per cent as possible the whole of the cost of providing free milk to necessitous children, and of the handling of the milk in the schools, was to be met by the Exchequer. With the help of the Minister of Food measures were being taken to facilitate the purchase of equipment, to ensure that the most necessary and suitable kinds of food were available in adequate quantities, and to remove difficulties which had stood in the way of rapid expansion of the service.

Mr. Butler told the press that at that date 300,000 meals were being served daily in grant-aided schools. He wanted that figure doubled within six months, and trebled within a year. As near as makes no difference, the latter ambition was realized ; early in 1943 the President was able to inform the House of Commons that in October 1942 896,236 children were daily receiving meals in grant-aided schools—elementary, secondary, and technical. A few weeks later the one million mark had been passed, and by April 1943 a million and a quarter children were having meals at school.

In May 1943 a third large advance was initiated. The President of the Board of Education announced that the rate of progress of the School Meals' Scheme, though striking, did not meet present needs and that it was necessary to aim at much more rapid development and a far higher target. One out of four children in State schools were taking meals ; the Government's objective would not be reached until that proportion was raised to three out of four.

To assist local education authorities in achieving this, plans would be circulated by the Board, and building work undertaken where necessary by the Ministry of Works. As from May 1 all capital expenditure to which authorities were committed would be met in full by the Government, and all kitchens and canteen equipment ordered after that date would be supplied to authorities free of charge. Mr. Butler added that the Minister of Food had guaranteed to safeguard supplies of food for school canteens even if the development of the offensive phase of the war necessitated curtailment of domestic rations.

Another important statement made by Mr. Butler in October 1941 was that the demand for school meals far exceeded the supply. A large and growing number of parents were glad to pay for the meals. This was particularly the case where industry was crying out for woman labour, but it was true everywhere. That statement has exceptional sociological significance. An institution which has become a habit is likely to persist in this country, however much the circumstances which induced habit-formation may alter or disappear. Communal school feeding, which previously 33 years had utterly failed to popularize, within two years became a habit very generally accepted by upwards of a couple of million parents and over a million children.

It is admittedly a habit not yet entirely agreeable to all of them. A Hertfordshire inquiry [1] in 1941–42 showed that while 31 per cent of boys and 35 per cent of girls preferred meals at school, 45 per cent of boys and 41 per cent of girls preferred home meals, 13 per cent of boys and 9 per cent of girls being indifferent. According to the children whose preferences were investigated, 38·5 per cent of their parents were favourable to the idea, only 22·5 per cent unfavourable or negative. Too much

[1] The School Child and the School Canteen. Hertfordshire County Council, 1942.

reliance cannot, of course, be placed upon a single sample inquiry of this kind, especially as evidence was taken only from children, but it does at least suggest that a considerable proportion of parents and children do not find the habit of communal feeding at school either a disagreeable one or one they would willingly relinquish.   This in two years is very remarkable in view of the fact that, prior to 1940 :

> The provision of meals at school had never been accepted as a normal part of the child's life.   Some *excuse* had always to be found—that the parents were on the verge of destitution, that the child lived three miles or more from its school, that foster parents would be relieved of an intolerable responsibility.   The school meal was looked upon as a substitute or a temporary convenience.[1]

The Government's food policy for children has during the past two years been most enlightened, and the continued good health of the children is a measure of its success.   But the matter goes deeper even than that.   It is safe to say that today the great majority of educationists are convinced that the midday meal at school should be an integral part of the school day, and that a considerable body of parents would concur with them in this opinion.   That body of parents may be expected to grow in size, for it has to be remembered, not only that the provision of school meals is still expanding rapidly, but that every term there enter the schools large numbers of children whose parents will have the advantage of the service from the start of their children's school life and who consequently will not have to grow used to the idea.

Educationists hold that the social training made possible by the School Meals Service is in its way as valuable as the un-questionable nutritional benefits.   Parents, too, are realizing this. The possible future effects upon our industrial economy remain to be seen, but it is clear that the communal feeding of children at school would do much to enable married women to continue full- or part-time employment after the war.   In view of the likelihood that many will wish to do so, and that their con-tinuance in employment would materially affect both production and conditions of labour, the School Meals Service may have very wide repercussions outside the schools.

[1] F. Le Gros Clark, in *The School Canteen, 1939–40.*

Camp Boarding Schools [1]

In November 1940 Mr. Malcolm MacDonald, then Minister
of Health, told the House of Commons that the Camp Boarding
Schools which had recently been opened as part of the war-time
evacuation scheme represented "one of the most significant
pieces of work that Parliament has lent its hand to in recent
times". After three years this judgment can be endorsed, and
the reasons for it somewhat amplified.

The camp boarding schools were brought into being by the
Camps Act, 1939. This provided for the construction, financed
by the Government, of camps of a permanent character, the
intention being that they should be used in peace-time as schoolchildren's camps, and in the event of war for evacuation purposes.
In 1940 they were put at the disposal of the local education
authorities. The first to be occupied was that at Kennylands,
near Reading, of which the boys' side of the Beal Central School,
Ilford, took possession in February of that year.

There are 30 camp schools in operation. Each is located
on a carefully chosen site of from 20 to 40 acres, amid beautiful
rural surroundings, and has residential accommodation for over
200 children, with the requisite staffs. The buildings, of cedar-
wood on concrete foundations, comprise, in separate units,
dining-hall and kitchen, assembly hall, class- and work-rooms,
dormitories, lavatory blocks, and hospital.

The "hotel facilities" at all the schools are provided by the
National Camps Corporation, which built the camps and owns
the land and premises. The teaching staff and the educational
equipment at each school are provided by the local education
authority which hires the camp and from whose area the children
come. The camps are occupied by 26 elementary schools (some
single-sex, some co-educational), two boys' secondary schools, a
school for physically handicapped children, and an orphanage.
All the children are 11 years old and upwards. At the outset
it was decided to exclude younger children from the scheme
owing to the heavier incidence of infectious diseases among
them.

In this setting between 6,000 and 7,000 boys and girls have

[1] The greater part of this section was published as an article in the *Christian Science
Monitor*, on December 29, 1942.

been living and being educated, some of them now for as much as three years. What lessons have been learned from this experiment, concerning which Mr. Chuter Ede, Parliamentary Secretary to the Board of Education, said in 1942 that he had not met a camp school teacher (and he has met most of them) who thought it other than a success?

It is unnecessary to stress the physical and mental benefits gained by city children, drawn largely from the poorer and more congested areas, of an ordered life, with good food, pure air, and abundant sleep, in an environment at once peaceful and secure yet novel and stimulating. These benefits have been enjoyed by many other evacuated children.

The clue to one distinctive contribution made by the camp schools lies in the fact that they constitute a novel social experiment as well as a valuable educational one. There have been boarding schools in England almost from time immemorial, but previously (with negligible exceptions) they have been strictly selective, and for the past century at least virtually confined to the children of well-to-do parents. For the first time in our history, the camp schools have made boarding-school education available on a considerable scale to children of parents in the lower income ranges. This has in numerous instances effected little less than a revolution in the conception of school in the minds of both children and parents.

The children have experienced, enjoyed, and profited from the closer-knit community life of a boarding school, which has given them an invaluable and unprecedented social training, developed their powers of initiative, self-reliance, and poise, and encouraged qualities of leadership and responsibility. The parents have learned a new respect and admiration for an institution capable of conferring such great and obvious benefits upon their children. New bonds of fellowship have been forged between children and parents, parents and teachers, teachers and children. Nor (incidentally but quite importantly) should it be overlooked that the local education authorities concerned have acquired a new sense of responsibility for the children whose schooling is their care.

In respect of the techniques of learning and teaching the schools have made an equally significant contribution. By affording an almost ideal controlled environment, they have enabled the teachers to break away from the academic curriculum, the instructional technique, and the mass-production methods which have been so long the curse of English education. The opportunity has been abundantly seized, and in some schools important advance has been made towards an integrated curriculum which provides, in the words of one of the head teachers, an " adjustment between the child and his environment, whereby he shall realize his one-ness with the community, rendering service to it and receiving support from it ". In other words, the camp schools are helping to point the way towards a truer conception of education for democratic living.

The content of education has been enlarged to include every aspect of value afforded by the immediate and neighbouring environment. Side by side with this has gone an intensive encouragement of children's interests, so that leisure has become invested with purpose—again, an entirely new conception in the minds of many of these children—and the line of demarcation between work and play happily blurred, if not obliterated. In teaching methods, projects are supplanting subjects, group work and individual study class instruction, and the Socratic quiz the teacher's monologue. Every school is adapting the traditional curriculum and technique in its own fashion, thus helping to create in fact that diversity within a unity of purpose which is a basic ideal of democracy.

It would be idle to pretend that everything has always gone perfectly smoothly in all the camp boarding schools. It would have been no less than a miracle had this been so, for almost without exception neither pupils nor staff had had previous experience of boarding-school life. But all the reports, and my personal investigations on the spot, suggest that the scheme has had an unexpectedly large measure of success, and has already been productive of profoundly important sociological and educational results. For this great credit must be given to the teachers who volunteered for this new service, and who have enabled thousands of children to enjoy and profit from a hitherto inaccessible experience—one which many hope all children may in the future enjoy during part at least of their school life.

THE SERVICE OF YOUTH

On October 3, 1939, the President of the Board of Education, Earl de la Warr, announced in the House of Lords that a committee had been appointed to advise the Government on problems of juvenile welfare in war-time, and that a special juvenile welfare branch, to deal with the work of organization, development, and administration of grants, had been set up in the Board of Education. Two months later, on November 27, the Board issued to the local education authorities for higher education circular 1486, entitled " The Service of Youth ", inviting their co-operation in this new field for which the Board had accepted responsibility.

At its inception, the Service of Youth was quite frankly envisaged as a preventative of physical, mental, and moral deterioration among young people who had left school but had not attained the maturity of adulthood. At the same time its establishment was an equally frank recognition that the social, recreative, and educational interests of young people had been grossly neglected in the past, and an acknowledgment that, for their own safety and for that of the nation, such neglect could no longer be tolerated.

In his' speech announcing the formation of the National Youth Committee, Lord de la Warr referred to the appalling deterioration among young people which, owing to the absence of adequate welfare provision, had taken place between 1914 and 1918. He admitted that even in peace-time the lack of provision of spare-time recreational and educational facilities for boys and girls between 14 and 18 or 20 was a grave defect in our social system, and he added significantly that what in peace-time was " merely a tragic wastage, in war-time became an open, festering sore ".

Circular 1486 stated the problem to be faced in somewhat more detailed terms.

The social and physical development of boys and girls between the ages of 14 and 20, who have ceased full-time education, has for long been neglected in this country. In spite of the efforts of local education authorities and voluntary organizations provision has always fallen short of the need, and today considerably less than half of these boys and girls belong to any organization. In some parts of the country, clubs and other facilities for social and physical recreation are almost non-existent. War emphasizes this defect in our social services : today the black-out, the strain of war and the disorganization of family life have created conditions which constitute a menace to youth. The Government are determined to prevent a recurrence during this war of the social problem which arose during the last. They have accordingly decided that the Board of Education shall undertake a direct responsibility for youth welfare.

The step was immediately recognized by the discerning as of the first importance and immensely significant for the future, and it was widely hailed as a genuine attempt to grapple on a nation-wide scale with a problem which, as circular 1486 put it, " challenges our whole sense of social responsibility ". Equally significant and important was the means the Board proposed for the development of the new service. For the first time in the history of this country all the statutory and voluntary bodies concerned were called to work together on a national scale in free and equal partnership.

The National Youth Committee had as chairman the Parliamentary Secretary to the Board of Education, and included members of local education authorities and voluntary organizations. Its functions were to advise the President of the Board and to provide central guidance and leadership. Circular 1486 suggested that as its counterpart in the localities there should be set up in all areas local youth committees representative of both the local education authority and the voluntary organizations, which would thus be closely associated " in full partnership in a common enterprise ". This, the Board added, need not " entail any loss of prestige or individuality on either side ".

The Board urged all local education authorities for higher education to take immediate steps to see that properly constituted youth committees existed in their areas ; and in order to impress upon them a sense of urgency stated that they would

be glad if local authorities for higher education will give this matter their early consideration, and will inform them, not later than 1st March, 1940, of the arrangements for constituting Youth Committees in their areas.

A specimen lay-out of a local committee, with notes upon its constitution, was provided for the guidance of the authorities, who were nevertheless given a wide freedom in this respect. In some areas, said the Board, excellent committees (the Juvenile

Organizations Committees) already existed, and nothing was needed save a change in name.   Some authorities might prefer to form a sub-committee of the Education Committee under Section 4 (5) of the Education Act, 1921, with adequate representation of the local voluntary bodies ; others to establish an advisory committee in close association with the local education authority.   But whatever the choice it was to be a proper committee, not merely a " body ".   " It is important," said the Board, " that from the outset the constitution and functions of the committee should be clearly defined."

Ample guidance was given concerning functions :

The first duty of the Local Youth Committee is to formulate an ordered policy, which shall provide for meeting the most immediate needs and which shall indicate the lines on which a real advance can be made under more favourable conditions.   For this purpose the committee should ascertain the local needs and decide where assistance can best be given.   In doing so, it should bear in mind that the better use of leisure, on which the welfare of youth largely depends, cannot be considered without reference to social and economic questions.   For example, when young people are living under unsatisfactory conditions and are employed for unduly long hours, often on work of a dull and arduous character, they cannot be expected to take full advantage of any facilities offered for the use of such leisure as is left to them.   The committee will also plan the lines of future development, showing clearly how the field should be covered and where the responsibility for any new facilities will lie.   In this way the foundations of an ordered scheme of local provision will be laid without imposing an undue strain on public and voluntary finance.

The Board laid it down specifically that " it is not the task of the local Youth Committee directly to conduct youth activities " —a direction which, however, they were subsequently to retract. It was their business " to strengthen the hands of local authorities and voluntary organizations ".   But, added the Board, in what was probably the most inspired passage in the circular—

co-ordination is not enough ; a new initiative is needed.   Young people themselves must be encouraged to find through the Local Youth Committees new constructive outlets for their leisure hours and for voluntary national service.

How the voluntary organizations were to make their contribution to the new youth service was, of course, their own business :

and the Board very properly refrained from offering them any advice on the matter. But the local education authorities were told in some detail of the part they were expected to play.

The principal directions in which local education authorities can assist financially are : first, in the provision of staff, office accommodation, and clerical staff : secondly, in making grants where necessary, towards the rent of buildings and salaries of full-time leaders, and towards the upkeep and maintenance of premises including the provision of equipment : and lastly, in providing competent instructors in such subjects as physical recreation and craft work in clubs and other centres.

Approved expenditure, under Section 86 of the Education Act, 1921, local education authorities were told, would rank for grant at the rate of 50 per cent. They were told also of other practical ways in which they could foster the work of youth welfare ; they could, for example, grant the use of their school premises free, or at reduced charges, offer the use of playing fields on favourable terms, and give facilities for the purchase of equipment.

The Service of Youth as thus envisaged was an ambitious project, but as the Board pointed out, one along traditional English lines.

The association of voluntary effort with the public system is typical of the history of the growth of the educational services in this country and will give the service of youth an equal status with the other educational services conducted by the local authority. In the Youth Committee the individual traditions and special experience of youth possessed by the voluntary organizations will be joined with the prestige and resources of the local education authority.

No less traditional and typically English was the unequal and generally cautious way in which the service bodied out in the localities. Some authorities—those for the most part who had been doing for years the sort of work advocated—took a deep breath and bit hard at once ; others began to nibble ; others again sniffed and didn't like the smell ; still others pretended not to have noticed at all. On January 6, 1940, *The Times Educational Supplement* commented that " there is little news as yet of the formation of the local youth committees for which the National Youth Committee has asked ", but added that " one county is reported to have allotted £2,000 to the work ".

The response of the general public was, to say the least of it, lukewarm. When circular 1486 was issued the King sent a letter to the Prime Minister expressing his pleasure at the appointment of the National Youth Committee, and adding :

> The need for leaders is specially urgent, and I hope that it will be met without delay. There must be many who are both free and well qualified by sympathy and experience to give help to clubs and other centres for young people. I appeal to them to do so ; they can be assured that service to youth is service in the cause of Britain.

Simultaneously there was published an appeal for leaders signed by the President of the Board of Education and the Secretary of State for Scotland.

Two months later it was recorded [1] that about 700 answers had been received in response to the Royal and ministerial appeal. About half of these were possibly definite offers of voluntary service. Some 250 replies came from men and women needing employment. Over 100 inquirers did not reply when further details were asked for. Ultimately 530 applications were passed on to various youth organizations.

Only just over 500 volunteers to an appeal sponsored by His Majesty for service to Britain ! Evidently youth had not as yet much glamour value. It was to be a different tale when youth was dignified with uniform.

On March 5, 1940, the Parliamentary Secretary to the Board of Education, Mr. Kenneth Lindsay, told the House of Commons that by the " appointed day " (March 1) 111 of the 146 authorities for higher education had informed the Board of action taken to carry out the policy recommended in circular 1486. From 65 schemes for the constitution of youth committees had been formally submitted ; in 44 schemes had been discussed and action was expected ; from 36 no information had been received.

Hardly an exhilarating response, though Mr. Lindsay professed to be pleased with it. Yet there were bright spots. Middlesex, for example, had allotted £10,000 for youth work in the coming financial year, Durham County had allocated £5,000 by way of initial expenditure, Cornwall, Nottingham-

---

[1] *The Times Educational Supplement*, February 3, 1940.

shire, and Wolverhampton £1,000 each. In some areas, notably Coventry, many new youth clubs had already been formed.

The following twelve months was a period of gestation, occupied chiefly by committee-making. It was not until 1941 that the Service of Youth got properly under way and the last recalcitrant authorities had been prodded and bullied by the Board into at least a tardy simulation of action. This is not to say that there was not much useful preparatory work done in 1940. There was ; and a considerable amount that was something more than preparatory.

In June 1940 the Board of Education issued circular 1516, entitled " The Challenge of Youth ". The text of the circular was hardly so arresting as its title—what a historic document this would have been had the fundamental challenge of youth to a disintegrating social order really been stated ! But all circular 1516 attempted to do was " to give some guidance on the general aim and purpose of the work " of youth service, and " to find, in the many and varied types of facilities provided, some common element, which will serve as a foundation for this new national movement ".

The general aim, it was stated, was to be found in " the social and physical training which links all youth organizations to one another and the schools ". The business of the youth service was to provide " appropriate means of bringing the child into a right and normal relation with his fellows and of developing bodily fitness through games and recreation ". Such means, said the circular, were already provided throughout the period of full-time schooling (were they ?) ; but ten years of life in the elementary school, said the Board, were insufficient to complete the process, which must now be continued through the years of adolescence.

On the crucial question of how it could be continued effectively when only the leisure hours of young people were available, and so long as their working hours were in general too long, and their employment frequently unsuitable, the circular was discreetly silent. That question was to remain unasked save by one or two lone voices until the registration of young people in 1942 thrust it into the foreground of the public consciousness. It still remains unanswered.

The overriding purpose of the social and physical training to be provided, said the circular, was the building of character ; and this implied " developing the whole personality of individual boys and girls to enable them to take their place as full members of a free community ". As a general statement this is unexceptionable ; but again, no indication was given as to how the whole personality could be developed by a half-time process, and one actually if not specifically divorced from the main formative influence of the working adolescent's life—the work environment.

Whether this fundamental issue was deliberately evaded or simply overlooked may never be known. It is of course true that it would have been virtually impossible to effect during the course of a war a major reconstruction of our educational system, still less of the entire process whereby youth graduates to full membership of society. (I say virtually, because in fact this has been done in recent years, in China if nowhere else.) But if the issue was raised and deliberately shelved, it would have been no more than honest (though doubtless impolitic) for the Government to have said outright that the proposed Service of Youth scheme was an admittedly inadequate and temporary war-time improvisation which must on the return of peace be at once replaced by a comprehensive and fully effective extension of the educational process to cover the years of adolescence.

No such statement has ever been made. The Service of Youth was introduced as though in itself a complete cure for the ills of adolescence. There has been a lot of talk since about weaving it into the fabric of the educational system—whatever that may mean—but no precise indication of how it is proposed to do this. The probability is that the Service of Youth as designed in 1939 represented the limits of the vision of its architects, who were genuinely incapable of realizing how circumscribed a scheme it was. The whole of its subsequent development justifies this conclusion. We are today in the most extraordinary tangle over the problem of the function and status of the adolescent in society, largely because we will persist in cutting his life into two parts, work and leisure, and trying to deal with each separately.

But even with fundamentals sidetracked, the Board found

abundant matter for discussion in circular 1516. First, bearing in mind the political outlook and influence of the disciples of voluntaryism, their particular bogey had to be banished.

Any attempt at a State-controlled uniformity or regimentation would be both stupid and perilous ; more than that, it would be wholly alien to the spirit of this country. The function of the State in this work is to focus and lead the efforts of all engaged in youth welfare ; to supplement the resources of existing national organizations without impairing their independence ; and to ensure through co-operation that the ground is covered in a way never so far attained.

Fine, bold, precise words ! But, alas, neither bold nor precise enough to liquidate the deep-rooted fear of " State-controlled uniformity or regimentation " which haunts the minds of so many, many people who cannot be brought to understand that no power on earth could ever regiment so individualistic a people as the English—let alone the Scots or the Welsh, whose individualism is even more pronounced.

The danger at present is all the other way ; lest the innumerable groups into which we naturally (and rightly) tend to split up will become so obsessed with their particularities and differences that they will be incapable of realizing that in spite of these we all have a common underlying purpose springing from a common ethos. England today is plagued with a multiplicity of voices, each claiming to preach the only way of salvation and each intolerant of all the others. A more catholic sympathy and a broader perspective are needed if the nation is to find its soul and realize its purpose.

Even had the words of circular 1516 quoted above been sufficient to still the fears of the voluntaryists, the very next sentences would have excited them again.

The function of the local education authorities is equally clear and essential. They are to take the initiative in their local areas. . . .

The voluntary organizations fiercely resented this. They had been in the field of youth welfare for many years ; they were the pioneers, and the experts, and, above all, the devotees. What did, or could, the local education authorities know or care about it ? Why should the initiative be handed to them ? Surely, in common justice, it should have been entrusted to the voluntary organizations, who had taken and, in spite of incredible obstacles, had maintained it single-handed for so many lonely years ?

For their part, the authorities replied, with some justification, that they held the purse-strings and that he who pays the piper calls the tune : that the voluntary organizations had never been able to provide sufficient money, premises, equipment or leaders to do the job properly ; and—less justifiably but with still some truth—that the ideas which the voluntary organizations had of administration were sketchy, of organization sloppy, and of finance chaotic.

So, in spite of the fervent appeal for good will and co-operation made in circular 1516, there was often " clash between statutory and voluntary effort "—in many places bitter and prolonged clash. Nevertheless, that did not prevent much useful work being done along the lines suggested in the circular.

Five main lines of practical development were indicated. These were :

(1) *Separate Clubs or Units*, belonging to a voluntary body, church, or works, and functioning on their own lines and in their own surroundings.
(2) *Youth Centres*, provided by a local education authority, by voluntary effort, or both, in which all local units could meet, and which all could share.
(3) *Recreational Evening Institutes*, such as had in recent years been developed by some local authorities.[1]
(4) *Old Scholars' Clubs*, meeting on their school premises, particularly those of the modernly designed Senior School.
(5) *Emergency Clubs*, described as a " means of combating the effects of war and the black-out ".

Broadly speaking, those are the lines on which the official Service of Youth has developed up to the present. The emphasis has been on (1) and (2), with this important reservation, that the Youth Centres provided by the local authorities have rarely become the meeting-place of units, but generally of young people *outside* the units. It may be suggested that therefore they more resemble (5), but those of us who saw the dreadful " emergency centres "—at best mere shelters from the street—which sprang up in some places in 1940, would hold it a discourtesy to find much connexion between the orderly and purposeful youth centres in, say, Manchester, Birmingham, or Tottenham, and

[1] Notably London.

the disorderly aggregations of young people in the " emergency " centres of the early days. Those constituted an " emergency " in more than one sense of the term ; thank goodness few of them now remain.

Some authorities have put their main effort into youth centres or recreational evening institutes, while some have concentrated on giving help to voluntary associations. Old Scholars' Clubs have remained a strictly localized provision, and it is doubtful whether even those bearing the name could strictly justify it. What sort of provision should be made for the welfare of youth is still disputed hotly. Battles royal have been (and still are being) waged over whether clubs should be single-sex, mixed, or " twin " (i.e. two clubs, generally separate but sharing some activities) ; whether young people should be given what they like or what their elders think they ought to like ; whether the emphasis should be on education or recreation ; and so on and so forth.

These disputes are doubtless inevitable concomitants of growth, particularly of a limited and frustrated growth such as the Service of Youth. What is more perturbing is the immense and complicated machinery which has been developed to run the Service. Authorities, having appointed their youth committees, discovered that they required salaried secretaries for these committees. Larger authorities split up their areas into districts, and discovered the need for organizers of these districts. Club and centre leaders and helpers were recruited, and it became obvious that they needed to be trained. When they had been " trained ", i.e. when they had attended a short course of lectures, they began to fancy themselves as members of a " new " profession, and to talk about status and salary scales and pensions and suchlike professional matters; and so on and so forth.

Had all this happened within the framework of a comprehensive system of education designed to meet the whole needs of the adolescent, no exception to it could have been taken. But it has not. The Service of Youth, however much politicians have asserted the contrary, has never been an integral part of the publicly provided system of education, and never can be so long as its operation is limited to the leisure hours of youth. In fact, it is today steadily marching away—or rather being pulled away—from the educational system, largely, it is true, because of the increasing demands being made upon the adolescent for voluntary national service, but also because of its very nature. Education concerns the whole of life ; the Service of Youth was deliberately restricted to part only of the life of the adolescent. Inevitably, the educational system and the Service of Youth were bound to drift apart.

The situation, it is to be hoped, will be very considerably clarified when the reforms proposed in the Government's White Paper on " Educational Reconstruction " are enacted. Any extension of the period of full-time attendance at school is bound to cut right across the Service of Youth. So, too, is a system of part-time continued education. There are some pretty problems ahead of us here ; but given courage and imagination, they are not insoluble.

What is ultimately far more important, and of fundamental sociological significance, is the intensely real challenge *from* youth which began to emerge in 1940. In a sentence this may be epitomized by saying that whereas the Government visualized and created in 1939 a welfare service *for* youth, by the middle of the following year the young people concerned were beginning to make it clear that what they most of all wanted was satisfying opportunity for service *by* youth.

This primary need of youth had, of course, long been recognized and met by some of the voluntary organizations. From the outset of the war many thousands of their members, as a result of the policy of the organizations to which they belonged, had been engaging in a wide variety of voluntary service in aid of the war effort. The Boy Scouts and Girl Guides Associations, who had amply proved between 1914 and 1918 how valuable (and reliable) the help of quite young boys and girls could be if trained and organized, had made their preparations before war broke out, so that, as a correspondent to *The Times Educational Supplement* wrote on November 11, 1939, of the Scouts :

. . . it is hardly going too far to say that on the outbreak of war all that was necessary in the United Kingdom was to issue mobilization orders ; and something approaching an actual mobilization of Scouts did in fact take place during the first week in September.

Thousands of Boy Scouts and Girl Guides played an invaluable part in the evacuation dispersal ; they carried luggage, conducted evacuees to trains, buses, and billets, made up emergency rations, collected and distributed bedding, cooking utensils, and other necessaries, scrubbed empty houses, cleaned barns, moved furniture. Other Scouts and Guides were attached to civil defence stations, hospitals, and first-aid posts ; or they filled sandbags, made splints and bandages, helped with the harvest, made and collected comforts for troops, assisted harbour masters and coastguards, helped with young children in reception areas, collected, sorted, and distributed clothing of every description for evacuees.

The uniformed Brigades gave similar service, the boys specializing in ambulance work but not confining themselves to this form of activity. They, like the Scouts, acted as orderlies at civil defence posts, manned telephone services, did farm and garden work, collected books and magazines for the Red Cross. The girls looked after children, assisted in hospitals, knitted garments for troops and evacuees. Members of other voluntary organizations did the same, though perhaps less as a matter of organizational policy and more by individual inclination. The National Association of Boys' Clubs began to train selected older members to take the places of the leaders called to the Services, as did later the National Association of Girls' Clubs. The Y.M.C.A. threw their centres open to evacuated schoolchildren, the Y.W.C.A. vigorously promoted clubs for girls and young women, especially in industrial areas. The Young Farmers' Clubs assisted War Agricultural Executive Committees, and initiated town children into the ways of country life.

But these acts of service were being performed by boys and girls already in youth organizations ; and two comments on this must be made. First, that at a generous estimate the voluntary youth organizations did not touch more than a quarter to one-third of the young people between 14 and 18 : and second, that their membership was very largely of children still at school. It is not unfair to say that theirs was service mainly by children, not young people.

In the summer of 1940 young people outside the voluntary organizations began spontaneously to manifest their desire for service. Three illustrations, very different in character, must here suffice. First, when the call was made after Dunkirk for Local Defence Volunteers (the Home Guard) very large numbers of boys of 17, and many who were not yet 17 but said they were, offered themselves for enlistment. Second, in July and August there came into being in East Suffolk the first Youth Service Squads. This latter is a fascinating story.

Rural areas present almost insuperable difficulties to youth organizations. East Suffolk overcame these in original fashion. Towards the end of July a poster was sent to every one of the 250 villages in the county urging young people to get together to form squads to do work of local and national importance. They were to do this entirely on their own, to elect their own leader and secretary, and then to apply to the county education office for advice.

The response was prompt and widespread. Nearly 100 villages replied almost at once ; in three months 142 squads had been formed, in six months nearly 200. And of the members about 70 per cent had never previously been in any youth organization. The squads, directed almost entirely by their youthful and self-chosen leaders, salvaged, did farm and garden work, kept stock, learned civil defence duties, organized concerts, ran small clubs, and generally made themselves useful in a host of ways.

East Suffolk was a significant pointer. So was Liverpool, where a Civil Defence Cadet Corps (later to do invaluable work in the blitzes) 2,000 strong sprang into being within a few weeks. So were other areas, rural and urban, which developed similar movements. But the full flood of youth's response to the call for service was not to come until the launching of the Air Training Corps in January 1941.

The story of the A.T.C. is told in the following section. Here I would only point out that since its initiation there have been running in this country two distinct youth movements. One, the Service of Youth, is heterogeneous, divided, and uncertain of purpose, hesitant in face of the apparently conflicting claims of education and recreation ; yet nevertheless consciously seeking a social objective of enduring value. The other, represented by the pre-Service organizations, the younger members of the Home Guard, the school harvest camps movement, and one or two as yet small associations such as Youth Service Volunteers, is homogeneous, certain of its purpose, united by the single desire to perform service of immediate value to the nation ;

yet by the very nature of this desire limited to a temporary
objective.

Neither movement can by itself offer a full solution to the
problem of giving the adolescent his rightful place in our society.
Even were the two movements fused, so that both purpose and
variety were present, that full solution would still be lacking.
Only a movement which embraces both the working life and
the life of leisure can do that. And, since the adolescent is a
being still under tutelage, this must be an educational movement
—in the widest sense of the term.

PRE-SERVICE TRAINING

On January 9, 1941, the Secretary of State for Air, Sir
Archibald Sinclair, announced a new and nation-wide Air Training Corps scheme open to all boys between 16 and 18. Its
purpose was to ensure an adequate flow of young men of the
right standard for pilots, air crews and the technical trades of
the Royal Air Force. It would provide facilities for general
education and Service training for boys between the ages of
16 and 18. The primary qualifications for membership were a
desire to serve in the Royal Air Force, or the Fleet Air Arm,
and physical fitness. The corps was to be organized on the
model of the R.A.F. in flights, squadrons and wings, and cadets
would wear the R.A.F. uniform, which would be issued to
them free.

As in all these war-time developments, the framework of the
scheme was far from new. There had been for years an Air
Defence Cadet Corps, a voluntary organization which had at
the time nearly 200 units in schools and universities. What was
new was that for the first time in our history the Government
made a direct appeal to the 16-year-old boy, and appealed to
him, not as a boy but as a *man*. It associated him with the
Armed Forces of the Crown, to strengthen which it needed his
services. New, also, was the deliberate creation of a State-
sponsored, State-financed, and State-controlled—but nevertheless voluntary—youth organization.

The Times Educational Supplement commented (January 18,
1941) :

This is far and away the most comprehensive attempt to capture the allegiance of British boyhood that has ever been made, and unless those in charge bungle badly (which is not likely) it is certain to succeed on a vast scale. There is already an immediate and eager response, and it will swell to a mighty torrent, because the appeal that has been made contains every element dear to the heart of a boy. A national youth movement, State-directed, State-controlled, regimented, uniform—everything, in fact, the critics said it ought not to be—has been created overnight ; and it will carry everything before it.

That prophecy has been abundantly justified. Those who launched the Air Training Corps felt at the time that their wildest hopes would be realized if they enrolled 100,000 boys within the first twelve months ; in fact, the Corps was 200,000 strong within six months, and, slight fluctuations apart, it has stood round about that figure ever since, in spite of the fact that the pre-service training organizations for the Royal Navy and the Army have since been largely expanded.

Air Force cadets have let no difficulty or obstacle deter them. They walk, cycle, or bus incredible distances (30 miles by bicycle is recorded) after the heaviest day's work to do the dullest and driest academic study in the dingiest surroundings. In the early days suitable premises were virtually unobtainable in many places, and welfare facilities non-existent. It did not matter : the cadets met in sheds, barns, basements, cellars, and derelict houses, unfed and after long hours of employment, to pore earnestly over the mathematics they had so loathed at school. And they have persisted : the enthusiasm to-day may not be quite so red-hot as in 1941, but it is still as real, the determination is as dogged as ever, and the percentage and standard of the cadets who qualify for the R.A.F. very high.

An equally overwhelming response to the call for service was manifested when early in 1942 the Admiralty decided to expand the Sea Cadet Corps from about 120 units to 400 units providing for 50,000 cadets. The Sea Lords could have got many times that number. In inland towns far from the sea units could have been filled five or six times over. The Sea Cadet's training is even duller than that of the Air Cadet ; no matter : the objective compensates for any conceivable drudgery. In the early days there were no boats (not even where there was a river), and equipment for practical work was hard to come by. No matter : the cadets carried on with their theory, confident that ultimately it would carry them to the land of their heart's desire. And it did.

Perhaps the expansion of the Army Cadet Force in December 1941 did not quite so wholly thrill the heart of the British boy. There were sound reasons. The term " P.B.I." is not unknown even to the 16-year-old. The Army was at that date still widely regarded as the least efficient of the three Services, and the most hidebound by traditions of the " spit and polish " order. It had taken some very nasty knocks, and had, to offset these, no glamorous success such as the Battle of Britain. It was not a new service, like the R.A.F., nor a mysteriously exciting one, like the Navy. And—no inconsiderable concern to a 16- or 17-year-old boy—khaki is not an attractive uniform ; at least, not the private's khaki. Moreover, by the time the Army decided to expand its Cadet Force, almost all the 16- and 17-year-olds of mettle were already in the Air Training Corps or the Home Guard.

Nevertheless, probably owing to the fact of its lower age of entry (14 as against 15½ [1] for the A.T.C.), the Army Cadet Force had by the end of 1942 enrolled 170,000 members.

When the Air Training Corps was launched *The Times Educational Supplement* wrote :

At present it is confined to boys, but it is not beyond the bounds of possibility that it will spread also to girls. Just as thirty years ago the sisters of the Boy Scouts compelled the formation of the Girl Guides, so may the girls of today compel the formation of a female A.T.C.

Again, a true prophecy—or very nearly so. In spite of all their efforts the girls have not succeeded in securing a " female A.T.C." But it has not been for want of trying. It was not very long before a Women's Junior Air Corps was in existence. This was a privately formed association, unaided by public funds —though it was reported in June, 1941, that at Wakefield the local education authority was co-operating by providing accommodation and other help, and similar help may have been given elsewhere. Meanwhile in various parts of the country other voluntary units calling themselves the Girls' Training Corps or some such name were banding together.

[1] The A.T.C. from the start enrolled boys from 15½ upwards, though until 1942 full membership was not officially granted until 16.

It began to look as though there might develop a number of separate unofficial " pre-service " movements for girls, all having generally the same aims, but all probably too weak to have effective appeal.   The Board of Education took the wise step of calling the various leaders together and suggesting amalgamation.   The advice was taken, and in February 1942 it was announced that a National Association of Girls' Training Corps had been formed, with a view to extending this movement which had been developing as the result of individual initiative, and to fit girls for entry into H.M. Forces, Civil Defence, and other forms of national service.   The minimum age of entry was to be 14, the essential conditions of membership physical fitness and the written consent of parents or guardians.   Units could be formed through local education authorities, schools, voluntary societies, or other bodies. There was to be a uniform (not provided) consisting of navy blue beret, white blouse, blue tie, navy blue skirt, and the G.T.C. badge.   The course of training included as compulsory subjects first-aid, hygiene, dispatch-carrying, a handywoman's course, squad drill and physical training.

The new association was not a government-maintained pre-service organization like the A.T.C., the Sea Cadets, or the Army Cadet Force.   It was described as a voluntary organization, supplementary to, and in no way a rival of, existing voluntary organizations (several of which, including the Y.W.C.A., the Girl Guides, and the National Association of Girls' Clubs, already had their own service training schemes).   The description caused some bewilderment at first in many quarters, particularly among members of the W.J.A.C. (which had refused to join the National Association, though it professed itself ready to co-operate with it).   The bewilderment was not entirely groundless ; voluntary organizations are not normally formed on Government initiative, and it was clear that the N.A.G.T.C. was receiving far more active support from the Board of Education (and it was suspected a far larger measure of financial assistance) than the ordinary voluntary organization might expect.

But the Board did well to take the initiative in the way they did.   The previous position was chaotic, and might have become cut-throat.   From the moment the National Association was announced it was clear that it met a deep-felt and widespread need among girls.   The Board were wise also to nurture its development carefully. The Corps might never have survived otherwise, for the response to its establishment was as overwhelming as had been that to the establishment of the A.T.C., and for a while threatened almost to submerge the tiny headquarters staff. Applications poured in ; units were formed all over the country ; requests for information and advice arrived in stacks. At the first national conference, held in March 1942 to discuss the formation, organization, and running of units, there were present 700 representatives of local education authorities, youth committees, voluntary organizations, schools, existing G.T.C. companies, and units of the W.J.A.C. Nearly every county in England was represented, and delegates came also from Wales and Scotland (which latter had already formed a comparable national association). Six months later the Corps had reached a strength of 100,000 ; by the spring of 1943 it numbered 130,000.

In June 1942 it was announced that the N.A.G.T.C. and the W.J.A.C. were to amalgamate. Existing units of the latter body and those in process of formation would affiliate to the reconstituted national body, but would retain their present title, and badge. No new units of the W.J.A.C. were to be formed. Thus there came into being what both the Board of Education and the Services desired, a single movement [1] providing a general pre-entry training for either military or civil defence service.

These pre-service training organizations have presented the nation with a formidable new problem, but throw valuable light on some old ones. It is beyond question that they have appealed to young people to a degree far exceeding that of any other youth movement in this country, and for very definite reasons. Their call is to the manhood and womanhood in youth (that of the Scouts and Guides, equally popular movements, is to the child rather than the adolescent) ; the objectives they present are clear-cut, and quickly to be attained ; they possess all those elements of glamour and of drama which delight the heart of youth.

Yet in their present form and with their present objectives they are clearly war-time phenomena, and cannot long survive— at any rate in their present state of vigour—the onset of peace. Can form and objectives be transformed to meet the needs of

[1] Now called the National Association of Training Corps for Girls.

peace ? Is it desirable that the attempt should be made thus to transform them, or should these pre-service organizations be deliberately disbanded when their objectives are no longer valid ? The Services have already given their answer to this last question ; they have announced their intention of continuing the organizations after the war. But will they offer for youth in peace a purpose as compulsive as in war ? Some such purpose must be found. That is the fundamental problem which faces us.

There are other questions to which perhaps even earlier answers must be found. Since 1918 there has been statutory provision for the part-time education of the adolescent up to the age of 18; and the Registration of Boys and Girls Order of 1941 (discussed in a following section), by handing over to the education authorities the interviewing and guidance of the young people registered, has been widely taken to mean that the responsibility for the welfare, education, and training of all young persons up to 18 has been vested in the Education Department. But the pre-service training of boys is directed and financed by the Service departments. It is true that these rely very largely upon the education authorities for such general education as they afford, and at present for much of the specialized technical training. They draw instructors, including instructors for physical training, from the education authorities, and use their buildings and equipment. But the responsibility for the training as a whole lies with them, and they finance and control it. Should this be so ? Should not pre-service training for national defence, when it is placed on a permanent basis, be regarded as an integral part of training for citizenship ; and as this latter is clearly an integral part of the education of the whole man, should not the ultimate responsibility lie with the Education Department, however much the day-to-day administration may be delegated to other departments ? The principle is observed in respect of the G.T.C., and this organization would appear to offer the most appropriate foundation on which to build for the future.

SCHOOL HARVEST CAMPS [1]

In 1942 over 30,000 boys and girls, most of them secondary school pupils between the ages of 15 and 18, spent the whole or part of their summer holidays aiding the war effort by helping to get in the harvest. During term-time elementary and secondary school pupils by the thousand engaged in part-time agricultural work. Altogether, it is estimated that during the year schoolchildren did about 3,000,000 hours of work on the land.

School harvest camps came into being shortly after the outbreak of war. A number of secondary school headmasters, desiring to give their pupils an opportunity to aid the war effort in a healthy and vigorous way, arranged summer holiday camps on their own initiative. The experiment was not an unqualified success ; many farmers doubted the value of inexperienced and youthful help and were reluctant to use it ; some camps were badly timed, being held too early or too late ; the possibility of bad weather was overlooked by some camp organizers, and consequently campers hung about idly ; camp conditions and catering were not always good enough.

Nevertheless the experiment was felt to be sufficiently encouraging to repeat on a larger scale the following year ; it was clear that it held great possibilities. Camp organizers analysed their mistakes with a view to avoiding them in the future. The Ministry of Agriculture and the County War Agricultural Executive Committees (W.A.C.) were found to be interested and ready to give valuable assistance. Consequently the camps in 1941 were a great advance on those of 1940 ; there was better liaison between schools and farmers ; more camp sites were made available ; transport and catering were improved.

But still it was felt that much more could be done. Systematized, and put on a nation-wide basis, the camps could make an invaluable contribution to the war effort. It was suggested to the Ministry of Agriculture that a committee be set up to survey the whole position. The Ministry agreed, and a committee representative of the schools, the farmers, the Ministry of Agriculture, and the Board of Education got to work, with Mr. R. R. Hyde, Director of the Industrial Welfare Society, as chairman.

[1] The greater part of this section was originally written as an article for the Ministry of Information, for publication overseas.

In March 1942 a detailed memorandum (H.C. I), based
on recommendations made by this committee, was circulated
by the Ministry of Agriculture to the schools, and a publicity
campaign opened up to encourage as many schools as possible
to join in. The memorandum was a first-class piece of work.
In three sections it dealt exhaustively with (a) details of camp
organization—site, equipment, catering, etc. ; (b) the arrangement of the campers' work, and (c) camp finances.

All camps, it was suggested, should be arranged in con-
junction with the W.A.C., which would advise about location,
dates, numbers required, and the nature of the work ; assist
in finding sites ; lend equipment, effect liaison with farmers,
and give on behalf of the Ministry of Agriculture guarantees of
work and financial assistance.

Camps of about 30 boys with two teachers, a cook, and two
or three camp orderlies were advised, though local conditions
might demand larger or smaller numbers. Emphasis was laid
on the necessity for ample, well-cooked meals, and consequently
for competent cooks and adequate cooking facilities. The
Ministry of Agriculture offered to contribute towards the cost of
staffing the camps, and the Ministry of Food arranged that camps
should be recognized as catering establishments in Category A
Industrial Group.

On account of the variability of the weather, wholly tented
camps were discouraged. Instead, it was suggested that some
permanent building—e.g. a large barn, a village hall or a rural
school—should be secured as a nucleus, so that meals could be
taken in comfort, and campers have a dry retreat for the evenings
and on wet days.

If schools were unable to provide the main items of equipment—marquees, tents, cooking ranges, palliasses, blankets, etc.
—the Ministry of Agriculture offered to loan them. If schools
used their own or privately borrowed equipment, the Ministry
would contribute at specified rates towards the cost of wear and
tear. Arrangements were made with railway companies for
parties to travel at very cheap rates, and the Ministry offered to
pay the first 7s. 6d. of the return fare and the full cost of baggage
and equipment, including bicycles—which campers were advised
to bring. Similar help was offered if campers came by road.

During their hours of employment in agriculture campers

would in the ordinary course be protected by statute and common
law in the event of accidents.   But it was felt to be essential
that boys should be insured against all kinds of accidents at
all times.   The Ministry therefore arranged a Special Personal
Accident Insurance Policy giving them complete cover in and
out of camp, at a cost of 9d. per week.   The policy did not cover
medical expenses arising out of accidents not causing disablement ; but the Ministry would pay the reasonable certified
cost of these.   Arrangements for quick admittance to hospital
were also made.

Minimum rates of wages were fixed at 6d. an hour for boys
under 16, 8d. an hour for boys over that age.   Teachers and
other adults joining in the work were to be entitled to the minimum rates for inexperienced workers—on the average about
1s. an hour.   Farmers could pay higher wages if they wished
(some did, or added a bonus), and schools were entitled to ask
for them if they had particularly heavy expenses to meet.

W.A.C's were authorized to guarantee that on an average
boys should have 30 hours' paid employment a week, provided
schools did their best to find work and kept adequate records
of the hours worked.   To help them to secure full employment,
liaison officers were appointed by the W.A.C's.   If in any week
the hours of employment fell below 30 through work being not
available, the W.A.C. would make up the balance of pay.   If
the hours worked exceeded 30, payment was made in full for
the extra hours—which were not used to cancel previous under-
employment.   Campers were not to be paid individually.   All
items of camp expenditure and income were to be pooled, and
the surplus to be shared out at the conclusion of the camp.
(On the average throughout the country camps paid their
expenses and 6s. a week to each camper.)

Under these arrangements 650 officially organized school
harvest camps were held in 1942.   Almost without exception
they were completely successful, so much so that it was necessary
only to make a few minor alterations in the arrangements for
1943, for which a target of over 1,000 camps, accommodating
50,000 boys and girls, was set.

Of the pleasure and satisfaction felt by the campers, and the
benefits they have derived from the vigorous work in the open
air, there can be no doubt ; and among the happiest camps in

1942 were those in which school boys and girls worked alongside young people released from shops and factories by their employers. Farmers have on the whole got over the suspicious attitude so many of them at first adopted. Many are loud in their praises of the boys and girls who have worked for them, and it is not unusual for a farmer to " book " a party from the same school for the following year. Some schools have indeed returned each year since 1940 to the same site.

The contribution to the war effort which has been made by the school harvest camp movement is already substantial. But the movement would appear to have in it the seeds of something more permanent than this. There are today many who believe that a period of national service should form part of the education of every citizen-to-be, and that this period should come at about the age of 18. Exactly how such a period would best be occupied no one yet knows. But it certainly looks as though the school harvest camps, together with comparable movements such as Youth Service Volunteers, offer a valuable pointer in the right direction.

Some idea of the response from young people may be gathered from the experience of Youth Service Volunteers. In 1942 they ran three experimental camps, doing forestry, munition salvage, and fruit-picking, and catering for only a few hundred boys. In the early summer of 1943 they announced a dozen camps, and told the press that they were ready to take on 4,000 campers within the following six months. Within a month they had had 20,000 applications, of whom nearly half were girls ; and further applications were coming in at the rate of 600 a day.

YOUTH REGISTRATION

On December 2, 1941, the Prime Minister announced in the House of Commons that, among other measures designed to secure the maximum national war effort, all boys and girls between the ages of 16 and 18 were to be registered and subsequently interviewed to discover how their well-being and training for national service could be advanced.

Mr. Churchill gave briefly the reasons for this decision. We had to think, he said, of the future citizens as well as of the business of carrying on the defence of the country. We had to be particularly careful that our boys did not run loose during this time of stress. So those young people who were not already members of a youth organization or doing useful work of some kind would be encouraged to join one or other of the organizations through which they could obtain the training required to fit them for national service.

There were fine opportunities, said the Prime Minister, open to strong lively boys of 16 to 18 for helping in the war. They could serve in the Army Cadets, the Junior Training Corps, the Air Training Corps, the Sea Cadets, or in voluntary organizations on the civil side. Boys of 17 might already join the Home Guard, and it was hoped to take some of the 16-year-olds in areas where the Home Guard would be entrusted with anti-aircraft and coast defence duties. But, added Mr. Churchill, in all these fields the well-being and training of the boys would be the prime consideration.

Winding up the debate which ensued on the Government's proposals, the Minister of Labour and National Service, Mr. Ernest Bevin, said that this move was the beginning of dealing in an organized manner with the adolescent. He ventured to prophesy that in a few years' time it would be discovered that they had not only done something for youth in the war, but had laid a foundation for developing the great educational system of the country. A few days later the President of the Board of Education spoke in similar vein at rather greater length. After declaring that he believed our young people were only too anxious to do their bit, that their response had already been magnificent, that new opportunities would now be open to the 16–18's through the expansion of the Cadets and the Home Guard, he added that he was not overlooking the interests of the younger boys and girls, but was asking local authorities to do all they could to increase facilities for training and service for 14–16's also. Mr. Butler then stated :

These steps are a first start towards building the arch from 14 to 18. They are not intended to take the place of Fisher's plans for continuation schools. We may hope to do more later. But our present scheme will certainly accustom young people to the idea that in their early years the path to manhood and womanhood lies through knowledge, work and service. Indeed, I sometimes wonder whether this may not be the beginning of a new social charter. From early youth the young citizen should learn that there must be acknowledged duties to be performed by the individual for the State, which should confer certain rights and privileges in return.

The Parliamentary Secretary to the Board of Education, Mr. J. Chuter Ede, also expressed high hopes of what the new move would effect.

We can now, he said, promote and encourage the well-being of our youths, and give them the training that will enable them to take an intelligent, active and constructive share in the citizenship of a free community. Suddenly, by the strange chances of war, the youth committees and the voluntary organizations have been presented with a golden and spectacular opportunity to prove their worth to the nation. If we seize it and make the outstanding success of it which with resolute effort we can, we shall have prepared for youth when peace returns an instrument for self-realization and self-expression from which will be fashioned a truly democratic citizenship.

What exactly was the plan which moved these government spokesmen to such confident assurances ? The scope and the details of procedure were given in the Board of Education circular 1577, issued on December 20, 1941. In this the Board stated that, while boys and girls between 16 and 18 still in full-time attendance at school were included in the registration scheme, the main object of this was to enable local authorities— for the first time—to make direct contact with all those young people of the ages concerned who had left school and were no longer under educational supervision and discipline.

The actual registration, which was to be compulsory upon all, was to be carried out through the machinery of the Ministry of Labour and National Service at their local offices, except that local education authorities who exercised their powers to deal with choice of employment might, if they wished, carry out registration at their own juvenile bureaux. At registration boys and girls were to be asked to supply, in addition to the essential particulars of name, age, and address, information concerning the nature and place of their employment, and whether they were members of a youth organization or junior Service unit.

The act of registration was to be the only compulsory feature of the scheme. No obligation was to be laid on boys and girls in this age group to undertake any specific form of training or national service. But it was desired to encourage all those who were not already fully occupied to link up and share with their fellows in the common endeavour; and the procedure subsequent to registration was devised to this end.

When the registration cards were completed, they were to be passed by the Ministry of Labour and National Service (where this was conducting registration) to the local education authority for higher education. This authority was to review the registrations, check up with the voluntary youth organizations and pre-Service units the declarations made of membership of these, and then to make arrangements for inviting to interview those young people registered who were not members of any voluntary or pre-Service organization.[1] The authority, it was suggested, might at the same time wish to review the facilities for training and service open to boys and girls in their area.

The circular indicated that the interviews were to be friendly and informal in character, and advised that care should be taken to enlist as interviewers men and women likely to command the confidence of boys and girls. It pointed out that it would be quite unreasonable to make further calls on the energies of the many young people working under considerable strain in industry, fully occupied with continued education or, in the case of girls, with domestic duties.

It cannot be stated too clearly that the object in view is not to apply methods of compulsion to the recruitment of the youth organizations, including those that provide pre-service training, but to give advice and encouragement to young people to play their part, and to secure contact between them and the Youth Service. (*Board of Education Circular 1577.*)

At the same time, however—

While young persons should be left free to express their preference for the type of training or organization for which they may volunteer to enrol, every encouragement should, in the present war emergency, be given to fit boys not already associated with some organization and not otherwise suitably occupied, to undertake some form of pre-service training. (Ibid.)

No advice was given as to what girls should be encouraged to do. The Government had clearly not yet made up its mind on this point; it proposed to defer the registration of girls until after that of boys, and promised that a communication regarding

---

[1] Some authorities interviewed *all* young people registered.

girls' interests would be addressed to authorities before this registration was due to take place.

The circular concluded by admitting that this new demand upon the local education authorities would entail extra work for them, but added that—

> Authorities will, however, recognize the significance and importance of this new development, which offers a new opportunity to establish more firmly and develop still further the Youth Service which is now taking shape under their aegis as the recognized medium for securing appropriate guidance and training for the rising generation.

Some at least, if not all, of the significance of the move was widely recognized. It was clear that the Board of Education and the local education authorities were confirmed in the responsibility for the welfare of boys and girls between the ages of 14 and 18 who had left school which had been tentatively entrusted to them by the establishment of the Service of Youth in 1939. Though it was nowhere officially so stated at the time, the implication was that, whereas previously the Education Department, in co-operation with the voluntary youth organizations, had been through the Service of Youth assigned permissive powers to look after the welfare of this age group, these powers had now been made obligatory.

But the same serious limitation of powers as had originally been imposed upon the Service of Youth remained. The Education Department was to concern itself with the leisure time occupations only of the young people interviewed. *The Times Educational Supplement* took up the point at once. " Is it not realized yet ", it asked, " that no full picture can be obtained so long as employment and leisure are treated as separate entities ? " And it continued—

> Those local authorities who desire to obtain a really accurate picture of their young people will be well advised to obtain also information about wages, hours of work (real, not nominal), reasons for choice of employment, numbers and duration of jobs held, and reasons for relinquishing situations or occupations. Only thus can the true value of recruitment to, and membership of, voluntary organizations be assessed. (31.1.42.)

Almost without exception, this is what local authorities did. Very great credit is due to them for the general arrangements they made for the interviewing of young people, and for the way in which most of the interviewing was carried out. The job was handled with all the seriousness it deserved, great care was taken to select the right people as interviewers, and full and valuable records were made. An equal tribute is due to the thousands of men and women who undertook voluntarily the arduous and prolonged task of interviewing. They did it con-scientiously, and they did it well.

Even more credit is due to the authorities for the courageous way in which they explored and exposed a grave defect in our socio-economic system—the legally permitted exploitation of boys and girls in industrial and commercial employment.

Registration took place between January and April 1942, and interviewing went on during these and subsequent months. From about May onwards local authorities began to publish reports on the results in their areas, and a number of them held conferences to discuss and analyse the information which had been obtained. Very soon an extraordinarily interesting fact began to emerge ; everywhere, in spite of the fact that particulars of employment were officially outside the terms of reference of the interviewers, the hours and conditions of employment of the young people interviewed had been a main, if not the main, subject of inquiry. Moreover, it was evident that what the interviewers had learned had deeply moved them. Report after report stressed the evil of the long hours boys and girls were working, and the heavy strain placed upon them by the great distances many had to travel to and from their place of employ-ment.

One northern industrial borough found that in the case of approximately one-third of the young people interviewed the interviewers found themselves unable to recommend the taking up of any extra activities.

In the case of the boys this was entirely due to excessive hours of work, which in the words of one interviewer resulted in many of the boys seeming to be " mentally and physically exhausted ". (*The Times Educational Supplement*, May 23, 1942.)

The City of Lincoln Youth Committee reported that—

Hours of work were recorded as appallingly long—50, 60, and even 70 hours a week—but it was disturbing to find on investigation that the statutory limit was not being exceeded. The maximum hours of work allowed in wartime seemed beyond the physical capacity of juveniles. Many of the boys admitted to a permanent feeling of fatigue. . . . (*The Times Educational Supplement*, June 27, 1942.)

Among girls, said Lincoln :

Cases of excessive hours were as bad as with boys, if not worse. Normal week-day hours in the foundries and engineering firms were 7.30 a.m. to 7 p.m. Many girls appeared tired ; cases of " bad legs " were viewed with concern, all the more so as it was only when questioned that they were admitted to, and the assumption was that this defect was not included in a health report. (Ibid.)

At a conference held in Surrey in June 1942 many people who had taken part in interviewing commented strongly on the instances of long hours they had come across. For example, Alderman F. S. Wagner, Mayor of Malden and Coombe, said that when youths were working 60 hours a week, as they were in his district, it was absurd to ask them to join an organization. Legislation ought to be introduced to stop such hours. Mr. T. Braddock maintained that the long hours worked by young people, far from increasing output, retarded it, and that if this was the case there was no argument, not even that of national necessity, to justify the injury being done to the young people. Others spoke in similar vein, and the meeting as a whole expressed its indignation at the state of affairs revealed and its conviction that hours of employment for young people should be reduced.

In Wallasey the interviewers found that between 10 and 20 per cent of boys were working long hours, as were girls employed in laundries, cinemas, and canteens—

. . . it was evident that some (girls) were tired out and unfit to undertake further activities, especially when they had to help at home after a day's work ; a heavy burden rested on girls in large families. (*The Times Educational Supplement*, August 8, 1942.)

In Northampton 13 per cent of those interviewed were found to be working over-long hours in industry (the criterion taken by the committee here was that any employment involving 10 hours' continuous absence from home was too long). In Southampton 25 per cent of girls were regarded as working long or difficult hours or engaged in exceptionally tiring work. In Hertfordshire, where between 8,000 and 9,000 young people were interviewed, 100 cases were reported where boys were working a 60-hour week.

The worst cases of long hours, stated this report, appear to be in work for their parents, either on the land or in small shops, and in restaurants, cinemas, golf clubs and so on, where some boys have a 12-hour day. (Ibid.)

In the London County Council area " long hours of work were given in an appreciable number of cases as a reason for inability to join an organization," and—

The general feeling was that the girls are in some respects bearing a heavier load than the boys, but with unfailing cheerfulness. . . . It was not uncommonly remarked that many looked tired. This was more noticeable in the industrial areas, and it seemed to be due not only to long working hours but to heavy work at which girls must stand all day. (*The Times Educational Supplement*, September 12, 1942.)

In the West Riding of Yorkshire about 25 per cent of the 48,610 young people interviewed were excused from taking up further activities, " mainly because of long hours of work, including in many cases travelling long distances, shift work, or the isolated situation of their homes ". In Coventry, a city in which problems of juvenile employment have for many years received sympathetic attention, " alleged excessive hours were in every instance in employment not covered by the Factories Acts ", but—

. . . factory workers showed evidence of nervous strain, probably due to the lack of sufficient sleep, or a general attitude of tiredness both physical and mental. (*The Times Educational Supplement*, September 19, 1942.)

The Middlesex authority, which made a valuable analysis of the occupations of young people in relation to their membership of youth organizations, reported that—

The plain fact emerges that, when meal times and time spent in travelling are added to actual working hours, many boys and girls of 16 and 17 are engaged for an average of 12 hours daily in the discharge of their occupational tasks. . . . Even in wartime there is little justification for the demands on young workers in some occupations. (*The Times Educational Supplement*, October 31, 1942.)

In Kent, " many boys could not be recommended to undertake youth activities because of long working hours or shift work ", and " a large number of girls could not be directed because they were fully occupied with home duties ". In Westmorland—

there was much evidence of the effects of war upon working conditions ; in particular, arduous journeys are a conspicuous factor. There is little need to query the " toughness " of Westmorland youth ; what is disquieting is the intensive drain upon their health and energies. (Ibid.)

The reports, it will be seen, came from all over the country, and from all kinds of areas both urban and rural. Everywhere, interviewers found evidence of this " intensive drain " upon the health and energies of young people due to excessive hours of employment.

Here, clearly, was a national problem which ought to be tackled without delay. "Apart from any other consideration," wrote *The Times Educational Supplement* on June 27, 1942, " we cannot from the point of view of national safety afford to run any longer the risk of devitalizing a whole generation."

The Government, after reviewing the reports sent in by the local education authorities, came to the same conclusion. In May 1943 they issued " Youth Registration in 1942 ", a White Paper (Cmd. 6446) summarizing the assessable results of registration and interviewing during that year. This showed that, of 610,619 boys and girls interviewed, on an average between 25 and 30 per cent could not reasonably be advised to undertake fresh voluntary activities, because their hours of work were so long or inconvenient as to leave them little leisure or energy, especially when—as was found often to be the case—much time was consumed by travel to and from employment, or the young people concerned were also engaged in part-time work or domestic duties in addition to their main employment.

Accordingly, the Government proposed—

(1) to review immediately, in consultation with representative organizations of employers and workers, all cases of wartime relaxations of hours of employment with the object of providing that (*a*) young persons of 16 and 17 years shall not be employed for more than 48 hours in any week except where the hours allowed were necessitated by the particular circumstances ; and similarly (*b*) that young persons of 14 and 15 years shall not be employed for more than 44 hours a week ;

(2) to arrange wherever possible for the transfer of young people

from an employment which necessitates travelling for more than one hour each way to other employment nearer home ;

(3) to develop as far as possible the existing policy of staggering hours of employment so as to facilitate the journeys of workpeople to and from their places of employment ;

(4) to review the arrangements for the feeding of young people in industrial and business establishments and, if necessary, to strengthen the existing Canteens Order ; and to call upon factory managements to give special attention to educating young people as to the necessity for taking adequate meals in the canteens ;

(5) to make it clear to Local Education Authorities and interviewing panels that young people should not be encouraged to participate in activities outside their ordinary employment to the extent that they have inadequate periods for rest and sleep ;

(6) to enquire into the question of double employment with a view to strengthening the law in respect of the employment of young persons by more than one employer.

The problem, it is important to note, is not specifically a war-time one ; on the contrary, though war conditions have undoubtedly exacerbated it, credit must be paid to the Ministry of Labour and National Service for the way in which it has persistently striven to keep the exacerbation within fairly moderate limits, and for the large measure of success it has achieved. There has been no unchecked illegal exploitation of the labour of boys and girls such as took place between 1914 and 1918 ; the regulations of the Factory Acts have been on the whole rigorously adhered to ; and the Ministry have, save at moments of acute national emergency, strenuously resisted attempts to increase the working hours of young people.

The problem is a long-standing one ; it dates from the beginning of the Industrial Revolution. It is a diminishing problem ; for a century now the permitted hours of employment of children and young people have been progressively, if slowly, reduced, and the conditions of their employment have been progressively, if equally slowly, improved. But though much has been done, much still remains to be done. By far the most valuable result of the registration of young persons is that it has focused public opinion on the conditions of their employment, and has not only moved the Government to action, but has effectively stirred the social conscience of many people who previously were ignorant of, or indifferent to, this particular problem.

TECHNICAL EDUCATION

At the outset of the war Britain found herself faced with a literally terrifying shortage of skilled workers. Fundamental among the causes was the fact that technical education had, from the onset of the Industrial Revolution, not only been grossly neglected but relegated to a position of social inferiority as compared with the more literary and academic types of education.

One writer not long ago went so far as to say that " most of the progress made has been the result of national crisis rather than of objective planning ", and while it is only fair to say that during the years immediately preceding the war there were many signs of a growing recognition of the place due to technical education in a highly industrialized country, it was still the fact that in 1939 the technical institutions which were really up-to-date in respect of buildings and equipment could almost be counted on the fingers of one's hands. Generally speaking, technical education, though in many places of high quality, was being carried on in inadequate buildings with obsolete apparatus and equipment by staffs that were too small in numbers, included far too high a proportion of part-time members, and were remunerated at rates comparing most unfavourably with those to be obtained in industry and commerce by workers of comparable ability.

Almost all technical education was being conducted in the evenings, during the workers' leisure time. Industry and commerce alike—with a few notable exceptions—resolutely refused to permit employees to participate in it during their hours of employment. Of, roughly, 2,000,000 employed juveniles between the ages of 14 and 18 less than 42,000 were in 1938 released by their employers during working hours for any form of education whatever. The number of adult workers released was negligible. As a result the technical institutions stood virtually empty during the daytime, though they were crammed to suffocation at night.

In 1939—or rather earlier, for the war cast its shadows before it—national crisis once again compelled the nation to turn to its technical institutions for help. In the first fortnight of September it was announced that, though all schools in evacuating areas were to remain closed, technical institutions might be opened for the training of members of the fighting forces and of workers engaged in industries necessary for the prosecution of the war. Where the request came from a government department the institution could be opened without reference to the Board of Education. A condition of reopening was that there should be adequate air-raid shelter, but a month later this condition was removed : an institution could be opened as soon as the work of providing protection was begun.

Even so, many of the technical institutions found it difficult to get going. A correspondent to *The Times Educational Supplement* wrote on January 20, 1940 :

The case is perhaps strongest for a review of the position of the technical colleges, with their important and advanced work in science and commerce, which have suffered a severe set-back. . . . Many of them had to endure long delays in opening. Some . . . have been either partly or wholly taken for military or civil defence purposes. Others . . . have had other schools dovetailed into them. All of them . . . have had to face alarming reductions in enrolments. . . . In most of them advanced courses have had to be discontinued. One wonders . . . how, with the advanced work in central and secondary schools also so much curtailed, the technical colleges will be able to maintain their normal courses at all.

Yet in spite of all obstacles the technical institutions did maintain their normal courses, and are doing so today. But much more than their normal courses was shortly to be demanded of them. Dunkirk saw to that. In July 1940 the Board of Education appealed to them to intensify the training of recruits for the war industries, and asked local authorities to give immediate attention to the supply of training staff.

In every institution, said the Board, it is expected that there will be enough new recruits to fill every place available for such crafts as machine-tool operation, instrument-making, fitting, welding, and sheet-metal working. Three shifts a day were wanted, and each shift would work 48 hours a week. Training courses were not expected to exceed three months and might be conside ably less ; on the average, probably about six weeks.

In dealing with the question of staff, authorities were not to upset existing arrangements. There must be no interference with the courses already being provided for employees of firms engaged in war work and the Army trainees who for some time had been coming in increasing numbers into the institutions. In fact, a larger number of instructors would be required for the latter ; the War Office was asking for a two-shift system. Moreover, skilled workers were not to be diverted from industry to training. The most important source of supply of instructors, suggested the Board, was the large number of handicraft teachers, drawn from the institutions and from schools, many of whom were now engaged on productive work in the institutions. Intensive short courses should be arranged for these to enable them to take up the task of training.

Production, insisted the Board, must in technical institutions always take second place to training. Nevertheless, the productive work already being undertaken in many schools and colleges was of great national value. As much should be done as possible. A good deal of it could be incorporated into the training courses ; for example, the manufacture of gauges and of components for war industry was useful practice.

Though it was hardly noticed at the time by anyone save a few far-seeing people, the Government's demands—all of which were complied with—effected nothing less than a revolution in the world of technical education. Previously, the institutions had done the bulk of their work in the evenings and but little during the day. They had been run in the main with skeleton staffs of full-time personnel reinforced by a large number of part-time instructors, most of whom regarded teaching in a technical institution as quite subsidiary to their main occupation. During the day the institutions had observed school hours, and they had, like the schools and universities, closed down for generous holiday periods. Their courses had been comparatively leisurely. They had rigorously eschewed productive work, both because they felt it was outside their scope and also to avoid conflict with the trades unions ; and, save in a few institutions doing advanced and specialized work, had little to show in the way of original research. Their relations with industry and the government departments concerned with industry were in a few places close and cordial ; more often they were distant if not chilly.

From now on all the institutions capable of responding to the Government's appeal were to become high-pressure factories, turning out at top speed two types of products : skilled workers and manufactured goods. Save for the statutory holidays, they were to be open every day in the year, and in many instances for twenty-four hours in the day. Staffs were to be enormously expanded, and the proportion of full-timers greatly increased. Curricula were to be drastically overhauled, teaching techniques drastically revised, courses drastically speeded up and intensified. Co-operation between the institutions, government departments, and industry was to become an intimate and daily reality.

In only one fundamental respect was there to be no change. It had been feared by some that the linking up of the technical institutions with the war industries and with the Ministry of Labour and National Service might mean that effective control of them would pass from the local authorities. This fear was dissipated in September by the Ministry of Labour itself. In a manual on the training of war workers it stated categorically that there was to be no disturbance of the control exercised by local authorities over technical colleges maintained by them. The collaboration of the Ministry was to consist in initiating the training courses in consultation with H.M. Inspectors of schools, in supplying the appropriate syllabuses, drawings and tests, correlating the supply of labour with the training facilities available, arranging for the recruitment of trainees and for their placing when trained. To effect this co-operation each institution was to have connected with it a local office of the Ministry. On the whole the arrangement has worked exceedingly well.

The technical institutions tackled their heavy new responsibilities with courage, determination, speed, and skill. I had the privilege of visiting a number of them during the autumn of 1940, and I was amazed at the transformation which had already been effected. A great deal of what I saw—and have since seen on subsequent visits—may not yet be revealed ; but I was permitted to disclose that—

. . . in the past few months men from the forces have been poured into the technical colleges and schools ; and right splendidly the colleges and schools have responded . . . rooms have been transformed, staff acquired, equipment secured, courses so skilfully conducted that efficiency has marched hand in hand with economy of time. Some institutions are working 24 hours a day ; shift succeeds shift of khaki-clad boys in endless procession ; course succeeds course with barely a breathing interval between. (*The Times Educational Supplement*, October 19, 1940.)

Nor, as has been indicated above, was the work of the institutions confined to the training of military personnel, for—

Industry too needs skilled and semi-skilled recruits by the thousand, and these too are to be found cheek by jowl with the boys in khaki or in blue—recruits in the same army, one might almost say, in spite of their civilian clothes, since all today are in the front line of battle. (Ibid.)

Everywhere there was going on the productive work of which I have previously spoken, and, as I constantly observed, many of the institutions were maintaining all, or nearly all, of their normal courses. But in addition another change had come about in the institutions, a change long desired by many engaged in technical education. Social and welfare activities—so often impossible in the past because students had to rush straight from employment to evening school, and were too tired later to do more than crawl home to bed—had become of necessity an integral feature of the life of the institutions, because—

It would be no fun to turn out daily at seven in the morning . . . to hack cold steel in a basement workshop, and at the end of eight hours of concentrated learning and doing to trek back empty-stomached to billet or barrack. (Ibid.)

Not only would it have been no fun ; it would, as the institutions realized, have been a positive deterrent to efficiency ; and so—

. . . the colleges are seeing that this does not happen. In case after case the bakery department has become a huge communal kitchen where hundreds of savoury meals are prepared and cooked each day. (Ibid.)

For the preparation, serving, and clearing of these hundreds of meals all the students in the various catering departments of the institutions were enrolled. Then, the pangs of the trainees' hunger satisfied—

The students' union, hitherto confined to entertaining its own members, and annually its friends, now deals daily with guests by the score ; the college library is full with khaki students ; the college gymnasium and playing fields resound to the commands of the physical training instructors or the shouts of the soldier guests at games in their spare time. (Ibid.)

In short—

The (technical) college has become . . . not merely a centre to which a soldier or an airman comes for a course, but a club of which he is a full, and knows himself a welcome, member. (Ibid.)

This has not happened everywhere, of course. There are many technical institutions where it is impossible for it to happen, because the essential facilities are non-existent and cannot even be improvised. But it is safe to say that it has happened wherever it has been humanly possible for it to do so. And the fact that it has happened is going to have a profound effect upon the future of technical education in this country. There is all the difference in the world between being a member of an institution which doles out dollops of vocational training and little else, and a member of a large and lively community, united in pursuit of one main purpose, but at the same time sharing a wide variety of diverse social activities.

The immense scope of the work being done in technical colleges for the Services, the Ministry of Labour, industry, and community welfare was well illustrated at an exhibition of the war-time activities of the four technical colleges in Essex which was held at the South-West Essex College at Walthamstow in October 1941. There were exhibits and demonstrations of fitting, turning, welding, instrument mechanics, radio mechanics, electrical installations, camouflage, war-time applications of science, testing of materials, foremanship, Civil Service courses, dressmaking and cookery, nursing and ambulance training, and posters and other publicity matter for the national Food and War Savings campaigns.

As the war has proceeded, further responsibilities have been laid on the technical institutions. The formation of the Air Training Corps led to a demand for facilities and instructors for various technical subjects, as did also a few months later the expansion of the Army Cadet Force and the Sea Cadets. The Home Guard has in places made similar demands. In September 1941 the lowering of the minimum age limit for State bursaries in radio and engineering, while it affected principally the universities and university colleges, brought yet more students to the technical institutions. In November 1942 the Government announced a scheme of engineering cadetships, open to boys between 16 and 19, and leading to technical commissions in the fighting services. This meant for the technical schools and colleges the provision of courses of 18 months', 2 years', or 2½ years' duration for the older cadets, and appropriate preliminary courses for the younger ones.

All these tasks have been undertaken cheerfully and are being performed efficiently. One can affirm unhesitatingly that the technical institutions of this country have, in spite of the gravest handicaps, risen to the very height of the occasion and played an invaluable part in safely bringing Britain through her time of greatest peril and placing her on the high road to victory.

This has immense significance for the future. Britain must, if she is to remain in the front rank of the nations, always remain a highly industrialized country. That means a regular inflow into industry of highly skilled workers, in all occupations and in all grades of employment. The technical institution is the training ground of industrial and commercial efficiency. Technical education must assume a place of far greater importance in our national economy than it has ever been accorded before and, equally essential, be fully integrated into the national system of education.

That this may happen there must be effective direction from the centre. By whom? That is not yet decided. At present there is every indication that a struggle for supremacy may arise between the Ministry of Labour and industry on the one side and the education authorities on the other. The Ministry of Labour has greatly developed its training centres during the war and has virtually taken command of the projected schemes for the higher education and training of demobilized persons after the war. Several leading industries, including engineering, coal-mining, building, and textiles, have said in so many words that they must be responsible for the training of their recruits in the future. The Luxmoore report on post-war agricultural education, published in March 1943, proposed a National Council for Agricultural Education, to be responsible to the Minister of Agriculture for all agricultural education. On the other hand the education authorities maintain that technical education is in its essence in no way different from all other forms of education and that therefore it is their business to supervise it.

At all costs conflict must be avoided. Technical education can only be successful if there is complete co-operation between the government departments concerned, the representatives of industry and commerce, and the education authorities. There must in the national interest be one body ultimately responsible, and logic would suggest that this body can only be the Education Department. Training for vocation is an essential element in education and must be closely co-ordinated with all the other elements. Divided responsibility could never effect that co-ordination.

University Education

The universities and university colleges did a considerable amount of provisional planning in anticipation of the war, based on the assumption that they would carry on their work in as near normal fashion as possible. When war broke out a University and Colleges (Emergency Provisions) Act was passed enabling various adjustments in administrative and financial matters to be made, including recognition of the war service of prospective scholars ; and to ensure that the best use was made of the services of resident graduates and undergraduates who desired to offer them, joint recruiting boards were set up at all the universities.

For twelve months at least the near normality which had been assumed did in fact obtain. London University was certainly dispersed to the four corners of Great Britain—its students were evacuated to Bristol, Cambridge, Manchester, Nottingham, Oxford, Sheffield, Edinburgh, Glasgow, St. Andrews, Aberdeen, Aberystwyth, Bangor, Cardiff, and Camborne in Cornwall—but the other universities and university colleges remained *in situ*, and life and studies proceeded without excessive change or dislocation ; in fact, with a great deal less of either than most people had expected.

This is not to say, of course, that neither change nor dislocation occurred. A measure of both was inevitable. A number of university buildings were taken over, in whole or in part, for hospital and other war-time purposes. Accommodation was further strained at the places mentioned above by the presence of students and staff evacuated from London. Many members of the teaching and administrative staffs were called up or transferred to other work. The numbers of undergraduates in residence declined. Though the 18–19 age groups were not immediately called upon, the lowering in September 1939 of the age of obligation for military service to 18 introduced a serious element of uncertainty into university planning, particularly as for some time there was no definite ruling as to how long undergraduates might expect to have their entry into military service deferred. Sir Richard Livingstone, President of Corpus Christi College, Oxford, pointed this out in a letter to *The Times*.

The latest official information [he wrote] is that undergraduates who are 18 will have one term certain before they are called up, probably two, and possibly three ; those who are 19 or nearly 19 will have one term certain, and possibly two. This information is not definite enough to enable us to make the most of our opportunities of education.

This element of uncertainty was to be recurrent for over three years ; and in fact it is hardly yet certain that it has completely disappeared. It appeared to have been cleared up in January 1940, when as the result of a test case brought by the Ministry of Labour and National Service it was ruled that—

A student will be granted postponement of military service if, after studying for at least one year, an examination vital to his career is due to be held within nine months of the date of his registration.

The exigencies of war were later to render this ruling meaningless.

Generally speaking, however, it is safe to say that until roughly the end of 1940 the universities and university colleges continued to function in remarkably normal fashion. The most noticeable differences were the reduced numbers of undergraduates (though the fall in numbers was not nearly so great as many had anticipated), the absence of many teachers and of a large proportion of the men of the senior years, a natural preoccupation with national service in hours previously devoted to games and social activities, and the seriousness with which the students in residence attacked their work. Realizing that they had at best little more than a year of university life before them, freshmen everywhere cast aside their traditional irresponsibility and devoted themselves to their studies with an earnestness which surprised everyone save themselves.

How the universities fared during the first year of the war may be illustrated by extracts from the Oration delivered on October 9, 1940, by the late Mr. G. S. Gordon, President of Magdalen College, Oxford, when he took office for a third term as Vice-Chancellor of that university. After saying that what had above all impressed him was the " universal vigour and good will " with which the situation had been met, he declared that, in respect of the structure and administration of university studies, on the whole—

. . . our improvisations worked well, and we continue to improve them. Time and experience have revealed defects in a machinery created almost overnight ; there has been some waste of effort . . . but the great thing is that the young men were swept along and kept interested, and that even their briefest incursions into the field of knowledge were given some sort of beginning, middle and end.

This happy experience, it is safe to say, was common to all the universities. There had, of course, been moments of difficulty. For example, on the outbreak of war, when everyone thought that the number of undergraduates in residence would diminish very materially, some resentment had been felt among senior members of the university that the Government did not immediately make use of their services in other capacities. But, said Mr. Gordon :

As the policy of the Government took shape, it became clear that university teaching must still be regarded as of high national importance. To deplete without check or calculation the teaching strength of the university at a time when young men were being encouraged, in the interval allowed them, to pursue their academic studies, when new courses had to be devised and new examinations, would have been the extreme of imprudence. This, fortunately, was seen in time, and an arrangement was presently made with the Ministry of Labour to ensure that the recruitment of temporary Civil servants should be subject, so far as possible, to a double control : the special suitability of a man for Government service and the needs of his Faculty or Department in the university.

The Vice-Chancellor continued :

It would be strange if it had never occurred to us to ask ourselves whether the life we are still trying, not unsuccessfully, to lead, as an academic and collegiate community, is any longer, perhaps, quite in keeping with events. Laudable and salutary as our studies and teaching may be, is there, on a general view, any longer a settled place for them among the growing distortions of war ?   Doctors and scientists must still, no doubt, be trained ; but need the list, it might be asked, go much beyond that ?

In view of the subsequent events, the answer Mr. Gordon was able to give has peculiar significance.

So far, this sort of question has been answered for us, and by national authority. *The universities of the country have been repeatedly and publicly encouraged by His Majesty's Government to continue their work, even if this meant, as for some it did, migration to other centres.* (My italics.)

But, persisted Mr. Gordon, things had moved on.   Was it possible, he asked, that a national policy until now unquestionably right was on the point of becoming antiquated ?   He had the highest authority for saying No.   He had just received a letter from the Chancellor of the University, Viscount Halifax, which commented that young men on leaving school would be faced by an awkward gap before the time when the country would call on their services, and that while no doubt they would solve their problem in different ways,

. . . *it is difficult to believe that any solution would be as satisfactory as that provided by the university.* (My italics.)

The calling-up age for men at that time was 20.   As Lord Halifax said, this left a gap between school and military service. Later that gap was to be closed by the lowering of the age, first to 19, and then to 18.   Then the question of the importance of university life and studies, and in particular of the humane studies, had to be faced again, this time in absolute form.   Not as a stop-gap occupation, but as an integral part of the national life.   Not nearly so satisfactory an answer was given.

On January 29, 1941, the application of the National Service (Armed Forces) Act was extended to include at the lower end of its age range men of 18 and 19, and while the 18-year-olds were told that their registration would be deferred, probably for some months, the 19's were instructed to register on February 22. At once there was re-introduced the element of uncertainty about the length of university life for all save those studying " to obtain certain scientific and technical qualifications that will fit them for important national work ", as the Ministry of Labour put it.

There was this time an added reason for uneasiness.   The Ministry of Labour and National Service, in a statement published

on January 29, after pointing out that the joint recruiting boards
had power already to defer the military service of undergraduates
studying the reserved subjects, added that the arrangement was
to be extended to cover young men at school who were studying
these particular subjects and likely to pass the Higher School
Certificate.   But nothing was said about those studying any other
subjects.

The Council of the National Union of Students saw the
red light at once.   On February 8, it passed a resolution re-
affirming its belief that " the maintenance of university education
is important to the community in war and peace ", and stating
its fear that—

. . . the Proclamation of January 29, 1941, will make impossible
the continuance of non-technical university faculties, with serious
effects both on the contribution which the universities can make
in the life of the community today and during the reconstruction
period after the war.

The fight for the humanities had begun.   Today, after
more than two years, it is still not won.   But it has one minor
success to record.

When the Air Training Corps was launched on January 25,
1941, it was announced that the Air Ministry was also arranging
at various universities a six months' course for young men who
wished to serve as pilots or navigators and who were regarded
as potential candidates for commissioned rank.   The course was
to be taken between the date of leaving school and the date of
beginning Service training, the age limits for nomination being
$17\frac{1}{2}$ and 18 years 8 months.   The subjects that could be taken
were limited to *such as were considered of value from the Service point
of view*, i.e., mathematics, mechanics, electricity and magnetism,
engineering, meteorology, and navigation.   In addition, those
undergoing the courses would, as members of their university
air squadron (henceforth to be affiliated to the A.T.C.), undergo
a course of instruction similar to that at the initial training
wings of the R.A.F.   In all other respects they were to be treated
as full members of the university.   They were even to be given
preference, if necessary, over the ordinary undergraduate in
that wherever possible they were to be allotted rooms in college
or accommodation in a university hostel rather than in lodgings.

Even such special consideration, however, could not conceal

the fact that a new and radical departure from university tradition was being made. In future, in addition to being homes of pure learning and research, the universities were to become occupational training centres giving strictly vocational courses. In war-time this could no doubt be reckoned a perfectly legitimate perversion of their purpose, but the extraordinarily interesting and highly significant fact about these short pre-Service courses (which incidentally the Army had already started and the Royal Navy was later to take up) is that before many months had elapsed the military authorities had discovered that, for the development of intelligent fighting capacity, technology by itself was not enough. Within a year the regulation that these university trained candidates for commissions must take only specified scientific and technical subjects was done away with ; and at the present moment roughly half the men taking these short courses are studying humane subjects.

The permanent value of six months' residence at the university, at an age below that of the normal undergraduate, is another question altogether. Upon this there is no agreed opinion. My own, for what it is worth, is that for the more retiring or introverted boy two terms at a university between 17 and 18 should prove a very valuable form of transition from the life of school to that of the armed forces. For the extravert the advantages are not so obvious, especially if he has risen to a position of leadership in his school. In any case a short course of this kind is a *pis aller*, designed to meet an emergency situation ; in the nature of things it cannot be wholly satisfying.

In September 1941 the Board of Education announced that in order to meet the prospective need for men and women trained in radio and in engineering the minimum age limit for applicants for State bursaries had been lowered. Boys and girls who had attained a sufficiently high standard in physics and mathematics in the Higher School Certificate examinations, and who were born between January 1 and June 30, 1924 (i.e. were between the ages of 17·9 and 17·3), would be considered : and it was added that it was urgently necessary in the national interest that as many as possible should make application. The intention was that they should have in the first instance two years at a university or technical college. So successful was the appeal that within a fortnight the Board and the Scottish Education

Department had to announce that no further applications could be entertained. The award of these " State bursaries in Science " has continued, and thus there has come into being a new type of undergraduate : the young scientist whose future services are already earmarked by the State, and whose period of residence at the university, while not likely to be less than two years, is of uncertain duration, the criterion being the nature and quality of the service it appears he will be most fitted to give and the consequent amount of university training he will need.

As the number of students of science and technology has increased, so the number of those studying the humane subjects has decreased. The reduction in December 1941 of the age of call-up to $18\frac{1}{2}$, and the Government's refusal to consider deferment save for students of " useful " scientific and technical subjects, could not fail to diminish the numbers on the arts side. Twelve months later the National Service Act, 1942, made men liable for military service on their 18th birthday, and in order that they might be immediately called up required them to register at the age of 17 years 8 months. In the debate on the Second reading on December 9, Mr. McCorquodale, Parliamentary Secretary to the Ministry of Labour and National Service, confirmed what many already feared, that this meant the end of the arts courses at the universities. It would not be possible, he said, to defer the call-up of students going to the universities beyond June 1943 to enable boys to study for an arts degree. In the present strenuous and serious position of the war they could not possibly continue these courses.

There the matter still stands. All protests, all suggestions that the Government reconsider this decision, have proved unavailing. In a leading article on December 22 *The Times* wrote :

There is universal agreement that it is essential not only to win the war but to win it quickly and very thoroughly. . . . The men must be found, in numbers and of a quality sufficient to launch and sustain the offensive by which alone the end can be attained. That is not in question. What is seriously disputable is whether the wholesale suppression of the arts courses . . . is inevitable in the extension of the call-up now enacted. The Act contains provision for amendment by Defence Regulations. Is it not possible that a proportion of the young men capable of profiting to a high degree from a course of university study in humane subjects, thereby equipping themselves to render invaluable service to the nation, may be allocated to this vital end ? Or, if that be not practicable, can they not after absorption into the forces be given appropriate educational opportunity ?

Neither alternative has found favour with the Government, nor any other compromise. The only crumbs of comfort in the present situation are that, as previously stated, many of the men on the six months' Services courses at the universities are studying the humanities, and that it is still possible for an able boy to come up at an early age and spend two, or in exceptional cases three, terms reading a humane subject. Women are still in somewhat better case, for they are not called up before 19, but even they have little chance of completing a full university course.

The position will persist only till the end of the war ; the Government have already said so in their published statement on education after demobilization. It will largely depend upon when the war ends how serious the loss to the national life. But even should the gap be no more than a year or two—and this seems hardly likely—it cannot be inconsiderable. Britain will need in the future every type of trained ability in the largest possible numbers. She cannot do without students of the humanities. The balance in education as between the sciences and the humanities undoubtedly needs adjustment, but the way to effect it is certainly not to dam up completely the flow of students of the humane subjects. A much more scientific allocation of brain-power is required. It is impossible not to regard the Government's policy as a mistaken one.

The future of the universities is a subject much too vast to attempt to discuss here. As yet, it is one too little explored. Two important books only have been published on it since the war began : *The Universities in Transformation*,[1] by Dr. Adolf Löwe, and *Redbrick University*,[2] by Bruce Truscot. More studies of the same calibre are urgently needed. Meanwhile, for the time being, the British universities have almost ceased to function as universities.

ADULT EDUCATION

Adult education in England before the war was a limited and imperfect growth. Though the statutory bodies responsible

[1] Sheldon Press, 1941.   [2] Faber & Faber, 1943.

for education had during recent years played an increasing part in its provision, even in 1939 it still owed its dynamic—as a century before it owed its birth—to voluntary effort and individual demand. It was still not regarded as in any sense an activity which was necessary to the well-being of the community, or one demanding much more than benevolent tolerance from the State. But for the sustained persistence of the University Extra-Mural Departments, the Workers' Educational Association, and other bodies, it is safe to say that it would have remained negligible in both quantity and quality. As it was, in the years immediately preceding the war only about half a million adults out of a potential field of recruitment of at least 18,000,000 were undertaking any form of organized education; and of the half-million three-quarters or more were doing so for strictly utilitarian reasons. The W.E.A., after nearly 40 years of indefatigable crusading on behalf of cultural study, could count only about 60,000 students in its classes.

How can one explain this state of affairs? There is no simple answer; it was the result of a complex of causes—economic, social, political, psychological. To attempt to analyse these out in detail would take up too much space; but some are obvious: poverty, bad living conditions, overlong hours of employment, and the inadequacy of the education given to children. To these I would add another; too much of the wrong sort of education.

I simply do not believe that the average English man or woman has ever been by nature antipathetic to education. All our history goes to disprove this theory—still so resolutely held in some quarters. The present war, I maintain, should kill it for ever. The English people have always at heart longed to be well educated, but the circumstances in which most of them have had to grow up and pass their lives have effectively prevented them from satisfying this desire.

It is important, though, to be aware of the nature of their desire and of the kind of education which meets their needs. The English are not, and I believe never will be, a race of potential intelligentsia. Though they throw up thinkers, scholars, and inventors in abundance, they are on the whole a practically minded people. Their instinct is to learn through action, not by the processes of abstract thought, and their genius has always lain in their capacity to act rightly without any apparent precedent intellectual activity.

The education of the future, for both children and adults, must have the strictest reference to this almost universal characteristic. It has been in the past woefully neglected, and nowhere more so than in the field of adult education. Happily, the past quarter of a century has seen a growing recognition of this ; but I do not think that even yet there is anything like a sufficient appreciation of how much the English love education —provided it be the right sort. I use the word " love " in all sincerity.

The London County Council were among the first to come to an understanding of the kind of adult education that appeals to the generality of English people. Their Men's Institutes, established shortly after the last war, and later their Women's Institutes, and their Junior Men's Institutes (for boys in the later years of adolescence), have had a resounding but in no way surprising success. In these institutes you can see men doing carpentry, metalwork, cobbling ; learning to look after poultry, pigeons, rabbits ; playing in bands and singing in choirs ; painting pictures and rehearsing plays ; debating politics and social questions. You see women absorbed in practice of the domestic arts, and not less but probably rather more so than the men in the practice of music, drama, literature, painting, sculpture, and architecture. You see boys rapturously busy with the pursuits dear to the heart of youth ; physical training, creative craftsmanship, song, dance, and debate. And in all departments you see the members forming their committees and electing their officers to run their departmental affairs.

But this is recreation, says the highbrow. Well, why not ? Must education be regarded as a sad and solemn business ? The crucial question is whether regular participation in such activities as those listed above enables the participants to live healthier, saner, and more intelligent lives. If it does, it is education. And to that question experience shows there can be but one answer.

Hitler has, without meaning it, been a great friend to Britain in more than one way. Among other benefits he has conferred upon us, he has compelled us as a people to take adult education seriously. Munich was the first important stimulus he applied.

As a result of that famous—or infamous—episode many thousands
of English men and women who previously had never dreamed
of subjecting themselves to any educational process became at
once ardent and determined students. They crowded into
classes to learn about war gases and how to combat them, about
first-aid and home nursing, about fire fighting and the duties of
a civilian in the case of invasion or an air-raid. All very
utilitarian, no' doubt. But many of them began also to apply
themselves to study on a higher level than this strictly utilitarian
one. Munich awoke in them an irresistible desire to know why
the world had fallen into so sorry a state. So, just as they crowded
into their gas lectures and their first-aid classes, they thronged
lectures and courses on international affairs, on politics, economics, history, psychology—anything which promised to supply
the answer to their insistent questions. The bodies concerned
to provide such lectures and courses were hard put to it to meet
the demand.

The outbreak of war intensified and broadened both kinds
of demand. More people began to learn A.R.P., first-aid, and
other matters appertaining to civil defence. War-time cookery,
housewifery, and handyman-ery were added to the list of " useful " occupations it had become desirable to learn. The thirst
for knowledge of the underlying causes of the world debacle
redoubled, and was among the causes of the speedy reopening
of many of the educational institutions the Government had
closed. Evacuation revealed to many people the need to inquire
into the effects of our social order ; and social studies of one kind
or another began to attract an increasing number of students.
The black-out and the closure of most cinemas left a serious gap
in the leisure life of scores of thousands of people ; the recreational
evening institutes, with their practical activities, and their
dramatic and music courses and circles, proved a boon to many
who previously had never entered their doors.

Then came the blitz. If anything could have been calculated
to arrest the spread of adult education, at least in the areas
concerned, surely it was this. On the contrary, it stimulated
rather than deterred both providers and recipients. I have
told how the evening schools, when it became too hazardous to
open in the evenings, held their meetings on Saturdays and
Sundays. It must also be recorded that in one or two places

at least, when driven from their buildings they went into the public air-raid shelters and carried on there. In Bermondsey, for example, the heads of two evening institutes organized in 1941 between 80 and 90 classes for 2,500 students. Practical activities predominated, dressmaking being most popular among women, shoemaking and handicrafts among men. But travel talks and talks on current affairs also had a strong appeal, particularly when accompanied by films. Many discussion groups were formed, and mobile libraries brought books for those who wished to study further the topics discussed. Plays were rehearsed and staged, concerts given by locally recruited talent, by the Pioneer Corps, and by C.E.M.A.

This seems the appropriate place at which to tell something of the story of C.E.M.A.—the Council for the Encouragement of Music and the Arts. It is one of the most enheartening of the war. Towards the end of 1939 the then President of the Board of Education, Earl de la Warr, approached the Pilgrim Trust to see whether it would make a grant towards the maintenance and encouragement of music and the arts in war-time. The Trust responded with £25,000, to which shortly afterwards the Treasury added another £25,000. A committee of four—Sir Kenneth Clark, Director of the National Gallery, Sir Walford Davies, Master of the King's Musick, Dr. Thomas Jones, Secretary of the Pilgrim Trust, and Mr. W. E. Williams, Secretary of the British Institute of Adult Education—was appointed to advise the Board of Education, which had been named as the recipient by the Pilgrim Trust, as to the disbursement of the money.

C.E.M.A. came into being in January 1940, with Lord Macmillan as its chairman and Miss Mary Glasgow as secretary. Its purpose was defined as the encouragement of musical, artistic, and other cultural activities outside the large and more prosperous organizations. Subsidiary but essential aims were quickly discovered to be the safeguarding of the livelihood of professional musicians and artists, the preservation of the standards of British art in music, drama, and painting, and the taking of good music, drama, and pictures into the towns and villages where such pleasures had been rare or unknown before.

The Council quickly got to work. Guarantee grants were made to the great orchestras, who were encouraged to give concerts in places where they had never previously been heard.

Travelling organizers were appointed through the Rural Music Schools' Council to foster music-making of all kinds in the country areas. Factory concerts were initiated. Assistance for the professional theatre was organized ; the " Old Vic " Company was given a guarantee to tour industrial areas, and, later, other companies received comparable guarantees. Pictorial art was encouraged by a large development of the " Art for the People " exhibitions which the British Institute for Adult Education had been for some years arranging on a small scale.

To attempt to assess the value of the work C.E.M.A. has done during the past four years would be futile. Suffice to say that it has brought new and joyful experiences into the lives of hundreds of thousands of people. Everywhere its touring companies and exhibitions have received a welcome far exceeding all anticipations. The London Philharmonic, the London Symphony, the Hallé and other well-known orchestras have had enthusiastic receptions throughout the industrial areas. The tour of the " Old Vic " Company, led by Sybil Thorndike, in 1940, through the mining towns of South Wales, will never be forgotten by any, either among the players or the audiences, who took part in it. Hundreds of villages first realized what drama meant when the Pilgrim Players came to their village hall or played upon the village green. 270,000 people visited the " Art for the People " exhibitions during 1940 alone.

What I personally shall always best remember is the service C.E.M.A. rendered in the air-raid shelters and emergency rest centres during the height of the blitz. Night after night—I believe many did it five nights a week for months—C.E.M.A. artists travelled by taxi, in buses, and on foot, often while the bombs were falling, to play and sing to audiences of people who had just lost homes and belongings, or who might lose them at any moment. I saw C.E.M.A. artists come into rest centres full of men and women stunned into apathy by their experiences (they had all been bombed out scarcely twelve hours previously), and, by the sheer grace and sympathy of their art, warm them first to clapping, then to singing, and—within an hour and a half—to joyous cheers and radiant laughter. If ever a body of men and women helped to revive and sustain the morale of the English people, during a time when this was most needed, those C.E.M.A. artists did.

C.E.M.A., which has now become an entirely State-maintained institution, has, I firmly believe, introduced into this country the germ of a new form of adult education. Not an entirely novel form, of course ; as I have insisted earlier in this chapter, not one of these war-time developments is altogether new. Concerts and dramatic performances of high quality as regards both matter and manner are in no sense new. Nor are exhibitions of fine art. But for the most part these used to attract the *cognoscenti* only ; the ordinary man or woman kept away from them, was indeed rather afraid of them. C.E.M.A. has brought them to the masses. That is both new and important. In so doing it has had to learn new techniques. You can open a concert at the Wigmore Hall with Beethoven, but you cannot in a munition factory, an air-raid shelter, or a remote country village : you have got to lead up to Beethoven. You can stage without explanation an exhibition of masterpieces at the National Gallery or the Royal Academy ; but you cannot do so in a small market town. C.E.M.A. has learned how to give concerts and show exhibitions as successfully in the depths of industrial or rural areas as in the West End. That, too, is new—and very significant for the future of education in England.

I have written earlier on in this chapter of the quite sensational developments in technical education which have taken place during the war, and in the second part of this section will sketch very briefly the equally sensational development of army education. I conclude this part with a brief note on residential adult education.

Before the war there were in Great Britain (outside the universities, the teachers' training colleges and other specialized professional institutions) places for less than 350 students wishing to undertake residential adult education. Today there are places for scores of thousands.

Taking the term in its widest sense, all the men and women who join H.M. Forces undergo a course of residential adult education ; but forgoing this wide interpretation, there are men from the Forces at the universities, men and women from the Forces at innumerable specialized residential courses, men and women from industry, or in process of being recruited into industry, at training centres with residential accommodation ; men and women from government departments at the univer-

sities ;   men and women who have come into the Service of Youth
or the pre-service organizations being trained at residential
courses.   There may well be other categories of which I have not
heard ; but the above list shows how extensively residential adult
education is being practised today.   And—an important point—
it has even developed into a two-way traffic between this country
and other lands.   Young men go from Britain to the Dominions to
learn to fly ; young men from the Dominions come to Britain for
part of their training.   Young men from India come here to learn
industrial skills ; men and women go from Britain to other
countries for a similar purpose.   It is proposed by the Government that after the war this exchange of students between Britain
and the Empire overseas shall be continued, at least during the
period of demobilization.

Residential adult education must become an integral part of
our educational system.   We cannot do without it.   There have
been published already government plans for sending, on their
demobilization, suitably qualified men and women to universities,
university colleges, and training colleges.   But that is not enough ;
the residential college for adults must become a permanent
institution, and open to all.

There will probably be the necessity for a variety of types of
institution for adult education.   But the provision of institutions
is in itself only the provision of a setting, a framework.   It is
necessary to inquire what is to be done in these institutions,
what is to be learned and taught, and how the matter learned
is to be taught.   On these points the Services have much to
teach us, as the following brief summary of the progress of army
education during the war will show.

Before the war each of the three fighting Services made
organized provision for the general education as well as the
specialized training of its personnel.   The specialized training
was naturally designed to meet specific needs and consequently
was very varied in each Service, and very different as between
the three Services.   The main aim of the general education
given was in each case the same : to make a better sailor, soldier,
or airman, and the main task of those administering it was found
to be to make good the shortcomings of an education which had
ceased at 14.   The Army Educational Corps, for example, was
chiefly preoccupied with elementary and secondary instruction

in the basic school subjects.   There was, in the Army at least, little or nothing of what is generally known as adult education.

On the outbreak of war the A.E.C. was virtually disbanded, most of its members being seconded for other duties, and general education in the Army came almost to a full stop.   But there were those, both in the Army and outside it, who realized that for general education to cease permanently would be disastrous. Early in 1940 a Services committee was set up, with General Haining as chairman, to study the problems of war-time army education.   The committee produced in the autumn of the same year a report which was never published but which nevertheless had a profound effect on future development.

Meanwhile the universities and a number of voluntary bodies, notably the Workers' Educational Association and the Y.M.C.A., which had previously been doing valuable educational work among the conscripted militiamen during their term of military service, had realized the need for effort on a national scale, and were striving with might and main to bring it about.   They succeeded in getting together in conference representatives of the three Services, the Board of Education, the local education authorities, the universities, and the voluntary societies concerned with the provision of adult education ; and from this resulted, towards the end of 1939, the Central Advisory Council for Adult Education in H.M. Forces.   This body invited Vice-Chancellors of universities and principals of university colleges to set up regional committees, constituted on the same model, in each of the 23 regions into which the country was divided, the purpose being that, under the direction of the Central Council, they should survey and endeavour to meet the educational needs of the Forces in their regions.

A start was made.   Volunteers who would act as lecturers and tutors came forward in encouraging numbers, and local education authorities offered facilities at their evening institutes and technical colleges.   But the obstacles were formidable ; the Central Council had neither money nor official status, liaison with the Services was difficult, and in many places co-operation not forthcoming.   For a while little real progress could be made. Then came the Haining Report.   As a result the Central Council received formal recognition, and funds were placed at its dis- posal by the Government and the Services.   At the same time the Army Educational Corps was returned to its proper function, and a Directorate of Army Education was established at the War Office.

It will be recalled that this was shortly after the disaster of Dunkirk. Among the lessons to be learned from that disaster was that in modern warfare the individual soldier had to be able to act with intelligence and initiative. The day of the automaton who blindly obeyed orders was over. The subsequent development of adult education in the Army shows a progressive appreciation of the implications of that lesson. Three clearly marked phases can be distinguished up to the present.

The first phase, which lasted for about a year, was one of encouragement of voluntary educational activities by the Army Command (though not, alas, always by commanding officers), and the provision of a profusion of facilities of the most varied kind. There was plenty of enthusiasm on the providing side, and in many places a welcome response from the Army ; but the programme was formless. It had no recognizable pattern, and there was evident in it no coherent purpose. Officers and men expressed their needs—real or imagined—and wherever possible those needs, which ranged from Hindustani to cobbling, from philosophy to elementary mathematics, were met. It was education very much à la carte.

In September 1941 there took place a significant advance. The Army Bureau of Current Affairs (A.B.C.A.) was set up. One hour a week of the soldier's training time was allotted to the discussion of current affairs—military and social, national and international. Three points in particular are to be noted about this most important development. First, a departure from the voluntary principle. It was officially recognized that education was not merely desirable but necessary for the soldier. Second, it was further recognized that the soldier was a citizen as well as a soldier, and that the better citizen he was, the better soldier he might be expected to be. Consequently, alongside his training as a soldier there must go education in citizenship. He might (or might not) continue his education for individual enrichment in his spare time, choosing his study or activity according to his bent. He would of necessity be compelled to continue his military, that is, his vocational, training. It was now thought fit that he should be compelled to begin, or continue, his training as a citizen, because he must know " the purpose behind his duty ". Third, this new form of army education was to be conducted, not by an instructional but by a discussional technique. Two pamphlets on topics of current interest were to be issued fortnightly, one dealing with the military course of events, the other with political, social, and economic questions. These pamphlets were to be used, not as lessons but as briefs. The regimental officers were to be in charge, but they were not to *teach* ; they were to lead the discussions of their men which arose out of study of these briefs.

The principles involved were of the first importance ; and they were laid down deliberately. They represented a very great advance towards the idea of democracy. It may well be that in the years to come the importance of A.B.C.A. will be seen to reside not so much in what it actually did as in what it pointed the way to—the purpose, the content of, and a technique for, the adult education of all in a mass society. Mr. Herbert Read has declared [1] that :

> The plain fact about democracy is that it is a physical impossibility. In an aggregation of millions of individuals such as we always have in modern society, we may get government *of* the people and even government *for* the people, but never for a moment government *by* the people.

The form of adult education which began in 1941 as A.B.C.A. may yet prove Mr. Read absolutely wrong.

The next step forward was taken a year later ; and again it was a very big one. From November 1942 to March 1943 three hours a week of training time, in addition to the A.B.C.A. hour, were set aside for the education of the man or woman (for the scheme included the Auxiliary Territorial Service) in the Army. The crucial importance of this " Winter Scheme of Army Education " lies, not in the extension of the time given to education, but in the fact that the scheme was a coherent and comprehensive pattern.

One hour each was allotted to the education of the man or woman as soldier or auxiliary, as citizen, and as individual. This implied a clear recognition of the fact that if a democratic society is to function each of its members must actively participate in

[1] In *The Politics of the Unpolitical*, Routledge, 1943.

a three-fold capacity, and therefore needs to be educated in each of these capacities.

By reason of this recognition, and by the provision made to translate it into terms of action, army education has forged ahead of adult education among civilians, and it is profoundly encouraging to learn that so outstandingly successful was the " Winter Scheme " that this has been extended to cover the summer months—though on a shorter time basis owing to the demands of military training.

It has to be admitted, of course, that it is the highly ordered and disciplined organization of the Army which has made this extraordinarily valuable experiment possible on so large a scale. In such an organization a system can be imposed—as this one was—by a stroke of the pen. That method obviously cannot be used in a civilian society which professes to respect the freedom of the individual. But the educational pattern is clearly a correct one, and the technique seems to be along the right lines. The problem to be solved is how to obtain general acceptance of the idea that some such pattern is also a necessity in civilian society.

CURRICULAR TRENDS

It had long before the war been a common complaint that curricula in both elementary and secondary schools were in many respects remote from reality ; and in increasing numbers enterprising teachers were experimenting to make school life and work more relevant to the life and work of society. The war has given them in a variety of ways an unprecedented opportunity to extend and develop such experiments, and has encouraged—and indeed compelled—many others to follow in their footsteps.

Evacuation brought hundreds of thousands of children and many thousands of teachers into intimate contact with a way of life and with activities of which they had had previously little or no experience. Interest attracted them, and circumstances made it obligatory on them to participate in this way of life and these activities. Innumerable town children, for example, began to garden for the first time in their lives, and many teachers were not slow to seize the opportunity thus offered. Some of the rural schools already had school gardens ; in other cases land was secured for the purpose.   School gardening became a regular feature of the curriculum.

The development of communal feeding in schools gave an immense impetus to the school gardening movement, for it supplied a clear and quickly realizable objective.   It became a matter of pride that the school supplied all, or nearly all, the vegetables for its midday meals.   The " Dig for Victory " campaign added a further fillip, and did much to introduce school gardening into urban schools, many of which took up allotments when (as was usual with elementary schools) ground of their own was not available.   Secondary schools in both rural and urban areas gave up part of their playing fields to food production.

In many instances stock-keeping has been added to gardening. A few rural schools did this before the war ; the number has been increased enormously during the past three years, and today it is not unusual to find hens, ducks, geese, bees, rabbits, pigs, or goats on a school " farm ".   Some schools have them all. Larger stock—horses and cattle—have been generally found beyond the capacity of schoolchildren, though there are some schools—notably those with Young Farmers' Clubs—which tackle even these.

School gardening, and even more so stock-keeping, demands equipment and apparatus.   Many schools have shown rare initiative and enterprise in providing both by their own efforts ; they have made cold frames, built tool-sheds, greenhouses, poultry houses, piggeries (with cement floors and brick walls), constructed beehives, broody pens, and incubators.   Where there is a craftsman on the staff the work is often of rare quality and finish ; and more than one evacuated teacher without previous experience has turned himself into a first-class craftsman during these war years.

It may be mentioned at this point that there are schools doing similar productive work not for themselves alone but directly for the war effort.   I have been in a senior school which at one and the same time was turning out components for the Navy, equipment for hospitals, and toys for nursery centres.

There are, it must be admitted, some schools where gardening has remained a more or less mechanical occupation, the production of food being the sole aim.   There are, more regrettably, a few schools where stock-keeping has become a mere money-making enterprise. But my information and experience lead me to believe that this is not usually the case ; so far as I have been able to learn, teachers generally are correlating these healthy outdoor activities with the more academic side of the school work and gradually establishing them as integral parts of a realistic curriculum. This is the case more particularly in the senior elementary school, but it is being done with conspicuous success —though naturally in a simpler way—in some junior schools I have visited. The process is less developed in secondary schools, for the obvious reason that the demands of the School Certificate examination severely limit the time that can be devoted to it. Yet even in secondary schools I have seen remarkable progress.

Some few schools have developed the study of rural science to a high degree ; the school garden and farm have become, so to speak, the outdoor laboratories, and all work done there is scientifically planned and subjected to scientific analysis. This is as yet rare ; but in very many instances there is close relationship between the farm and gardening activities and the work done in the science lessons. Botany and animal biology have become live subjects, and some of our perhaps over-academic advocates of sex instruction in schools would be surprised (and maybe a little startled) to discover how fully many quite young children are informed about the " facts of life ", and how perfectly naturally they treat them, as a result of their having been allowed the care of animals. The most important and beneficial advance in sex instruction ever made in our schools was initiated when in 1942 the Board of Education urged them all to keep rabbits.

The arithmetic and English in many schools have been improved out of all recognition and made infinitely more attractive to children and more realistic because of the necessity—if the job is to be done properly—of keeping full, accurate and legible records and accounts for the garden and farm. Drawing and painting, too, have achieved new meaning when used for the making of hen-house plans, of diagrams to illustrate the anatomy of animals seen in the flesh each day, or sketches of the animals themselves.

This applies also to the study of wild nature, both plant and animal, which has formed so valuable an element in the lives of many schoolchildren during the war years. A whole fascinating chapter could be written on this topic ; but it must suffice here to say that the joy children have experienced in learning to love the flowers, fruit, grasses, trees, birds, and animals of the countryside has been expressed in innumerable artless (and not infrequently highly artistic) narrations, written compositions, poems, songs, plays, drawings, and paintings. On the scientific side the study of botany and biology in particular, but also in some instances of geology, meteorology, and even astronomy, has advanced very materially. There are some schools where field work goes hand in hand with laboratory work, and where the laboratories are genuine houses of scientific experiment and research.

It may be appropriate at this point to say a word about the agricultural work which schoolchildren of 12 and upwards are permitted, and indeed enjoined, to do in aid of the war effort. Local education authorities have been asked so to arrange school holidays that children may help in gathering the various harvests and assist in other farming operations within their capacity. In addition these older children may be excused up to 20 sessions (10 days) of schooling a year to help on the land in seasons of pressure.

Many worthy bodies and individuals (chiefly, one suspects, with an urban background) have protested, some of them violently, against this alleged exploitation of child labour. They ignore, or do not realize, that the country child has always worked on the land from a tender age, and what is more has always loved it—it is part of his way of life ; and it is almost impossible, provided the hours of work allowed by law are reasonable, to " exploit " the labour of children (or of adults, for that matter) in agriculture, in the sense of overdriving them, simply because it is impossible to maintain a factory supervision in the open fields ; and that the permitted absences from school are in fact the surest preventative of more frequent or prolonged illegal absenteeism.

The use of child labour on the land is, of course, open to abuse, both wilful and through negligence. But the regulations under which the children may work are strict, and there is no evidence of abuse on any large scale. I personally cannot feel uneasiness about the present position, but rather the reverse.

The children, except in rare instances, suffer no harm and get much good through being in the open air.   Their help is urgently needed to get in the crops upon which we depend, and it is being used in ordered and humane fashion—which was not by any means always the case before.

Another type of activity which has been developed with great profit and enjoyment by not a few schools is the local survey. The possibilities inherent in this are almost limitless, for a survey of a parish or a district can include study of all its history and its geography and of every aspect of the life of the people in it.   Not many schools have pushed the matter thus far, though one camp school has made an amazingly complete survey of the neighbourhood in which it found itself.   Generally speaking, the school surveys which I have seen and of which I have heard have had a markedly historical and archæological or architectural bias, though some have paid considerable attention to rural industries and crafts.

The extent and thoroughness of a survey naturally condition to some extent the influence it has upon the rest of the school work.   But it is safe to say that in all instances, in addition to the primary benefits it confers upon the children by opening their minds to a wide range of interests and giving them opportunity for creative activity in a variety of media, it improves their handwriting and powers of composition, gives them an incentive to draw and paint, teaches them much history and geography and incites them to learn more, often introduces them to the study of archæology, geology, meteorology, and biology, and in a few instances to sociology.

There are quite a few schools which have seriously taken up the practice of rural crafts, and it is probably no exaggeration to say that in some instances they will literally save these from dying out.   What is to my mind equally interesting is the extent to which homecrafts of various kinds have been forced by circumstances upon so many children.   In many a rural school today you will see boys cobbling their own and their sisters' shoes, girls mending their own and their brothers' clothes.   The reason is simple ; the flood of children evacuated into the district overwhelmed the local cobbler and seamstress ; the school took on the task of repairs and has continued at it ever since.   Many of the children now expert with the last or needle would—as was made only too evident in the first days of evacuation—rarely, if ever, have touched either in the whole of their lives had they not been evacuated. You will find also laundering being done in places—for the same reason and with the same beneficial results.

The rapid expansion of the school meals service during the war has had to be built up on the minimum of expert and adult help.   So children assist regularly with the preparation, cooking, serving, and clearing of the meals.   Some schools have carried the interest aroused by these new activities over into the arithmetic lessons, where the accounts for the meals service have been made out and checked.   The children get a great thrill out of this, and no better way of learning household marketing and budgeting could be devised.

But probably the greatest enlivener of the arithmetic lesson has been the War Savings campaign.   The amount of money which has been raised for War Savings by schools is stupendous ; by the end of 1942 it exceeded £15,000,000.   During the " Wings for Victory " campaign of 1943 the schools, which had been set a target of £3,000,000, actually raised over £10,000,000.   Of course the existence of a savings group in a school may mean no more than a weekly collection of contributions by the teacher. Even so, one cannot but feel that the regular habit must have a beneficial effect upon the children—and upon their parents, who supply the bulk of the contributions.   But in many, many schools War Savings has meant far more than this.

Those who visited the exhibition of children's posters held at the Royal Academy in 1942—the first time in history that children's art had ever been hung there—must have felt amazed at, if not overawed by, the fertility of invention and the skilful technique evident in the hundreds of posters by children of all ages from 4 to 18.   Those posters were but a tiny sample (admittedly a selective sample) from the hundreds of thousands which have been produced by schoolchildren during the past four years.   Go into any school, and you are almost certain to see somewhere some home-produced War Savings posters.   They may be crude.   That is not so very important ; what is important is that children have had the opportunity to create.

A few schools have found in the War Savings campaign an opportunity for valuable experimental work on a much larger scale.   One London school spent a term in preparation for

" Warships Week ". They traced the history of ships right back to the days of the log with a hole burned in it ; they made drawings and models of all sorts of ships ancient and modern— exploring museums and dredging libraries to get their data ; they studied trade routes and followed commerce round the globe. The work led them into innumerable fascinating fields of scholarship and activity ; and there is every reason to believe that some of the children at least have in consequence developed worthwhile interests or hobbies that will stand them in stead throughout their lives.

Other schools have experimented with this " project " method without even the excuse of a War Savings or other campaign. One girls' school holds a yearly " week " devoted to a single field of learning ; one year it was a " Greek Week ", the next, a " French Week ", during which plays were performed, poems and prose recited, pictures and models shown to illustrate the language, literature, and ways of life of the people under study. A boys' school has done the same, but stuck to French each year. Naturally, such projects demand weeks of intensive and co-operative planning and work.

These last two schools were secondary schools, which generally speaking have done far less in the way of experimenting with the content of the curriculum or methods of teaching and learning than have the senior elementary schools. But the active way in which the secondary schools have responded to the appeal to study more American and Russian history must be recorded, as must also the growing practice of Sixth and Fifth form seminars on " Current Affairs ". Between them these two developments may revolutionize our teaching of history—which needs it—and perhaps of geography also. Mention must be made also of the rapidly increasing interest shown and attention given in Sixth Forms to the elements of sociology, economics, and politics. That may portend a further revolution.

I do not pretend that all these developments are necessarily good. Many undoubtedly are ; others present potentially dangerous characteristics. Some have combined with other war- time developments in the educational situation to present the teachers with a pretty—and embarrassing—problem : what is the teacher's job ? Is it to teach, or to do a multitude of other jobs as well ? During the past few months much has been heard of the " extraneous duties " of teachers, and more will yet be heard. The clerical work expected of heads has increased inordinately ;   assistant teachers have been asked to supervise school meals, to look after children in the evenings, during week-ends and, latterly, during school holidays.   They have to serve milk, collect War Savings, check clothing coupons, manage school funds, arrange school entertainments.   They feel morally bound to become officers in the A.T.C., the Army Cadet Force, the Sea Cadets, or the G.T.C., or to run the local youth centre. And so on and so forth.   The matter was, I think unwarrantably, complicated in 1942 when in awarding a war bonus to teachers the Soulbury tribunal indicated that consideration had been taken of the " extraneous duties " performed by so many teachers.

The question of the duties of a teacher is of great professional interest, but it is a secondary issue only.   It is bound up in the larger question which I have tried to indicate in this section ; and this again is but part of the still vaster problem which I trust this whole chapter has illustrated.   Our conception of education is changing.   We debate its purpose, its function, its scope, its content, its administration, its techniques and methods. While we debate, the scope, the content, the technique, and the methods .are being changed before our eyes, not for the most part deliberately to suit our ends and purposes, but by the sheer force of circumstances.   How much with the grain, how much against it ?   Some light, but I fear not nearly enough, may be thrown upon the question by the next chapter, in which I attempt to present the debate.   Meanwhile, it is gratifying to note that in one respect at least all these curricular trends are along the right lines.   They all point towards the school as a society, a community of human beings learning and living co-operatively.

CHAPTER IV

FERMENT

SIX CATEGORIES

In presenting any outline of the great movement for reform in education which has arisen during the years of war it would be ungracious and unjust not to pay tribute first to those rare minds which for long previously had striven to penetrate into the future and to discern something of the shape of things to come. Nor less is tribute due to those who by courageous experiment—pursued oftentimes in face of discouragement, handicap, and obstacle—paved the way to reforms which are today either in being or universally advocated, but which have been made practicable only by reason of their initiative and resolute endeavour.

To mention names would be invidious. Many, perhaps most, of these pioneers—of both kinds—have remained unknown to more than local fame. Let thanks be recorded, without distinction, to all.

It is impossible to say just when the idea became articulate that there must be after the war a new order in English education. By the end of 1940 it was being canvassed in many quarters, though as yet in terms rather of vague aspiration than of practical politics. But months before this forward-looking educationists had begun to try to hammer out the principles upon which reform should be based, and even to put forward proposals having some measure of definition.

In 1941 the ferment spread rapidly, and it soon became possible to see definite forms and patterns emerging. There were early to be distinguished six main categories of thought : the philosophical, the religious, the professional (i.e. representative of the views of teachers and administrators of education), the political, the industrial, and that of the general public outside these specialized groupings.

Save for the last, which has remained diffuse, incoherent, and to a large extent inarticulate, these categories, though constantly impinging upon each other and often to no slight degree overlapping, have yet been throughout differentiated. The

163

ultimate aims which have inspired their representatives have
been different, and so too has been the emphasis each has laid
upon certain aspects of reform.

It would appear the most helpful plan to consider these
categories under separate headings, in the hope that the reader
may thus be enabled to obtain a clearer picture of the extraordinary variety of influences, aims, and emphases which have
gone to make up the reform movement, to assess the nature and
value of the contribution made by each category to the sum-
total of thought, and to form his own judgment as to the probable
effect of that thought upon the future of education and of society
in Britain.

As my analysis of these matters is an entirely subjective one,
it is of course liable to be biased, and I certainly cannot expect
that everyone will agree with it.   All I will say is that any bias I
may have introduced is entirely unintentional, and that I trust
this will be corrected by the factual story of the movement which
follows in this chapter.

One exception will be made to the procedure of treatment
under separate headings.   The professional and political categories have throughout acted and reacted upon each other so
continuously and in so intimate a fashion that to deal with them
apart would be almost meaningless.   They are accordingly placed
together under a single heading.

Philosophical thought has concentrated in the main upon
endeavouring to elucidate what should be the purpose and the
scope of education in a fully democratic society.   It has paid some
attention—though I think not enough—to the content of the
curriculum, but has concerned itself little with the structure and
administration of the educational system.   This I hold to be a
defect, for I believe purpose, content, and structure to be indis-
solubly related, and that consequently none of the three can
properly be examined without full reference to the others.

In seeking to discover the purpose of education, philosophical
thought has inevitably found itself driven back to examination
of the nature and purpose of a fully democratic society.   It has
made valuable explorations in this hitherto almost unexplored
field, but, with the exception of one or two thinkers—notably
Karl Mannheim and Sir Fred Clarke—the philosophers have
tended rather to overlook the importance of the setting—that

of mass industrialization—in which our democracy of tomorrow will have to be worked out. Consequently, their deductions concerning the relationship between education and the social order as a whole have not got much beyond the stage of statement of general principles applicable to any kind of democracy. Little attempt has been made so far to examine in detail the implications of these principles in the light of modern socioeconomic trends, and so to translate the principles into terms of action relevant to the state of society today.

For example, it is generally agreed that education should be the basic activity of the State in a democratic society, and universally agreed that the potentialities of each individual member of the community should be developed to the full. These principles demand for their implementation staggeringly revolutionary action ; but hardly a single thinker has yet dared to advance proposals which would come anywhere near implementing them to the full.

Religious thought has, unhappily, been hopelessly confused, and consequently lamentably undirective, because of an almost universal failure to distinguish between three quite distinct and separate issues ; the purely religious one, the denominational, and the administrative.

Even on the religious issue there has been a regrettable lack of clarity of thought. To seek to base all education upon Christian principles and to permeate it through and through with the spirit that was in Christ Jesus is a very noble aim— perhaps the noblest by which man at this era in our civilization can be inspired. Had the religious thought of the past three years consistently and undeviatingly pursued this aim, its contribution to educational reform would have been invaluable, for it is beyond question that the direst need of man today is for a compulsive and overriding sense of spiritual purpose and direction.

Unhappily, even where this aim has been pursued singlemindedly (and this has been exceedingly rare) almost without exception there has been made, not the correct assumption that it is *desirable* that education shall be based on Christian principles and permeated with the Christian spirit, but the dogmatic assertion that it *must* be. Consequently, little attempt has been made to do what most needs to be done—to demonstrate that Christianity offers a purpose, a directive, and criteria of conduct, such as to compel the allegiance of men and women seeking to live their lives on a higher moral and spiritual level.

The denominational and administrative issues are almost inextricably interrelated in the minds of most people. They are of course rooted in the very fabric of our educational history. They derive from the fact that it was denominational bodies which first provided educational facilities on a large scale for the mass of the people and thus established for themselves an interest and an ownership which could not in justice be expropriated and which the denominations would not relinquish when the State system was founded.

It seems impossible for many people to distinguish between the interest and the ownership, yet they are in reality quite separable. The separate issues can be stated in two simple questions : (1) Have parents (not the Churches, but the parents) the right to expect that in the schools provided by the community denominational religious instruction shall be given ? (2) Have denominations the right to ownership of buildings and a say in the administration of schools which are integral parts of the publicly provided system of education ?

I have my own answers to these questions ; but any answers I might give would be merely expressions of an individual opinion, and so of slight value and little interest. In a democratic society the only answers which can be regarded as valid and conclusive are those given by the community as a whole. Scotland has given such answers ; England has not yet managed to do so. We shall not do so until we are prepared to distinguish between the two issues, and to consider them, not only as separate but as on different levels.

As will be seen from the narrative in this chapter, professional thought was in the first instance stimulated to intense activity by political statements and action. It was most unfortunate that this resulted (though it need not have done) in the level of professional thought being decided by the politician, who naturally thought mainly in terms of legislative and administrative action, and not in terms of the social philosophy which should direct action. The fundamental defects of professional thought have throughout been that it has been recapitulatory rather than progressive, that it has concentrated upon the structural aspect of reform, and that it has shown a fatal fondness for compromise. Its proposals have never lived up to the principles upon which they were supposed to be based. In all these respects it has taken its cue from the political platform, and in the game of ball which has been played for the past two years or more between the politician and the professional, the former has consistently dictated the boundaries and the standard of play. At no time have the representatives of organized education insisted that the level of the discussion should be raised to a higher plane and made to embrace the whole range of educational problems.

" The wrong battle is being fought," the late Dr. H. G. Stead said to me a few weeks before his death. His words were profoundly true. Professional thought has succeeded in achieving a remarkable unanimity of opinion on a great many important questions, chiefly in the sphere of structural reform, but it has hardly begun to touch the fundamental problems of education in a democratic society. It has as yet no real answer to the question of purpose ; it has been content to pay more or less sincere lip-service (much of it admittedly sincere) to slogans the full meaning of which it has not troubled to analyse out. It has evaded the question of the scope of education, in that, first, it will not tackle seriously the problem of the relationship between the education of the young and their initiation into the world of adult labour and citizenship, and second because it burkes the issue of a comprehensive system of adult education—though this is beyond doubt the most immediately urgent educational issue before the nation at the moment. It has shied away from the problem of the content of the curriculum, because the internal vested interests which are antipathetic to change are too well placed strategically and too strongly entrenched to allow consideration of the radical changes that are required. And it has almost completely ignored, except in respect of the matter of entry thereto, the entire field of university and comparable forms of higher education.

This drastic criticism must not be taken to imply any lack of appreciation of the genuine contribution towards reform which professional thought has undoubtedly made. It has been the spearhead of that body of opinion which has convinced the public that there are grave defects and deficiencies in both the publicly provided system of education and in the educational set-up as

a whole. While it has never had the courage to state frankly
and fully the implications of the principle which it has made
its battle-cry—" equality of opportunity "—it has succeeded in
getting the idea generally accepted that there must be a very
considerable levelling up of opportunity. Though it has not yet
fully grasped the idea that the educational process is a continuous and all-pervasive one embracing the whole of life and
conditioning every activity of the individual and of society, it
has established a widespread conviction that education is immensely important, that its period must be considerably extended,
and that the process, to be effective, must be linked up and
co-ordinated with the other social services.

In brief, professional thought has laid a foundation for educational advance. If all the reforms it has so strenuously advocated
were to be carried into effect simultaneously we should at least
be in a position to consider a genuine and substantial educational
advance. It may be that this process of recapitulatory reform,
of stopping the gaps and repairing the defects in our existing
system, was inevitable, that public opinion (which ultimately
must be decisive) could not have been brought up to the pitch of
demanding both reform and advance at one and the same time.
I believe it could, and I am profoundly concerned lest this preoccupation of professional thought with recapitulation shall have
induced public opinion to be satisfied with too little. These
are no days for compromise, especially in education ; for the
future of our country literally depends upon the quality of our
post-war education.

What of the sixth category ? I have had some opportunity
to assess the state of mind of the ordinary citizen, for I have
travelled the length and breadth of Great Britain during the
past three years, and have met him at meetings, in conferences,
and at training centres ; and have listened to his conversations
in railway trains, hotels, clubs, the Forces, factories, business
establishments, and private houses. I admit that in the main I
have met only the interested citizen, the one who is making
some effort to understand this business called education because
he believes for one reason or another that it is much more important to him and his children than ever he imagined until
quite recently. I know there is a vast mass of people who are
not interested—at least not openly and actively interested—

though I believe that even among them there is latent, and not too deep below the surface, an uneasy feeling that all is not well which could be without difficulty quickened to a live interest.

Two characteristics are outstanding in the interested average citizen ; a desire for extension of educational opportunity which is pathetic in its intensity, and an ignorance which is equally if not more pathetic. He does not know in any detail what he wants, and he has no reason beyond the purely utilitarian one for wanting it. For him the educationist's slogan " For every child a chance in life " means, quite openly, " For my child a better job in life ". It is a tragic reflection upon the state of our society, but it is completely understandable in the individual, as the following section in this chapter shows only too clearly. And it is not only understandable ; it merits every sympathy.

But the matter cannot be left there. We cannot press for educational reform on a purely material basis—important though that aspect is. Nor do I think we need act as though the matter must be left there. Social security is the indispensable pre-requisite for the success of educational reform ; but given that, given even the guaranteed promise of that, I am confident that the great mass of the people of England would respond imme-diately and enthusiastically to a call on the moral and spiritual level. But that call must be such as to fire their imagination, and the action upon which it is based must be the work of creative and imaginative minds. Educational reform on the gradualist, compromising scale will strike no fire from the average citizen ; educational reform on the grand scale, linked with social reform of comparable magnitude on other fields, will mobilize in a flash a vast army of red-hot supporters.

Towards a New Philosophy

So far as I am aware, the first important contribution to the literature of post-war reform in education was a supplement to the *Christian News-Letter* entitled " Educating for a Free Society ", written by Mr. Geoffrey Vickers, and published on January 31, 1940. It was important for two distinct reasons : it laid down educational principles which have not only been accepted by but have since governed the thought of many other educational reformers ; and it showed clearly the relationship between education and the social order.

The crisis of which this war is a symptom and a part [said Mr. Vickers] is a challenge to men to show wisdom commensurate with their power . . . the new society, of which both politicians and common men are beginning to talk, will not come of itself. It must be created by the wisdom, the courage, and the self-sacrifice of men. . . .

People today are challenged to choose within the limits of the possible the conditions of life which they most want to preserve or create ; and in this process education has a double part to play. It can clarify the choice, and it can enlarge or narrow the limits of the possible.

Education cannot fail to reflect each generation's conception of what matters most and to imply its ideals for the future. . . . What is being done in education reflects the qualities and limitations of today. What is being attempted foreshadows the society of tomorrow. *Education is social philosophy in action, and as such it can express better than words the choice to which each generation is willing to commit itself.*[1] At the same time, to an extent at present unknown, education determines what kind of a society it shall be possible to create.

Mr. Vickers pointed out how difficult it was to fit men and women to form a free society, and the increasing demands such a society makes on ordinary men and women. They must become more and more sensitive to truth, more informed and intelligent, more independent and courageous.

Above all, they must have a common faith, for, " If men are to find their individual freedom in a common society . . . their respective ideas of what matters most must be consistent in essentials."

Therefore, said Mr. Vickers :

. . . education, if it be given a meaning as wide and as deep as it deserves, cannot escape—and should not seek to escape—the responsibility of playing a central part both in shaping the ideals of today and in making the community of tomorrow. It is not the State's gift, but the State's need. It is the most conscious part of the living tradition which links the future to the past. It is the most conscious channel through which each individual receives his share of the common inheritance and his opportunity to add to it. It can never be more important than at this time and for this generation. . . .

This, said Mr. Vickers, was a concrete task, concerning, not education generally, but education in Britain today. It involved solving a complex of specific problems. In particular, there were

---

[1] My italics, H. C. D.

three major issues before the country : to equalize the educational opportunity ; to extend the educational period ; and to deepen the educational purpose.

Wealth, argued Mr. Vickers, carried a greater privilege and poverty a greater handicap in England than in the systems of most civilized countries. The public schools remained the preserve of the rich and produced a recognizable class which got a better chance both socially and economically than the rest. If a public school education had the peculiar quality claimed for it, it should be made available to all who could profit from it, irrespective of wealth, on the ground of national interest no less than of social justice.

But, however adequately this issue were met, educational equality would remain an illusion so long as 85 per cent of boys and girls began whole-time wage-earning at 14. There was an irresistible case for raising the school age to 15, and ultimately to 16, and for extending part-time education until 18. The primary purpose of this extension should be, not to protect the young from conditions of life adults had an equal right to resent, but to maintain educational direction and control throughout the adolescent years and thus make this whole period a planned transition from childhood to manhood, citizenship, and work.

At 18 another even more neglected educational field opened —that of adult education. Nor should an earlier gap be forgotten—that which the nursery school was learning how to fill. Education, declared Mr. Vickers in a truly inspired passage—

has no boundaries. It will not be contained within particular age-groups, as ministries or categories of thought. It overflows from the mental into the physical and the spiritual. It is concerned with politics and midwifery, with philosophy and with drains, with religion and with milk supply. The unity which it needs can never be imparted by institutions, but only by an underlying unity of vision, of purpose and of faith.

When education became universal, traditions largely of aristocratic and clerical origin were carried over into a democratic world. They had not yet been unified and enlivened by a sufficiently clear and widespread vision of the task which education has to perform in a self-governing State today. Three traditions hindered the development of a philosophy of education fit to inspire the education not merely of a class but of a people : the critical tradition of the public schools, the instructional tradition, and the individualist tradition. The first, which preserved the supremacy of an education based on critical appreciation of the written word, tended to beget a bookish attitude to life which produced critics instead of creators. The second kept physical, recreational, and character training on the periphery of the educational field. The third tended to divert attention from the value in education of collective activities.

All three issues, Mr. Vickers added, are controversial. The first raises controversies in the political field, the second in the economic ; the third in an even wider sphere. He continued :

What should be the content of education and what its object ? What should be the place and scope of religious teaching ? Apart from religious teaching, how can the schools best contribute to the training of character ? What kind of activities should make up part-time training of the young during the transition period ? What is the educative value of collective activities and in what sort of communities should children experience them ?

These issues are much wider than the domain of education. They go to the root of the question—for what are we trying to educate ? In what kind of world do we expect them to live ? What are the essentials of that specific common faith which alone can make it possible for human persons to live significant lives in and through a coherent society ?

It is time to face these controversies, for education more than any other social activity can shape the future, and Britain is bound to be faced within a few years with the need for radical re-shaping. (My italics.)

There followed a merciless analysis of our present social order, which was declared to be made up of :

. . . increasingly powerful and autonomous vested interests . . .
. . . an urban proletariat without roots in the past, without a share in the present, and without a hope in the future . . .

With in between :

. . . the bulk of the population, highly stratified in classes and divided economically into categories, some . . . as rigid as Hindu castes.

In this order, power :

resides with an industrial plutocracy, which has inherited and still preserves some of the mentality and some of the institutions of feudalism.

Its only rival being :

a labour party which has been content for long to take an ever higher price for its continued acquiescence in the pace set by the governing class.

And its principal cement :

. . . the dividend from a golden age which is abruptly passing away.

To end this state of affairs, said Mr. Vickers, there must be profound change ; and the nature of the changed Britain that will emerge may depend on how the educational issues are faced now. Two policies, he urged, are needed : a long-term and complete one, and an opportunist and fragmentary one. The second would seize every opportunity war presents to establish bits of the long-term plan, and to prevent those opportunities from being misused in the service of temporary need.

To do anything adequate to the situation, concluded Mr. Vickers, there was required activity in five fields :

1. The purpose of education must be re-examined in relation to the changing social and political order—a task for all who share the same social ideal.
2. The policies must be worked out in accordance with the needs and opportunities of today—a task primarily for educationists.
3. Public interest and support must be mobilized, both generally and in particular among the leaders of the business world and of organized labour—a task for a non-political agency, formed if necessary for the purpose.
4. Parliamentary support must be won—an all-party committee of members was suggested.
5. The policies must be carried into effect. This involves the lively activation of local education authorities through the Ministry of Education and probably action by other Ministries.

Finally, Mr. Vickers pointed out, " mere planning for ' after the war ' is not enough ". The transition from war to peace may take longer than the transition from peace to war : and " after the war " will be too late.

The moment following . . . a successful war is always a psychological trough, without vision or energy. The beginning must be made now, while habits are shaken, and the economic system is accustomed to take orders based on national need ; while a common purpose seems something worth making ; while we are trying to describe to each other and to ourselves the kind of society we claim to be fighting to create.

I have presented thus fully the argument of this profound and penetrating essay, not primarily because of its intrinsic merits —remarkable though these are—but because it includes almost every point which philosophical thought on education has elaborated since. The voluminous literature (chiefly in pamphlet form) which has been published, and the innumerable public conferences and private discussions which have been held have advanced the philosophy of education little, if at all, beyond the point reached by Mr. Vickers in this summary statement. It will suffice therefore to indicate briefly a few of the more important contributions falling within the philosophical category which have been made.

In March 1940 Mr. T. S. Eliot contributed a Supplement to the *Christian News-Letter* [1] in which he attempted to discover the chief values at which education in a Christian society should aim, and suggested that these should be Wisdom and Holiness. Much contemporary discussion of education, he argued, was impaired by lack of any clear notion of what end was desired. " Equality of opportunity ", and " the democratization of education ", he said, were in danger of becoming uncriticized dogmas.

They can come to imply, as an ultimate, a complete mobility of society—and of an *atomised* society. . . . the individual in isolation, apart from family and from local milieux . . . having certain intellectual and spiritual capacities to be nurtured and developed to their full extent . . . a system of education as a vast calculating machine which would automatically sort out each generation afresh according to a culture-index of each child. The result might be to produce a race of spiritual nomads.

The scope of education, said Mr. Eliot—

is no longer the task of merely training individuals in and for a society, but also the much larger task of training a society itself—without our having any fundamental accepted principles on which to train it. The scope of education has been rapidly expanding as social organisms have broken down and been replaced by the mechanisation which increases, as it manipulates, the atomisation of the individual.

The warning was very apt ; but it has been largely ignored. " Equality of opportunity ", and " the democratization of education " are in the mouths of all too many people wholly uncriticized dogmas.

[1] March 13, Supplement No. 20.

Three weeks later an anonymous writer, in a further Supplement [1] probed further the question of the relationship of the educational system to the social order.

. . . in any free society the school system must learn to be *responsive* before it can become *directive*. It is a mistake to suppose that schools and universities, except on a very long and ill-defined view, can initiate great social changes. They can do only what the society they serve permits them to do. Sensitiveness to felt needs is their first essential. If they are thus sensitive they can do the great service of defining needs in terms of a concrete plan of training, and of so criticizing and refining the often crude indications that society offers as to make the society more fully aware of its own better desires. They are refineries of the product of the social soil, not experimental forms for the propagation of quite new species.

The second half of that excerpt is particularly valuable.

Meanwhile Professor (now Sir Fred) Clarke, Director of the University of London Institute of Education, had been attacking the problem of education and society from a different angle, in a little book called *Education and Social Change*.[2] Education must be seen, said Clarke, not only against the background of society but as an integral part of it. To do this involves looking into the past as well as at the present. So Clarke's book opens with an exploration of the " historical determinants of English education ", as a result of which he comes to the conclusion that there is an English tradition of education which can be adapted to and reinterpreted in terms of the age of the aeroplane —provided always, as he paradoxically put it, that we are conservative enough to be radical. In particular, he pleads that we strive to build a new synthesis out of the literary and the scientific conceptions of culture, and to sweep away the wholly artificial distinction—exaggerated if not created by the progress of mechanization—between " cultural " and " vocational " education.

One of the two important works on university education which have been published in this country during the war [3] appeared early in 1941. This was *The Universities in Transformation*, written by Professor Adolf Löwe,[4] who argued that whereas during the

[1] No. 23, dated April 3, 1940.
[2] *Education and Social Change*, by F. Clarke, Sheldon Press, 1940.
[3] The other is the valuable study of the modern university and its problems, *Redbrick University*, by Bruce Truscot (Faber), published in July 1943.
[4] *The Universities in Transformation*, by Adolf Löwe, Sheldon Press, London. Macmillan Co., New York, 1941.

50 years preceding the war of 1914–18 there had been at Oxford and Cambridge a " happy synthesis " in the education of the " ruling type ", a synthesis " not only between cultural and technical education but also between spiritual and material civilization ", since that time there had arisen a lack of harmony between the universities and society, due to social and economic causes, to " change in the general social background ".

Assuming that there would be in the future no radical social changes in the structure of society, Professor Löwe anticipated that there would be a period of transition lasting over a generation or more, in which our task would be that of adaptation to a planned society. The special task of the universities would then be the education of what he called " social functionaries ", a new élite of " enlightened experts " who would hold the key administrative posts and direct the planning. Professor Löwe examined in some detail the nature of the required curriculum, and indicated a new humanist " synthetic " education, having the social sciences as the central synthesizing subjects. This education should produce the " enlightened expert " who would understand the processes and the development of society.

There is a great need for more studies of this kind, and not merely of university education. To build an education that shall be a unity and completely relevant to the life and purpose of society we must examine in closest detail the specific tasks of the primary and the secondary school, and of institutions for adult education. And that implies also a rigorous investigation into the content of the curriculum for each.

In much more popular vein Francis Williams, in *Democracy's Last Battle*,[1] was about the same time analysing the influences formative of British public opinion. The greatest, he said, is the daily life of the people ; apart from that the most powerful direct influences are the educational system, organized religion, and the Press ; and of these the most important is the educational system. Of the English educational system he said :

There can be few more open manifestations of class distinction than British education, which makes of privilege and inequality a religion and which maintains and guards, as its most important

---

[1] *Democracy's Last Battle*, by Francis Williams, Faber & Faber, 1941.

characteristic, the perpetuation of social differences. For the most significant thing about it is that it is not one system but two—a State system of public education and a private system of Public education, spelt with a capital to distinguish it from the other.

Many other writers—in fact almost all who have written on any aspect of education—have commented on this dichotomy, and no question has been disputed more acrimoniously or with less effective result than that of the public schools. No solution of this problem is yet in sight.

During this same winter there appeared also a slim volume of which one reviewer commented that it " may well reorient all our thought ". This was *The Future in Education*,[1] by Sir Richard Livingstone, President of Corpus Christi College, Oxford. It achieved the triple distinction—almost unprecedented for a treatise on education—of being reviewed in almost every newspaper and periodical of standing, being widely quoted on public platforms, and being a best-seller.

This was not surprising, for Sir Richard propounded a revolutionary theory. The problem of national education, he said, of transforming the English from an uneducated to an educated people, could not be solved by any extension of educational facilities to the young, but only by an extension of adult education, because " you cannot study fruitfully certain subjects . . . unless you know something of life ", and " our school population has hardly any experience of life ". Education up to 14 was not education at all, but only a preparation for it ; even at 16 education was only just beginning. There must be " cross-fertilization of theory and experience ", and until we recognized and acted upon this principle we should never solve our educational problem.

Sir Richard advocated the introduction into this country of a system of residential adult education, comparable with that of the Danish People's High School, in which he would have given a liberal education such as would enable a man or a woman to become a " complete human being ". In one of the noblest passages of a book replete with distinguished passages he thus defined his complete human being :

[1] *The Future in Education*, by Sir Richard Livingstone, Cambridge University Press, 1941.

Human beings have bodies, minds and characters. Each of these is capable of what the Greeks called " virtue " (ἀρετή), or what we might call excellence. The virtue or excellence of the body is health and fitness and strength, the firm and sensitive hand, the clear eye ; the excellence of the mind is to know and to understand and to think, to have some idea of what the world is and of what man has done and has been and can be ; the excellence of the character lies in the great virtues.

Sir Richard Livingstone's book had a profound and far-reaching effect, though it is to be feared that neither it nor his subsequent ceaseless advocacy has yet moved the nation to regard the provision of universal adult education as a first priority in plans for post-war reconstruction.

In *Education for the People*,[1] published in the summer of 1941, Dr. F. H. Spencer, a former chief inspector to the London County Council, presented what was becoming by this time the conventional case for educational reform with more eloquence, and in more biting phrases, than any other writer during the war. Popular education, he said—

has been successively for the governing class and many others a matter of philanthropy, a measure of " ransom ", an insurance against the dangers of an illiterate democracy, a necessary consequence of developing industrial methods and increasing and transformed office employment. *It has never, by our statesmen, been conceived as the most important means among others of producing a noble race.* (My italics.)   Our new society will recognize this, or it will fail and fade like the shadow of another dream. It will care for the child, train youth to strength and goodness, and *never let go*.

If only Dr. Spencer's proposals for action had been as revolutionary as his thesis !   " It is time ", he said, " we had a principle which applies . . . at least to the social aim of this great and vital process that we call education." That principle, he rightly concluded, " must be the old, trite and true principle of equality of opportunity ", but when it came to listing the reforms necessary to implement this principle Dr. Spencer had to offer nothing beyond the conventional ameliorations of the existing system so many other people were advocating—more nursery schools, an enlightened junior school, secondary schools of various types, day continuation schools, and a broader path to the university, with improved school buildings, a better medical service, more

---

[1] *Education for the People*, by F. H. Spencer, Routledge, 1941.

communal feeding, and better trained teachers. All very desirable and necessary, but inadequate in themselves to carry out the revolution his earlier chapters demanded. To do this a unifying conception was needed.

In June and July *The Times Educational Supplement* published a series of four leading articles in which was outlined in general terms a conception of educational reform more far-reaching than any which had previously appeared. In the first, " Bases of Reform ",[1] it was declared that—

. . . before we can demand, and before we can have any certainty of securing, equality of opportunity for all our children, we must each one of us ask ourselves two questions and, though it cost " blood, toil, tears and sweat " (as it will), compel ourselves to give absolutely honest answers to them. The first question is, What does equality of opportunity mean ? ; and when we have answered that comes the much harder one, Do we really desire it ?

It was supremely important, continued the article, that we made absolutely certain that we realized fully and precisely the implications of " this most revolutionary principle ".

Do we understand, for example, that it means that there can be no such fact as a " school leaving age" in the sense that we understand the term at present ? . . . There can be no full equality of opportunity so long as there is a school leaving age which means for one section of the adolescent population an obligatory transfer from school to gainful labour, while for another section it means precisely nothing and involves no handicap whatever ? Do we understand also that true equality of opportunity must completely reverse the present conception of the day continuation school as a place which young wage-earners are permitted by their employers to attend for a brief period (or a long one, it matters not) each week ? There can be no equality of opportunity so long as one section of the adolescent population is free to choose whether to continue its education or not, while another is bound hand and foot to the wheel of industry, and must obtain " release " in order to obtain a modicum of education of probably inferior quality.

The bases of the conception of equality of opportunity, concluded the article—

. . . must be that citizenship begins at 21 ; that up to that age all boys and girls are wards of the State, and are to be regarded as in a state of tutelage ; and that during those 21 years no effort

[1] June 28, 1941.

must be spared to give each one, according to his or her capacities, and limited by no other consideration, the fullest opportunity to develop every innate power. Only thus can we hope to produce a noble race.

The following week, in an article entitled " Quality of Reform ",[1] the leader writer contended that those who accept as basic the principle of equality of opportunity—

. . . realize that its full implications cannot be worked out in the field of education as at present delimited, but they realize also that the working out must start from there. So they aim not merely to extend that field but to make it central and pivotal in the social order. They demand that childhood and youth shall be regarded as a unity, and that until the age of citizenship is reached boys and girls shall remain under the aegis of the education service, which shall have full responsibility for their welfare, education and training —individual, vocational and civic—till they reach the threshold of adult life.

In " The Function of Education "[2] the writer maintained that it should not be supposed that the sole function of an educational system was to act as a reflector of society ; it had also to help shape the future. But no system of public education such as the existing one in England, even if amplified and extended as people were suggesting, could " undertake any notable part in shaping the social order ". The English system did not deal with the child until the vital first five years of life were over, it relaxed its hold at 14, 15, or 16, and thereafter did " no more than throw a net full of holes blindly and feebly at random . . ."

Nothing less than a service which provides for all ages, which is given full responsibility for and control over the entire period of childhood and youth up to the age of citizenship ; a service of such prestige that it can attract to itself the ablest, most clear-sighted, and most forceful minds the nation possesses, and which is endowed by the community with resources commensurate with the magnitude of its task, could possibly hope to succeed.

And, added the writer :

Such a service is the condition of the continuance of Britain as a leader among nations and, more important, of the preservation of those values, tested and tried through long centuries of experience, upon which all that is finest in Western civilization has been built, and of the stabilizing of other values yet to be fully discovered.

[1] July 5, 1941.   [2] July 12, 1941.

In the concluding article of the series [1] the leader writer endeavoured to link the present with the future, asking what immediate steps could be taken towards realization of such a conception of education as had been expounded in the previous articles. "The opportunity is at hand ", he said, "to guide present developments in the light of future aspirations and needs," and he cited a number of developments in various branches of the educational service which, properly directed, should lead in the right direction. A synthesis, he said, was emerging :

Full and proper provision for the pre-school child, the closer relation of the schools to further education, and of both schools and universities with the outside world, the co-ordination of cultural and vocational training, and of the two with the transition to gainful occupation, the encouragement of a dynamic and forward-looking youth movement, and the development of adult education on a broader basis to cover all ages and all sections of the community—all these are already foreshadowed and their realization already beginning.

That was two years ago. "Education is changing, growing, developing before our very eyes," said the article. It is still doing so, but the warning with which the leader writer concluded is still valid.

A strong lead and a clear directive purpose will ensure that all these gains are consolidated and brought into harmony along the lines that will be most fruitful for the future. But an all-inclusive framework is needed, and no partial vision will bring success.

He would be a bold man who would say that in 1943 the lead is strong enough, the purpose sufficiently clear, and the vision full. [2] But the ideas expressed in these articles have not only gained a wide acceptance ; they have also influenced the minds of many, inside and outside the world of education proper, who would hesitate to accept them in all their fullness. Among those who welcomed them unreservedly was the late Dr. H. G. Stead, whose untimely death early in 1943 was such a tragic loss to the cause of educational reform. He literally killed himself for the cause ; despite physical enfeeblement due to a grave illness some years previously, he spent the last twelve

---

[1] "Present and Future ", July 19, 1941.
[2] I still hold to this, though the publication on July 16 of the Government's White Paper, " Educational Reconstruction," certainly altered the position very materially. See pp. 222 et seq.

months of his life travelling incessantly to spread the gospel of purposeful and comprehensive reform. In addition to numerous newspaper articles he left behind him a full-length book, *The Education of a Community*,[1] in which he analysed the defects of the existing educational system, and outlined his idea of the system for tomorrow.

Stead was a thinker who strove at all times to relate the purpose of education to the problems of society. Education, he said, was an expression of the basic values of society. These must be examined and criticized, and the principles on which the society of the future is to be based must be formulated. Then the educational system must be examined to see to what extent it is expressive of these new principles, and to what extent there must be change to enable it to sustain and develop the values of the new society. In making changes, Stead always insisted, equal attention must be paid to purpose, content, and structure, and he deplored the current tendency to concentrate upon structural change and to ignore purpose and neglect content.

Ernest Green, General Secretary of the Workers' Educational Association, in *Education for a New Society*,[2] declared (quite rightly) that we had not yet succeeded in making education attractive to the ordinary man. So, with the help of Mr. Harold Shearman, Education Secretary of the Association, he set out to show that :

. . of all the constructive tasks on which the nation is engaged, modern education offers scope for the most exciting adventure and promises the greatest social gain for the effort and expenditure involved.

In common with almost all other authors who have published books on education during the war, Mr. Green is bitterly critical of the existing system :

The educational provision of the 19th century was short-measured. That of the 20th century has been short-sighted.

He pointed out that " It is now nearly 40 years since we affirmed, in principle, a doctrine of equality of educational opportunity ", and added :

[1] *The Education of a Community Today and Tomorrow*, by H. G. Stead, University of London Press, 1942.
[2] *Education for a New Society*, by Ernest Green, Routledge, 1942.

What a different world we might have been living in had that principle been carried into practice. If children had *not* been denied educational opportunity because of the poverty of their parents the whole social structure of society might have been different. It is conceivable that had our practice been as good as our precept we might have had today a generation of young and middle-aged people capable of understanding and effectively working the machinery of political democracy.

There must be, declared Mr. Green, not only quantitatively more education ; that education must be relevant to the needs and the ideals of society.

That conclusion was the theme of my book, *A New Order in English Education*,[1] in which I outlined a scheme of education "from the cradle to the grave". The most important passage in that book, in my opinion, is that in which I attempted a definition, in general terms, of the ideal democratic society, with a view to discovering what should be the purpose and function of education in such a society. "The essence of democracy", I said, "is belief in the sanctity, the value, and the significance of the human personality ; and that this can only find full expression in community with its fellows." The ideal democratic society I described as :

. . . a self-orientated, self-governed, self-disciplined community, which accords to every one of its members the utmost possible personal freedom compatible with the general interest, and is, indeed, dependent for its health, vigour and dynamic upon their full exercise of this ordered freedom. The community as a whole, and the members as individuals, find their happiness in living together in a willed, and willing, state of harmony on the basis of each for the good of all and all for the good of each ; and their purpose in a gladly co-operative endeavour to bring about a continuous enrichment of human life and its direction towards an ever closer and deeper understanding of those enduring spiritual values upon which any free, positive and progressive society must be established.

It was upon that definition, and upon the thesis that the individual has a threefold value and significance, " as a human personality, as a citizen, and as a producer of wealth ", that I built the system of education for the young and for the adult which occupies the second half of the book.

[1] *A New Order in English Education*, by H. C. Dent, University of London Press, 1942.

The weakness of the definition quoted above is, of course, that it is entirely general ; it makes no reference to the nature of the civilization to which the democratic way of life is to be applied. I attempted to make good this defect to some extent in the concrete proposals I advanced, but I did no more, I admit, than scratch the surface of the colossal problem which the harmonizing of the democratic concept with the fact of mass industrialization presents. I hope I may later further explore this fascinating if fearsome problem—which indeed will demand for its solution the most earnest and sustained efforts of every able mind we possess.

Space will not permit more than the barest reference to a few among the many other writers who have made some examination of this fundamental problem of education in a democratic society.[1] Reginald Lennard, in *Democracy, the Threatened Foundations*,[1] bases his argument on the statement that " the future of democracy lies with education ". Sir Richard Livingstone has recently published another book,[2] the theme of which is that—

> We have to transform a world with uncertain standards and vague values, with many virtues but no clear philosophy of life, into one which knows how to refuse evil and choose good, clear in its aims and therefore in its judgments and action.

Mr. Herbert Read, in *The Politics of the Unpolitical*,[3] and in greater detail in *Education through Art*,[4] pleads the case for a de-intellectualization of education and for more attention to the education of the senses and the emotions. " The whole balance of education ", he says, " as between intellectual and instinctive activity, must be redressed ", because " the whole of our educational and moral outlook must be reorientated away from intellection towards sensibility."

Miss A. P. Jephcott, in a most valuable sociological study, *Girls Growing up*,[5] points the moral of her story at many points. So do also the authors of *Our Towns*,[6] the research into the condi-

---

[1] *Democracy, the Threatened Foundations*, by Reginald Lennard, Cambridge University Press, 1942.

[2] *Education for a World Adrift*, by Sir Richard Livingstone, Cambridge University Press, 1943.

[3] *The Politics of the Unpolitical*, by Herbert Read, Routledge, 1943.

[4] *Education through Art*, by Herbert Read, Faber & Faber, 1943.

[5] *Girls Growing Up*, by A. P. Jephcott, Faber & Faber, 1942.

[6] *Our Towns : A Close-Up*, Oxford University Press, 1943.

tions revealed by evacuation which has been referred to earlier in this book. Karl Mannheim, in his collection of war-time essays, *Diagnosis of our Time*,[1] subjects the problem of education to sociological analysis, and contributes what is, so far as I know, easily the most brilliant and profound essay on the place of youth in modern society that has yet been written ; an essay which sheds more light on the problem of adolescent education than many a pretentious tome.

Almost all the numerous memoranda on educational reform which have been issued by professional and other bodies during the past two years make some reference, however slight, to the philosophical aspect, but there is one which stands out from all the rest by virtue of being almost wholly a philosophical treatise. This is the first interim report [2] of the educational sub-committee of the Central Committee on Post-War Problems set up by the Conservative and Unionist Party Organization in 1941. In this report the sub-committee set out to answer the question : What should be the purpose of an efficient system of national education, both absolutely and in relation to post-war national requirements ? The attitude with which they approached their task may be judged from the statement they made of their conviction that " of all the State's activities, education is the basic activity, because it conditions the future character of the community ".

The report raised four major issues : the relation of the individual to the State ; the place of religion in the national life ; the creation and sustenance of " civic " morale ; and the leadership of the nation. On all these issues the committee gave precise and considered judgments. " The individual ", they said, " must surely be regarded as the recreator of society." Education must be regarded as a two-way service : to the individual pupil on the one hand, to the community on the other. Service to the pupil, they asserted, was understood in all competent schools, but service to the community " is only now beginning to be fulfilled in the State schools ". Thus they reached their first conclusion, that, as it had become a " matter of life and death that the nation should command the service of all its citizens " :

[1] *Diagnosis of our Time*, by Karl Mannheim, Kegan Paul, 1943.
[2] Educational Aims, 24, Old Queen Street, Westminster, 1942.

it must be a primary duty of national education to develop a strong sense of national obligation in the individual citizen, to encourage in him an ardent understanding of the State's needs, and to render him capable of serving those needs.

It was unfortunate that the sub-committee omitted to define anywhere in the report their conception of the State ; it was equally if not more unfortunate that, not only did they not define what they meant by " national education ", but they appeared, in another section of their report, to draw a distinction between " national education " and publicly provided education, when they said that—

. . . the special contribution made by the public and preparatory schools to . . . the education of talent and the development of leadership . . . would be jeopardized if they were to lose their independence and become *a mere part* (my italics) of the State system.

With regard to the place of religion in the national life, the sub-committee declared that :

. . . religion in the United Kingdom needs to be conceived, politically and administratively, in general terms as a basic and vital element in the national life, to be deliberately encouraged and fostered.

Consequently, in the nation's schools—

The State must do its best to ensure that every child is given every opportunity and help towards the awakening of its religious sense (though) it matters much less to the State what the particular dogmatic teaching given to the child may be.

With respect to the existing situation, the sub-committee concluded that :

. . . the need for effective practical agreement between the State and the churches is great and immediate—and not less immediate on the side of the churches than on that of the State.

In discussing the question of " civic " morale the sub-committee started from incontestable premises. " The stability of every State ", they said, " rests finally upon the moral quality of its citizens " ; and they asserted—what few would deny—that there had been an " extensive decay of the secular moral tradition " in modern communities of the democratic order ; that the slackening of moral fibre was common to all classes (though the result of different causes) ; and that " of all the immediate educational problems with which the nation is confronted, the problem of restoring and recreating civic morale is the greatest and most urgent ". But then came a most contentious passage :

The nature of our failure is indicated by the excessive emphasis placed in our present educational system (as in our social life) upon the ideal aim of individual happiness. To set up " the healthy and happy life " of the whole man, body, mind and spirit, as the objective of education, is to pre-suppose a state of affairs which has never existed anywhere, and can scarcely take immediate shape at the end of an immensely destructive war. Disease, disablement, pain, death ; inherited defects ; limited capacities ; misfortune, unhappiness, and the sense of guilt or sin—all these are a necessary part of man's life.

" We do not mean to suggest ", said the sub-committee, " that education must therefore have a gloomy colouring." But they did suggest that " it must be a prime object of education to fit the child to face and overcome trial and hardship ". Character, they asserted, must be " tough " as well as " good ". Education had aimed " mainly at the limited ideal of the well-behaved citizen ", to the neglect of " the qualities without which the community itself must fall to pieces—the bold qualities of adventurousness, initiative, enjoyment of difficulty and danger, the fighting spirit—in a word, grit ", together with equally necessary qualities which had also been steadily losing ground— " the will to work, pride in occupation regardless of its social or monetary reward, the self-discipline acquired through submission to discipline, and the desire to find salvation from selfishness in service ".

Education had yet a further task : to " detect and bring to fruition exceptional qualities of mind and character ". The sub-committee felt that the public and preparatory schools had a special contribution to make to the education of talent and the development of leadership ; but however that might be—

. . . the State system cannot leave a need of such magnitude to be met by others, or by pure chance. It must provide its own answer and give its own directions . . . however the educational system is governed and staffed, it should always be a matter of the most positive direction by the highest authority to all other authorities and to all teachers that children exhibiting signs of unusual ability should be watched with the utmost care and, if necessary, exempted from the customary requirements.

The Conservative report was the subject of much criticism from many quarters. It was most heavily criticized by sections of the Conservative Party, who according to their particular brand of conservatism variously described it as " pale pink slosh " or undiluted Fascism ! It is certainly open to criticism at many points, but the fundamental criticism which must be made of it is not in respect of what it said, but of what it did not say. The main contentions it advanced were essentially sound ; and despite defects here and there in the argument it is on the whole an essay in political and educational philosophy of a very high order, unique among the host of memoranda on post-war educational reconstruction in that it analyses and seriously grapples with fundamental issues. But most regrettably the sub-committee completely ignored one fundamental statement that they themselves made, that :

. . . the more the State has to require from its citizens, the more it should seek to give them in return ; and the more it enables them to " find themselves " as complete individuals, the more will its enrichment be.

If only the Conservative sub-committee had examined in-dividual rights with the same thoroughness that they did obliga-tions, their report would have been a contribution to educational reform of the highest order.

RELIGIOUS EDUCATION AND DUAL CONTROL

On December 21, 1940, there appeared in *The Times*, under the heading " Foundations of Peace ", a letter signed by the Archbishop of Canterbury, the Cardinal Archbishop of West-minster, the Moderator of the Free Church Council, and the Archbishop of York. In it the signatories declared their con-viction that " No permanent peace is possible in Europe unless the principles of the Christian religion are made the foundation of national policy and of all social life ", and offered a list of ten principles which they felt confident " would be accepted by rulers and statesmen throughout the British Commonwealth of Nations and would be regarded as the true basis on which a lasting peace could be established ".

The first five of these principles had previously been for-mulated by Pope Pius XII as a basis for the ordering of international life. To these the signatories added five " standards by which economic situations and proposals may be tested ". The latter were :

(1) Extreme inequality in wealth and possessions should be abolished.

(2) Every child, regardless of race or class, should have equal opportunities of education, suitable for the development of his peculiar capacities.

(3) The family as a social unit must be safeguarded.

(4) The sense of a Divine vocation must be restored to man's daily work.

(5) The resources of the earth should be used as God's gifts to the whole human race, and used with due consideration for the needs of the present and future generations.

If only religious thought had remained on this level there would have been no " religious question " in education in England during the past three years. Educational reform was here placed in its proper setting as an integral part of an all-embracing scheme of universal social reform.

Unhappily, the next official move made by religious leaders was as deplorable as this one was propitious. On February 12, 1941, the Archbishops of Canterbury, York, and Wales issued a statement the first paragraph of which ran :

There is an ever-deepening conviction that in this present struggle we are fighting to preserve those elements in human civilization and in our own national tradition which owe their origin to Christian faith. Yet we find on every side profound ignorance of the Christian Faith itself. There is evidently an urgent need to strengthen our foundations by securing that effective Christian education should be given in all schools to the children, the future citizens, of our country. The need is indeed so great and so urgent that former denominational or professional suspicions must be laid aside, and that all who care for the place of Christianity in our common life should stand together.

There may be elements in that preamble which are disputable, but its sincerity is beyond question and the level of argument high. The Archbishops went on to point out, quite rightly, that much more was involved in Christian education than " religious instruction ". It was a matter of the " whole tone and aim of the school life ". They were specially concerned, they said, with the sphere of elementary education, in which they regarded " our own Church schools as a trust which should be preserved for the sake of the ideals for which they stand ", though they felt that it was " difficult to exaggerate the importance of religious teaching " in the secondary schools, from which " many of the leaders in the public life of the country must come ".   Their one desire was that in all types of school Christian teaching should be secured and made effective.

To all this, little exception could be taken, save by bigoted anti-Christians.   But when it came to concrete proposals, the Archbishops completely forgot their own definition of Christian education, and descended to one of the most controversial of all spheres, that of religious instruction.   For they proposed that :

1. In all schools a Christian education should be given to all the scholars (except, of course, in so far as any parents may wish to withdraw their children from it).   The religious instruction should be entrusted to teachers willing and competent to give it.   We desire that no teacher should be prejudiced in his professional career by his unwillingness to give this teaching, but all teachers will agree that it is a sound principle of their profession that the teaching of any subject should be in the hands of persons qualified by personal interest, by knowledge, and by training to give it.

2. We urge that religious knowledge and the imparting of it should be an " optional subject ", not merely an " additional option ", in the course of training for the Teacher's Certificate.   This means that it should count in the gaining of the certificate.   We also urge that the local education authorities should further develop the post-certificate training courses in this subject arranged by them and should actively encourage teachers to attend these courses.

3. Where only one or few teachers in the school are duly qualified to give Christian teaching we urge that it should be made permissible to give this teaching at any period within school hours so that the same teacher may teach several classes at different periods.

4. In order that the importance of the religious teaching may be recognized we urge that it should be inspected in respect of its methods by H.M. Inspectors, or by some other duly authorized persons.

5. We urge that in all schools the timetable should be so arranged as to provide for an act of worship on the part of the whole school at the beginning of the school day.

The Archbishops added that they regarded the development all over the country of the " agreed syllabus " as one of the most hopeful signs of the times.   They hoped that a good agreed syllabus might be used in Church schools, and that accredited Free Church teachers would be welcomed in these schools to give special instruction to Free Church children at times when distinctive Church teaching was being given.

" We believe ", concluded the Archbishops, " that if these steps are taken grave hindrances to real Christian education will be removed and great progress will be achieved. But ", they added, " in the end it is the desire and purpose of the people that prevail ", and accordingly they called upon all Christian people in England and Wales to unite in promoting the reforms they outlined, and " to make a sustained endeavour at this fateful time to secure that the education which is provided for the youth of our country should be an effective training for Christian life and citizenship ".

The strategy was excellent ; the tactics disastrous. Had the Archbishops' proposals been up to the level of their preamble and their epilogue they might well have initiated a genuine crusade on behalf of true Christian education. But the " Five Points " did no more—and could have done no other—than resuscitate all the age-old controversies concerning religious instruction in schools which had riven English education from the moment when the first attempt was made to create a publicly provided national system. By implication these brought once again into undesirable prominence the equally aged problem of the dual control of the elementary school, a problem which for 70 years had effectively blocked any major educational advance along the whole front.

No intervention could, indeed, have been more ill-conceived or ill-timed. There was every reason to believe that the controversies about religious instruction had worn themselves out and were at long last peacefully dying a natural death. There was reason also to believe that the time was ripening for a solution of the hitherto insoluble problem of the Dual System. Not only had the number of children in Church schools been declining for many years ; the schools themselves were being closed at the rate of over 100 a year, and so bad was the condition of the majority of them that any considerable building programme (such as would be inevitable in any scheme of reform) would have swept most of them out of existence. The denominations could not possibly have replaced these ; they had not even been able to keep them in repair. Thus administrative control would necessarily have passed to the local education authorities

—to whom, as the representatives of the community, it properly belongs.

The publication of the " Five Points ", among other evil effects, once more confused the denominational and the administrative issues. The crusade to which the Archbishops called Christian people thus became—most unhappily—a crusade for vested interests rather than for Christian education. Naturally, profound suspicion and acute resentment were felt throughout the teaching profession. The Church, it was said, was taking advantage of a moment when the teachers were least able to defend themselves to impose upon them measures they had always stoutly (and successfully) resisted. It was manœuvring for position in order to buttress up the Dual System. Its " Five Points " carried implications which were grossly unfair to the teachers in the provided schools, and which revealed a lamentable ignorance of what actually took place in these schools. Religious instruction *was* in the hands of teachers " willing and competent " to give it, and it was certainly as good in provided as non-provided schools. A daily act of worship was almost universal in all provided schools where the accommodation made it possible, and in many where, humanly speaking, it was not. And teachers would not submit to the " religious tests " which inspection implied.

There were not wanting in the Church itself those who viewed with gravest apprehension the policy indicated by the " Five Points ". There were others who felt that the time had come to terminate the Dual System through the abandonment by the Church of the ownership of school buildings. In his book *A Policy in Religious Education*,[1] which was published only a few weeks after the " Five Points ", Canon Braley suggested that the Church of England should offer to the State all her elementary schools on condition (1) that religion should be taught as an integral part of the curriculum in all government-aided educational institutions, and (2) that it should be taught by people who were able and willing to do so, and (3) that the instruction should be inspected in schools and training colleges by H.M. Inspectors specially appointed for the purpose.

There were, too, Churchmen who, while prepared to support,

---

[1] *A Policy in Religious Education*, by E. F. Braley, Principal of the College of the Venerable Bede. University of London Press, 1941.

and even to advocate, the "Five Points", were yet deeply conscious that these did not and could not go to the root of the matter. In July 1941 the newly formed Christian Education Movement issued (with the approval, be it noted, of the Archbishops and the Acting Moderator of the Free Church Federal Council) a pamphlet entitled "Why Christian Education Matters",[1] in which they stated concisely the fundamental issue.

On all hands there is talk of a New Order. . . . Is this New Order to be Christian, in the sense that those who plan it understand and accept the Christian view of man's nature and destiny ; and recognize that an educational system which is Christian in that sense is an essential factor in securing it ? To put it bluntly, do we or do we not care whether successive generations of children are taught to understand and accept the truth of God made known in Christ, and the practical implications which follow from that belief ?

The " Five Points " were set out in the pamphlet, and the conviction was expressed that they were " useful and necessary " because " their adoption would remove certain definite defects in the existing situation ". But, it was added :

. . . by themselves they will not give us a system of education which really deserves the name Christian. For the achievement of that there is needed a thorough re-thinking of the philosophy and the social implications of education.

The authors of the pamphlet urged the formation up and down the country of groups fully representative of all concerned with education, including parents ; and gave their reason finely, as follows :

The ultimate aim of all such investigation and discussion is not merely the removal of existing defects and anomalies, but the awakening of the public conscience to realise the vital issue which is at stake. The past has been largely a phase of controversy : the present is one of negotiation and, it may be hoped, co-operation. But neither of these will achieve the real revolution which needs to be effected. That can only be done when the people of this country face the *decision* which has to be made upon the one crucial question which now confronts us. We know now that it is a choice between two conflicting and contradictory estimates of human nature. The one regards man as a creature of this world, finding the satisfaction of

[1] " Why Christian Education Matters ", a Statement issued by the Christian Education Movement. Press and Publications Board of the Church Assembly, 2, Great Peter Street, Westminster, S.W.1.

his nature in obedience to state-loyalties, and the enjoyment of state-rewards. The other regards him as a child of God with spiritual endowments which demand both training and freedom of expression. That choice radically determines our whole conception of education. . . . Neutrality is no longer possible. If God matters at all He matters more than any other fact in human experience.

Again, I cannot help insisting, if only the Church had consistently given a lead on this level, the administrative question of dual control, and the denominational question of religious instruction would have been seen for the utterly secondary issues they are, and would have been settled without controversy and almost without negotiation. But, unhappily, while voices, including, notably, that of Dr. Temple since his accession to the Primacy, have continued to be raised, both within the Church and outside it, on behalf of spiritual values, they have been too sadly drowned by the louder and more clamant voices raised on behalf of temporal and vested interests.

Needless to say, the Free Churches and the Roman Catholics, both of whom are in respect of the publicly provided educational system in this country rather in the position of not too well treated minorities, joined in the fray. The Nonconformists played on their major grievance, the fact that in so many districts the only public elementary school available was a Church of England one, the Roman Catholics stressed that they had to pay rates and taxes towards the provision of schools to which they could not send their children, because of the religious instruction there given, and yet were denied adequate financial aid to build their own schools.

By the summer of 1941 the battle for denominationalism and dual control was fully joined. In May the Convocation of Canterbury approved the " Five Points ", despite protests by the Bishops of Gloucester, Oxford, and St. Albans, and in June the Church Assembly not only approved them, but unanimously insisted that it " strongly urges " (the words were inserted in place of " earnestly hopes " of the original resolution) that speedy effect be given to them. Accordingly in August the Archbishop of Canterbury led a large deputation, including representatives of the Free Churches, to the President of the Board of Education (Mr. R. A. Butler, who had been in office less than a month), to impress the importance of the " Five Points " upon him.

The deputation found the new President completely in
sympathy with the aim of securing that effective Christian teaching be given in all schools, but markedly non-committal about
the " Five Points ".   Mr. Butler emphasized that before giving
any formal answer he must, of course, consult the local education
authorities and the teachers, and suggested that, even if he came
to the conclusion that the existing law required amendment,
legislation would be deferred until the time came for a measure
of general educational reform.   The deputation, so I have been
told, retired somewhat abashed.   This may be an exaggerated
description, but there were certainly some people who thought
that the mere presentation of the " Five Points " by a representative deputation should have ensured their immediate acceptance
by the Government.

From that date there began, behind the scenes, a long,
arduous, and wearying process of negotiation which continued
right up to the moment of the publication of the Government's
White Paper on Educational Reconstruction in July 1943.   I
do not know anything like the full story, but I do know that
compromise after compromise (some were of almost unbelievable
complexity) was presented, discussed, and scrapped or modified
again and again, and that there were several dramatic reversals
of policy by various interested bodies during the ensuing two
years.   Of these quite the most important was that of the National
Society in 1942.

In his presidential address to the Society in June 1942 Dr.
Temple, who had recently become Archbishop of Canterbury,
strongly defended the Dual System, and declared that the Society
could not agree to anything that constituted the wholesale
transfer or surrender of their Church schools.   They were prepared, he said, to consider specific modifications of the system,
but anything like wholesale surrender or transfer they would have
to resist.

This certainly suggested that the attitude of the Society was
wholly intransigent.   Four months later there appeared in
The Times [1] a leading article containing the following :

" No surrender of the Church's schools ! " has been used, and
may be used again, as a rallying cry.   Yet has not the time come

[1] On October 10, 1942.

when the Church of England might well reconsider this matter ? . . .
A national Church has to care for the children of the nation. Its
leaders may well ask themselves whether a frank readiness to surrender
the dual system at this stage might not best serve the interests of
their own Church, of religious education, and of Christian unity.

Coming events do sometimes cast their shadows before them.
Less than three weeks later the National Society issued a report [1]
in which it was admitted that serious objection was taken on
administrative and professional grounds to the Dual System,
and that therefore the Society was prepared to enter into negotia-
tions about such modifications as would relieve difficulties
without nullifying the essential character and traditions of the
schools. In a foreword commending the report to the consideration of the Church and the general public the Archbishop
of Canterbury declared that the policy proposed represented a
genuine recognition of the changed circumstances of the time
—which indeed it did.

On November 18 the report was submitted to the Church
Assembly. The debate was prolonged over two days. Sir
Robert Martin, who moved that the report be received, said
that the National Society had come to the conclusion that where
the managers of non-provided schools could not fulfil their legal
obligations in regard to repairs, alterations, and improvements,
there must clearly be a wide measure of public control. The
Society considered that this could be met by an arrangement
whereby these obligations of the managers as well as the appointment of teachers could pass to the local education authorities,
subject to the appointment of reserved teachers to such an
extent as might be necessary for the giving of denominational
teaching as set out in the agreed syllabus.

For the National Society this was indeed a revolution in
policy. The diehards rose in arms to protest, to be reminded
by the Archbishop of Canterbury that of the 753 schools on the
Board of Education " Black List ",[2] 399 were Church of England
schools. " That," said Dr. Temple, " is a situation profoundly
discreditable to us." They could not, he continued, continue a

---

[1] Interim Report on the Dual System. Published for the National Society by
the Press and Publications Board of the Church Assembly, 2, Great Peter Street,
S.W.1, and by S.P.C.K., Northumberland Avenue, W.C.2.
[2] Of schools considered either too bad to repair or in need of extensive structural
alteration. The list was compiled in 1925.

policy of bringing schools up to a point at which they would pass muster for another 10 or 15 years. " I am not going to pretend," concluded the Archbishop, " that this is a policy which is likely to arouse the enthusiasm of a crusade, but I believe it to be a wise adjustment to the situation in which we find ourselves, and which leaves us a great opportunity of serving the religious life of the community."

The Archbishop's intervention decided the issue. Despite the efforts of the Bishop of Chichester, who wished the Assembly to consider whether the Scottish solution could not be applied to England, and despite some plain speaking by the Bishop of Oxford, who said that the new policy of the Society would preserve nothing but the name of the Dual System, and that seven out of eight of the Church schools would have to be surrendered, the Assembly decided to approve and support the policy outlined in the National Society's Report.

This decision virtually put an end to any prospect of serious obstructionism by representatives of the Church of England when the expected Education Bill was introduced into Parliament.

There remained the Roman Catholics. They wanted at least a 75 per cent grant-in-aid for their schools ; the President of the Board of Education was determined not to go beyond 50 per cent. In the White Paper they have been offered a valuable concession in the revival of the relevant clauses of the Education Act, 1936, for they proposed 289 agreements under that Act. All these they can revive, and receive on them up to 75 per cent grant. This, I am told on unimpeachable authority, will cover their post-primary school problem. At the moment of writing it is not possible to say what attitude they will take if this proposal is incorporated in the Bill. At present they reject it. They have pressed and will no doubt continue to press, their case indefatigably in every possible quarter. But it is surely inconceivable that they will be allowed, or in the last resort will desire, to wreck the measure.

THE TEACHER AND THE POLITICIAN

So far as I know, one of the first teaching bodies to open public discussion on post-war planning was the National Council on Commercial Education, which at its annual conference on June 1, 1940, allotted considerable time to the problems of the future. In a message to the conference the Home Secretary, Mr. Herbert Morrison, who had been elected president of the Council for the ensuing year, wrote :

> You, as teachers and organizers of commercial education, will, no doubt, bend your energies to devising means of training the personnel of commerce, both to meet the present emergency and to face the new world which will emerge after the war. . . . The times call for a fundamental review of many educational problems of general and vocational education.

Mr. W. T. Chalk, Principal of the Highbury Commercial Institute, London, took up the theme. Describing the existing educational system as a " thing of shreds and patches ", he urged among other measures that no one should be allowed to enter the world of commerce in a clerical occupation before the age of 16 and without having had three years in a commercial school. At 16 those considered fit for a higher course should be sent to a commercial college, which Mr. Chalk visualized as a local university for commerce.

In the summer of 1940 *The Times Educational Supplement* began to throw out ideas on reform which it was later to develop more fully. On July 27, speaking more particularly of the generation growing up during the war, but evidently looking also to the future, it said :

> Our care must be made comprehensive. It must cover every aspect of the health and strength of body and mind and spirit, at all ages from earliest infancy—indeed, from before birth—to the attainment of manhood or womanhood. . . . In the opinion of very many wise and competent people the years from birth to the attainment of citizenship cannot but be regarded as a single whole, and they believe that therefore there should be not many authorities, but one single authority responsible for this care.

On September 14 it wrote :

> Unhappily, there is a tendency in some official quarters to defer consideration of questions of social reform until after the war. We deplore this tendency. . . . The spirit of reform is abroad ; it cannot—and should not—be checked. . . . This can be done without impairment of the war effort ; indeed, to neglect to do it implies impairment. . . .

From about this time onwards articles sketching in outline an after-the-war educational system began to appear with increasing frequency in the educational press. The schemes put forward were as a rule general in character, suggestive rather than definitive. For example :

End of the war ideals should mean a truly national system, embodying in it every child born into the land ; these children should be taught in open-air surroundings, in schools possessing—not as a happy chance or a remarkable example, but of right—playing fields, gardens, handicraft and science rooms, studios for art and music, libraries, gymnasia, cinema projectors, and up-to-date equipment of every sort. There should be widely differing types of schools . . . with associated adult and youth clubs . . . staffing should be sufficiently generous to allow of small classes . . . there should be for teachers grace-years, study-terms, refresher courses . . . camps, boarding houses, and hospitals should be a permanent part of the education system . . . factory owners, employers, workmen, and clerks should regard the school as a club, to which all their children belong. . . . (*The Times Educational Supplement*, Oct. 5, 1940.)

Post-war reform of education began to figure in the list of political issues towards the end of 1940. Curiously enough, it entered so to speak by the back door, by way of protests from the educationist against alleged retrograde utterances by the politician. Statements made in the autumn by the President of the Board of Education [1] excited in the minds of some educationists the suspicion that he was retreating from the Government's pledge (made shortly after the outbreak of war) that the suspension of the Education Act, 1936, was for the duration only, and that he was beginning to think in terms of substituting for the raising of the school leaving age which it enacted the day continuation classes of the Education Act, 1918. Even a categoric denial—" We have not retreated from that pledge "—made by the Parliamentary Secretary, Mr. Chuter Ede, in the House of Commons on October 16, was insufficient to dispel this suspicion. On November 30, the executive committee of the Workers' Educational Association adopted a number of resolutions on educational policy, one of which read :

The Central Executive Committee of the Workers' Educational Association, having noted recent speeches by the President of the Board of Education at Manchester and in the House of Commons indicating that the establishment of day continuation classes may be given preference over the policy of raising the age of full-time atten-

[1] Mr. H. Ramsbotham.

dance at school, and of providing for all children secondary education
of varying types as recommended by the Consultative Committee of
the Board of Education in the Hadow and Spens Reports, declares
that, while welcoming the proposal to require attendance at continuation schools for young people over the age of 16, it cannot accept
the President's proposal as a substitute for the raising of the school
leaving age. It urges the Board of Education to take steps to bring
into force the Education Act, 1936, at once in those areas where
full-time attendance is now possible, and to prepare plans for raising
the school leaving age to 16 as an essential part of the Government's
measures for post-war reconstruction.

A second resolution read :

The Central Executive Committee of the Workers' Educational
Association warmly welcomes the declaration of the Minister of Labour
(Mr. Ernest Bevin) at the Trades Union Congress Meeting at South-
port on October 9, 1940, that if the boys of the secondary schools
had been able " to save us in the Spitfire, their brains can be used
to produce the new world ". It also cordially approves the Minister's
speech in London on November 20, when he urged that " every
citizen should be directing his mind not to tiding over an immediate
difficulty, but to beginning the building of new foundations now ".
It urges the Government to make such immediate changes in educational policy as will prepare the way for the realization of this fundamental democratic principle. In particular, it demands that access
to secondary education should not be dependent on the ability of
parents to pay. Accordingly it calls upon the Board of Education
to take steps to apply forthwith the principle of 100 per cent special
places in secondary schools provided or aided by local education
authorities. As a further guarantee that no child shall be debarred
from taking advantage of such special places it asks that the Board
should secure revision of income scales to ensure that a reasonable
and uniform standard is adopted as a minimum by all authorities.

The President, Mr. H. Ramsbotham, gave his answer to the
first resolution in a speech to the Incorporated Association of
Assistant Masters in Secondary Schools on January 2, 1941.
Asking the question : What are our plans for the future of
education when peace returns, and even before then?, he replied :

First, to put the 1936 Act into full operation and raise the school
leaving age to 15. Second, to provide and develop types of post-
primary education on the lines of the Spens report with no question
of prestige or fallacious distinction between so-called liberal and
vocational types of education. Third, to restore the day continuation
school programme on the lines of the Fisher Act for the age group
15 to 18. Reform of the School Certificate might be undertaken

before the end of the war, and a committee of the Secondary Schools Examination Council had been set up to go into the problem. Finally, there were the recommendations of the Spens Committee in regard to medical inspection, school dinners, physical and mental fatigue, and physical exercise and games. A move might be made in these directions.

It will be seen from the above that the post-war reconstruction the President had in mind at that time amounted to nothing more than the statutory enforcement of reforms already enacted but inoperative, together with, possibly, some improvements which had been authoritatively recommended to the Board of Education two years previously, but had hitherto been officially ignored. There was in his speech not a hint of creative reform, of genuine educational advance, or of any awareness of the philosophical issues thinkers had been formulating and discussing for at least twelve months.

Political thought on educational reconstruction thus began on a level which was not only far lower than that of philosophical thought but also different in kind. It was recapitulatory and remedial, not progressive and creative. It looked to the past, not the future, for inspiration, and thus had no reference to the new problems of a society obviously in the throes of vast social changes. It had reference only to the improvement of an instrument devised to serve a social order that was already in its death agony.

This was to have the most unhappy repercussions on a very great deal of the strenuous and undoubtedly sincere professional thought which was to be put into post-war planning during the following two years, because the lead in planning was given by the Board of Education, and this lead was followed by the representatives of the teachers and educational administrators. In theory, it was ideal that the Board should give the lead ; but, regrettably, the wrong lead was given : it was one which ignored completely the fundamental issues involved.

It was, of course, to be expected that the Board of Education should concentrate upon the legislative and administrative aspects of reform, because the Board is specifically constituted to deal with these aspects, and the officers of the Board have always shown themselves reluctant to seek advice upon the educational aspects of any change. But one would have thought that even so the significance of the social changes taking place or clearly imminent at the present time would have overridden all other considerations and compelled the Board's officers to regard the question of educational reform from an unaccustomed point of view. They cannot have been unaware of the philosophical and sociological issues which were being raised ; and it must surely have been obvious to them that reform in terms of the past was inadequate to meet the needs of the future. Yet they chose to ignore this fact.

Philosophical thought, as has been seen, had been concerned to examine the conception of education in the light of a changing conception of society. It had therefore sought first to envisage the shape and form of the desired society of the future, and then, since it recognized that education is a main instrument for conditioning the development of any society, to discover what kind of education might be expected to effect a desirable conditioning. It stated its conclusions in general terms only, no doubt considering (quite rightly) that it is the job of the teacher and the administrator, as the experts, to work out in detail the technical problems involved.

Had the representatives of the teachers and the administrators taken their cue from the philosopher the story of the reform movement during the war would have been very different—and a good deal happier. Regrettably, they took it from the politician. They did indeed accept from the philosopher (as did the politician) the general principle of " equality of opportunity ", but instead of courageously analysing its implications and attempting to give expression to these in concrete proposals, they were content to accept as a basis for discussion the modest programme of remedial measures which the Board of Education put before them.

Deplorable though this was, it was perhaps hardly surprising. For many years the professional associations had been advocating —with singular lack of success—these very measures which were now offered to them, and which were, to say the least of it, long overdue. Their minds had become obsessed with the necessity of securing them, and the prolonged, arduous, and disappointing struggle to do so had doubtless robbed them of something of their power to think creatively. When at long last the politician showed himself favourably disposed, and when simultaneously there began to emerge, what had always been lacking before, signs of widespread public interest and support, what more natural than that the representatives of the teachers and the administrators should think solely in terms of the reforms for which they had so long pressed ?

The interesting question—not yet fully answered—arises as to what extent the executives of the associations represented the majority opinion of their members. It is significant that at all the annual meetings of the major associations in 1942 and 1943 there have been strong minority movements in favour of more progressive and radical reform which have only been held in check with the greatest difficulty by the executives. (In at least one instance the minority became the majority and imposed its policy.)

In fairness to professional thought in general, it must be added that it was subjected to a prolonged process of pre-conditioning by the Board of Education. In February the President told a deputation representative of the Workers' Educational Association, the Trades Union Congress, and the Co-operative Union that the Board was planning a " new testament of education ". At Morecambe shortly afterwards he told the Lancashire branch of the N.U.T. that he and his senior officers were devoting. a great deal of time to the ideal lay-out of education in the post-war world, and were forming provisional views on the changes, legislative and otherwise, which would be needed to put our educational system on the soundest and most enlightened and most democratic lines. He added :

When this task has been completed, and it is nearing completion, I propose to bring all our partners in education—teachers, the education officers, and the major educational organizations—into consultation.

On May 12 Mr. Ramsbotham told a large gathering of London teachers that he had already indicated three main lines of advance to be undertaken as soon as possible : the raising of the school leaving age to 15, without exemptions ; the establishment, concurrently if possible, of day continuation schools ; and the reform and expansion of the secondary school system so as to provide a secondary education suitable to varying capacities from the age of 11. Then he said :

It is my personal belief that the country will expect the planning of our education for the post-war world to be conceived on bold and generous lines. I do not think that the proposals, when they see the light of day, will be deemed to err on the side of timidity or excessive caution. You will look, I think, for something more than mere developments within the existing framework, and will expect that education shall offer an equality of opportunity really consonant with the ideals of our democratic society.

This statement raised high hopes. It gave the idea that the " three main lines " were part only of a much larger scheme which would transform the whole educational set-up. And rightly or wrongly, the phrase " when they see the light of day " was widely understood to mean that the Board's proposals were to be made public—in the ordinarily accepted sense of that term ; and teachers and administrators, keenly stimulated by Mr. Ramsbotham's suggestion that they embodied a really radical reconstruction, awaited the event eagerly. The entire scheme of reform, they imagined, was to be the subject of general discussion. Imagine the sense of frustration and resentment which arose when it began to be known not long afterwards that, far from there being any question of general publication, the proposals were being circulated only to the executives of certain professional and other bodies, and that they were going out marked as highly secret and confidential.

What was in this famous *Green Book*, as the Board's memorandum came to be known ? (It was bound in a green wrapper.) I cannot say, because I was not a member of any of the bodies [1] to which copies were sent. I have, like many other

---

[1] The *Green Book* was circulated to the Association of Education Committees, County Councils Association, Association of Municipal Corporations, Federation of Welsh Local Education Authorities, London County Council, Association of Directors and Secretaries for Education, Federation of Part III Education Committees, National Union of Teachers, Incorporated Association of Headmasters of Secondary Schools, Association of Headmistresses of Secondary Schools, Incorporated Association of Assistant Masters in Secondary Schools, Association of Assistant Mistresses in Secondary Schools, Headmasters' Conference, Association of Principals of Technical Institutions, Association of Teachers in Technical Institutions, Association of Technical Institutions, National Society of Art Masters, Tutorial Classes Joint Advisory Committee, Joint Standing Committee of the Training College Association and Principals of Training Colleges, Universities Consultative Committee of Vice-Chancellors and Principals, Association of Principals of Recognized Training Colleges of Domestic Subjects, National Foebel Foundation, National Society, Catholic Education Council, National Free Church Council, Central Welsh Board, Workers' Educational Association, Trades Union Congress, British and Foreign Schools Society. See answer by the President of the Board of Education to Mr. Wilson, in the House of Commons, July 31, 1941.

interested people, a fairly full summary of the document, but it would be most improper of me either to reveal how I obtained this or to use it for the illumination of those to whom the Board of Education, in its wisdom, decided not to make known its contents. Nor is it really necessary to do so. On October 23 the President of the Board of Education, Mr. R. A. Butler,[1] who had been insistently pressed both inside and outside Parliament (and had consistently refused) to publish the proposals, circulated in the Official Report a list of the major subjects and questions covered. These were :

1. The raising of the school-leaving age. Should there be exemptions after 14 as contemplated by the Education Act, 1936 ?

2. The need for redefining elementary education. Should the appropriate division of full-time education be primary up to the age of 11 and secondary thereafter ?

3. Such a redefinition would give rise to the following questions : (a) Would the retention of separate local Education Authorities for elementary (i.e. primary) education be justified ? (b) Would it be necessary to make the provision of secondary education a duty and not a power as at present ? (c) Should all schools at the secondary stage be administered under one Code of Regulations and be free ?

4. The need to review the method of the distribution of children at 11 to the different types of secondary school. Should there be a further review and redistribution at the age of 13 ?

5. The contribution that might be made (a) to maintaining the mental alertness and physical welfare of young people ; (b) to the improvement of their vocational training related to their employment ; and (c) the development of their social and recreational interests by a system of part-time day continuation schools up to the age of 18 following full-time schooling.

6. The relation of the Youth Service to any such development in order to build up a complete system covering the social, physical, and educational welfare of adolescents.

7. The need for an improved and extended system of technical, commercial, and art training, and for establishing closer relations between education and industry and commerce.

8. The establishment, in order to secure equality of opportunity, of a unified system of aid to enable students to proceed to the universities.

9. With a view to making the school medical services fully effective : (a) Should local education authorities be under an obligation to provide for the treatment for certain specific defects in the case of children in both primary and secondary schools ? (b) Should the responsibility of local education authorities, hitherto confined to

[1] Mr. Butler succeeded Mr. Ramsbotham in July 1941.

children attending school, be extended to include all children, say, from the age of two, through the provision of nursery schools and nursery classes ? (c) Is further provision desirable for handicapped and maladjusted children ?   (d) Should an obligation be laid on local education authorities to make or otherwise secure the provision of meals and milk for all children for whom such provision is necessary in order that they may derive full benefit from their education ?

10. The need to review the methods of recruiting to and training for the teaching profession, especially in the light of any decisions that may be taken as to the general framework of post-war education.

11. The question how the dual system can be adapted to a reformed system so as to secure equality of opportunity and sound and economical organization.

12. The possibility of establishing (a) a more uniform system of remuneration of teachers, and (b) a more equitable distribution between national and local finances of the cost of education.

The details can be filled in by anyone with a gift for analysis and the time to study comparatively the more comprehensive among the many memoranda (not far short of 100 in number) on post-war educational reconstruction which were published, issued or circulated during the following 18 months or so.   With rare exceptions, and excluding a number of specialist memoranda covering only a limited portion of the educational field, these have all been commentaries on the proposals in the Board's *Green Book*.

Extremely interesting commentaries, many of them ; for in almost all cases the authors made some attempt to state the general principles and criteria on which their proposals were professedly based.   It is possible here to illustrate this by only one or two examples, but the following are indicative.

The National Union of Teachers agreed [1] with the Board that the purpose of education is in this country regarded as having a twofold aspect : " the training of every child as an individual, and his preparation for life as a member of the community."   That facilities capable of implementing that purpose were not equally available to all children, said the Union, was common knowledge.   The Union was

profoundly convinced that equal educational opportunity for all must be an essential characteristic of any State system of education for this country if it is to continue its democratic form of government.

---

[1] In Educational Reconstruction. A Report of Proposals by the Executive of the National Union of Teachers, 1942.

And, that there might be no misunderstanding what the Union meant by " equality of educational opportunity ", it was defined, as :

. . . the application of the principle " that the accidents of parental circumstances or of the place of residence shall not preclude any child from receiving the education from which he is best capable of profiting ".

The Association of Directors and Secretaries for Education, in a memorandum [1] containing many pungent observations, pointed out two obvious causes of inequality of opportunity :

There exist side by side, each with its own virtues and defects, two systems (of education) which are sharply differentiated by their method of recruitment. On the one hand, there is the education offered by the public schools and the private preparatory schools, which is available almost exclusively only to those who can afford to contract out of the educational provision made from the public purse. On the other hand, there is the public system of education.

Of the latter, the Association said :

This public system is not so much an organic unity as a collection of parts, each of which retains to a greater or less extent the imprint of the state of social development which attended its birth. Thus the elementary school and the schools and institutions of higher education, instead of representing successive stages, remain, to a large extent, parallel ; and, to the extent to which this parallelism still persists, they perpetuate within the educational system a differentiation by caste which has no educational justification.

The Association were insistent that the reformed system must be based on " educational principles which have regard only to the nature of the individual and to the needs of the community ", and that the educational service of the country was still regarded in too restricted a light. Its duty was " only partially discharged when it has provided for the instruction of the children of the community ".

. . . the educational service has a contribution to make to the general development of community life and also a duty to provide for men and women in maturity as well as in childhood and adolescence.

And further :

As the general view of the place of education in social life has been too restricted, so has the duty of the educational system to

[1] *Education.* A Plan for the Future, Oxford University Press, 6d.

children and adolescents. . . . It is fundamental to a sound educational system that the health and well-being of growing children should be recognized as elements in their educational progress.

The Workers' Educational Association, which (as during the period preceding the Fisher Act of 1918) has played a prominent part in advocating reform, set out [1] its main principles in a five-point " Educational Charter ".

1. Equal opportunities for every child to develop his personality and abilities, so that he may grow up healthy in body and mind and ready to make his full contribution to the life of the community.

2. A " common school " system, in which social distinctions and privileges no longer play any part.

3. An education in which the full achievement of personality and the idea of service to the community will replace the competitive motive as the main principles of school life.

4. Lifelong education, the preparation for citizenship to be no longer limited to a brief period of childhood but extended to the threshold of adult life, with every opportunity for its renewal in a voluntary adult education movement growing out of social life and experience.

5. Education to be recognized as the central constructive service of society and provided accordingly on a more generous scale, adequate to the vast and inspiring task of creating for the first time in history a genuine social democracy.

In a foreword to a memorandum [2] adopted by the Trades Union Congress in 1942, Sir Walter Citrine declared that thorough revision of post-primary education was needed. It was not merely a matter, he said, of improving an existing system.

A new scheme of education must be devised if we are to give these older children a fair chance and fit them to be worthy citizens of a democratic society.

The education committee of the T.U.C., which prepared the memorandum, addressed itself particularly to the problem of the transition from school to employment and in this connexion made an outstanding suggestion. They said :

There is one point of common application which should receive the consideration of anybody formulating training schemes. From the point of the training facilities to be given to, and the experience

---

[1] In Plan for Education. A W.E.A. report on Educational Reconstruction, 38A, St. George's Drive, Victoria, S.W.1, 1942.
[2] T.U.C. Memorandum on Education after the War, Smith Square, S.W.1, 1942.

to be gained by, the young worker, it may often be desirable that he should not be bound to a particular employer. The alternative would be to bind apprentices and trainees to the joint body responsible for the training scheme in the industry concerned. This would enable young workers in training to extend and specialize their studies and to be transferred from one employer to another in the course of their training. Where there are recognized training institutions such as specialized technical schools, the trainee might well regard the school as his " home base ". *Thus the present practice of employers allowing apprentices to go to school would be reversed, and the schools would allow apprentices to go to employment.* (My italics.)

The principle that the school (i.e. the education authority) should control the allocation of the young worker's time has not yet received formal approval from any official or industrial authority, but that of apprenticeship to a responsible training body rather than to a single employer was advocated by the building industry in their report [1] on the recruitment and training and accepted by the Government in a White Paper [2] outlining the measures they proposed to take in respect of this industry.

As the number of memoranda multiplied, it became clear that, despite the diversity of sources [3] from which they came, there was a large measure of agreement on a very considerable

[1] Report on Training for the Building Industry, H.M.S.O., 1942.
[2] Training for the Building Industry, H.M.S.O., February 1943.
[3] Among the bodies which have issued reports or memoranda covering the whole or most of the educational field are : The Conservative, Liberal, and Communist Party organizations (the Labour Party have approved a summary statement of policy) ; the Trades Union Congress ; the Workers' Educational Association ; the Co-operative Union ; the Friends' Education Council ; the National Council of Women ; many branches of Rotary ; the National Union of Teachers ; the National Association of Head Teachers ; the Incorporated Association of Headmasters in Secondary Schools ; the Incorporated Association of Assistant Masters in Secondary Schools ; the National Association of Schoolmasters ; the National Federation of Class Teachers ; the Association of Education Committees ; the Association of Directors and Secretaries for Education ; the National Association of Juvenile Employment and Welfare Officers ; the National Council of Labour Colleges ; the Federation of Education Committees (Wales and Monmouth) ; the Contemporaries (a group of younger men with experience in educational administration) ; the West Riding Education Authority ; the Sheffield Education Authority ; the Bristol Education Committee ; various local teachers' associations.
Memoranda covering specialist aspects of education have been issued by the Nursery School Association of Great Britain ; the Independent Schools Association ; the National Council on Commercial Education ; a Joint Committee of the Association of Technical Institutes and the Association of Principals of Technical Institutes ; Nottingham University College and associated training colleges ; the Federation of Part III Authorities ; the British Association ; the Institution of Electrical Engineers ; the Institute of Physics ; the Grocers' Institution ; the National Society ; Nuffield College.

number of points. The following points were universally, or pretty well universally, accepted by mid-1943 :

Principles

There should be equality of educational opportunity for all children, and a wide diversity of provision to meet the diversity of needs.

Nursery ·Education

It should be made obligatory on local education authorities to provide nursery education in nursery schools or classes for all children from the age of 2 whose parents desire it. This provision should be a part of the State educational scheme and as such within the purview of the Board of Education. The provision should include an adequate medical service.

Note : There is division of opinion as to whether nursery school education should cover the period 2–5 or 2–7.

Primary Education

The term "elementary school" should be abolished. There should be instead a stage of primary education, which would be a common form of education for all children of the appropriate age.

Note : There is not agreement as to whether the primary stage should end at 11, 12, or 13.

The chief needs of the primary school are reduction in the size of classes, improved buildings and staffing.

Secondary Education

All forms of post-primary education should be regarded and treated as secondary, and as equal in status.

Note : There is difference of opinion as to whether or not fees should be abolished in secondary schools.

There should be one code of regulations for all types of secondary school, and equivalent conditions in regard to buildings, amenities, and facilities should be granted to all.

There should be considerable variety of courses at the secondary stage to meet the varied interests and capacities of the adolescent.

Note : There is divergence of opinion as to whether these courses should be provided in a single school (the multilateral school) or in separate schools, e.g. grammar, technical, commercial, modern.

The "Special Place" examination for selection for entry to secondary schools should be abolished, and pupils should be allocated to the type of secondary education judged most fitted for them.

Note : Opinions differ as to what precisely should make up the basis of allocation, but there is a very general feeling that much reliance should be placed on the record of the pupil's work and progress in the primary school. If allocation to secondary education takes place at 11+, the curriculum in all secondary courses should be the same for two years, and there should be re-allocation of pupils at 13+.

The school leaving age should be raised to 15+, without exemptions, immediately on the conclusion of the war, and to 16+ as soon as practicable thereafter.

Note : Many memoranda demand that the date for the raising of the school leaving age to 16+ shall be appointed in the Act, and there is a strong body of opinion which holds that this date should be not later than three years after the conclusion of hostilities.

Part-time Education

There should be compulsory part-time education for all young persons from the time when they cease full-time attendance until the age of 18.

Note : The generally accepted allotment for part-time education is a minimum of two half-days or one whole day a week ; but demands range from six hours a week up to half the working week.

Technical and Commercial Education

There should be a wide extension and great improvement of the facilities for technical, commercial, and art education. These facilities should include both whole- and part-time courses, and day-time release from employment should be granted for the latter.

University Education

Access to the universities should be available to all boys and girls capable of profiting by a course of university study. Financial considerations should be no bar to entry to a university course.

Note : As with secondary education, there is not agreement that fees should be abolished.

Adult Education

There should be a wide extension of facilities for adult education.

School Medical Service

The School Medical Service should be enlarged, given wider and more specific powers for treatment, and extended to cover all young people up to the age of 18. More and better provision should be made for physically and mentally handicapped children.

The Service of Youth

The Service of Youth should be closely linked up with the educational system, and co-ordinated with the arrangements for placing and training young persons in industry and commerce. Leaders in the Service of Youth should be regarded as equal in status with teachers.

Recruitment and Training of Teachers

The recruitment of teachers should be placed on a much wider basis. The present system of early option for a teaching career, with consequent financial aid during a secondary school and training college or university course, should be abolished. The training of teachers should be radically overhauled.

The Teaching Career

All salaries should be substantially raised, and a single salary scale should operate in all types of schools. There should be considerably increased mobility inside the teaching profession ; and it should be easier for teachers to move from teaching to other parts of the education service, e.g. administration or the inspectorate, or into other occupations ; and vice-versa.

Buildings

There should be a comprehensive building programme to eliminate all inadequate schools.

Finance

The system of grant-in-aid from the central exchequer to the localities must be so revised that all local education authorities may be enabled to make adequate provision of facilities in their areas.

Private Schools :

All schools outside the publicly provided system should be licensed by the education authority.

The list is imposing, in spite of the fact that I have limited it strictly to items on which there is complete, or virtually complete, agreement. It could have been made considerably more imposing had I included items, such as the abolition of the School Certificate examination or the general provision of midday meals at school, on which there is a very large measure of agreement. But even when these are excluded, it is still safe to say that at no time in our history has informed opinion been so united on both the main lines and the details of educational reform.

Yet I must point out, as I have consistently done, in print and on public platforms during the past two years, that the proposals for reform do not fully measure up to the principles on which they are supposed to be based. Effect everything in the list above, and we are still a long way from either equality of opportunity or a system of education adequate for a fully democratic society.

As the Association of Directors and Secretaries for Education, and many other bodies, have said, there can be no equality of opportunity so long as there exist side by side two systems of education sharply differentiated by their method of recruitment. Nor shall we have an adequate system of education until we have worked out an orderly and progressive transition for the adolescent from the world of school to the world of adult labour and citizenship. To tack a scheme of part-time continued education on to a scheme of full-time education is by itself quite inadequate to meet this situation. Nor, again, shall we have an adequate system of education until we have provided for the adult a range of facilities as comprehensive as that we provide for the child and the adolescent. Nor, finally, shall we have an adequate system of education until we have grappled, at all stages and in all its aspects, with the problem of the content of the curriculum. This huge problem has hardly been mentioned in any of the memoranda except the few dealing specifically with a specialist sphere of education. And it cannot, of course, be properly approached until we have at least a working definition of the purpose of our education.

However, on a large number of points we are all agreed. On what are we not agreed? There are three outstanding issues : the Dual System, the Public Schools, and the units of educational administration.

There is a strong body of opinion that the Dual System should be abolished, but many of the stoutest adherents to this belief doubt whether in fact abolition could be achieved without resort to methods abhorrent to democracy. The National Union of Teachers, for example, have stated their opinion that :

The only fully satisfactory solution would be the achievement of a national unified system of education by means of the transfer of *all* non-provided schools, whether included at present in the elementary or secondary system, to the control of the local education authority.

But the Union have from the start been prepared to compromise. So have all the political parties except the Communist Party, which advocated " the complete removal from the schools of the religious questions in any form, whether of teaching or of control of the schools ". In view of the fact that the authors of almost all the other memoranda state their conviction that religious education should be an integral part of the curriculum of every school, there is little chance of the Communist Party's view commanding any considerable measure of acceptance.

The Trades Union Congress hold that :

. . . the time has come when they (the denominational schools) should be incorporated in the State system of schools, except in so far as denominations may themselves be able and willing to bear the whole cost of their separate institutions.

This view is flatly opposite to that of the Roman Catholics, who maintain that the State should pay the whole cost of denominational schools.

The compromise offered in the Government's White Paper is probably about as near as we shall get to a solution of this most intractable problem.   In so far as the persistence of controversy is evidence of genuine and deep religious conviction, one can respect if not welcome it ; but there is all too sad reason to believe that it is kept alive nine-tenths by vested interest, and one-tenth only by religion.   That is a deplorable and discreditable situation.

The public school controversy is, like that of dual control, rooted in our history, and appears equally if not more intractable. Opinion on the matter ranges from an uncompromising demand for the abolition of the public schools—which, as I ventured to point out in *A New Order in English Education*, is merely silly— to the equally uncompromising demand that they be preserved just as they are—which is wholly undemocratic, if not worse.

There is no controversy about which more muddled thinking is done, or in which a vested interest is more stoutly defended. The fundamental question at issue is not that of high fees, nor even of exclusiveness, though both these factors are involved. It is simply this :   should there exist in a democratic society a group of schools having, for social rather than educational reasons, an implicit lien on most of the key points in our national life ?   But practically no one on either side fights on this issue. Consequently, almost all the proposed solutions of the " public school problem " are quite beside the point.   To offer a percentage of free or special places, as Winchester and other schools have done, is worse than no solution.   It merely introduces a little new blood to the privileged caste (and this is being done in other ways all the time), or, more likely, produces outcastes acceptable to neither the privileged nor the unprivileged.   Even to make all the places free or special would not necessarily effect a solution. To do that the social " pull " of the schools must be eliminated. One of the most interesting proposals is that made in the privately issued memorandum "A Democratic Reconstruction of Education," [1] where it is suggested that the public school buildings should be used to house something after the nature of the Danish

---

[1] "A Democratic Reconstruction of Education", by Four Headmasters of Secondary Schools, 1942.

People's High School. It may even be the right one ; it may
be that, instead of trying to incorporate the public schools in the
secondary branch of the publicly provided educational system,
it would be better to lift them right out of it into another branch.

The controversy over the units of educational administration
blew up to white-heat on publication of the White Paper. It
was always smouldering, and was bound sooner or later to break
out violently. Here again prestige is involved, though of a very
different sort. The problem dates from the unfortunate division
of local education authorities, made in 1902, into Part II and
Part III authorities, the former responsible for the provision of
all forms of education below the university level, and the latter
for elementary education only. Obviously, if the elementary
school system is to disappear, the Part III authorities as such
will cease to exist. Equally obviously, authorities which have
exercised powers for 40 years—in many cases extremely efficiently
—are not to be expected to relinquish willingly those powers,
especially if—as is often the case—they are larger, wealthier, and
more competent than the authorities to which their powers
would go. Pending reorganization of the entire structure of
local government (which must come in the not too distant future)
the plan proposed in the White Paper, modified to allow for
mutual agreement on division and delegation of powers and
responsibilities, would seem as good an interim arrangement as
possible.

None of these three problems is insoluble ; but each demands
serious sacrifice of long-cherished interests and traditions. When
those concerned are prepared to make, in the general interest,
such sacrifices, the problems will quickly disappear.

INDUSTRY TAKES A HAND

For many years before the war educationists, especially those
engaged in technical or commercial teaching, had been urging—
with little success—that there should be far closer co-operation
between education and industry, and that industry should pay
much more attention to the important questions of the recruitment, placing, training, and welfare of its young recruits. It
was not surprising to find them redouble their voice from 1940
onwards. What has been, if not altogether surprising in view

of all the circumstances, nevertheless profoundly gratifying, is that during the last twelve months large sections of industry have taken up the cry.

There had, of course, always been a few enlightened industrialists who realized that the care and training of young workers is not only a humanitarian but also a strictly businesslike proceeding. To what extent the industries which are today busily planning training and welfare schemes for their juvenile employees-to-be are actuated by humanitarian motives is doubtful, but there is no question that they have realized the business end of it. They have had to. Coal-mining, branches of engineering, building, textiles, agriculture, and other industries and trades have been compelled to acknowledge that young people simply will not come in under the existing terms and conditions, and they are being forced by sheer necessity to make conditions more attractive and progressive training available.

Speaking at a conference on recruitment and training in Manchester on March 24, 1943, Sir Raymond Streat, Chairman of the Cotton Board, said that :

Nobody from London or the Government has suggested that we should hold a meeting or take some action. The initiative has arisen in Lancashire, and it has grown out of a general realization of some very serious facts. The chief of these is that the number of juveniles seeking a career in the cotton industry has fallen away disastrously. This, taken along with the obvious probability that there will be great competition for juvenile recruits in post-war years, has led many of us to realize that there is no time to lose in putting our house in order.

Twelve months previously a government committee had been set up, under the chairmanship of Sir John Forster, to examine the questions of the recruitment and training of boys for the coal-mining industry, where also entry has been diminishing rapidly recently. It is said, for example, that in Barnsley, a district wholly dependent on coal, not more than a third of the boys leaving elementary school go into the mines, and not more than two or three in every hundred of those leaving secondary school. The building trades and the moulding section of the engineering industry are other instances in point.

A report issued late in 1942 by a Special Committee set up by the Council of the Textile Institution, after analysing the reasons

why the industry was not proving attractive to boys and girls
and making suggestions on this point, added :

The responsibilities of the industry do not end in the providing
attractive conditions of work and directing its recruits into the jobs
for which they appear to be fitted.   They include the training of
young workers, and the proper discharge of this duty is of paramount
importance, since it is vital to the efficiency of industry.

A similar acceptance of responsibility—admittedly based on
self-interest—has been made by a number of other industries.

From the point of view of this study one of the most interesting features of this change of heart in industry is the attitude
being taken by industrialists towards the nature, and particularly
the control, of training.   The Textile Institution say :

It is neither possible nor necessary for industry to undertake the
whole of the necessary training, but it must be responsible for laying
down the main lines of the training it requires for its various workers
and for directing, supervising, and helping them in the process.
Industrial and educational authorities might co-operate in a new
form of apprenticeship so that training in the works and training
in the technical college are co-ordinated, and the youth's progress
viewed as a whole and not in two separate, unrelated parts.

That is a relatively enlightened statement, though even so
there are phrases in it which arouse some apprehension.   It is
easy to see the education authority, which ought properly to
be acting on behalf of the community as guardian to the young
person, becoming instead, under the conditions outlined above,
merely a servicing body for the production of more efficient
industrial units.   Other industries have made it clear that this
is their aim.

The building industry have proposed, and the Government
have accepted the proposal, that there should be established a
Building Apprenticeship and Training Council, representative
of the industry, and of the professions and government departments concerned, with the Minister of Works and Planning
taking the initiative in establishment and his department finan-
cing, initially at least, the Council secretariat.

This Council, it is suggested, should be an advisory one
only, and its membership voluntary, but it would have reference
to a number of matters believed by many people to lie properly
within the purview of the Board of Education, e.g. education

and training, vocational guidance. The Luxmoore Committee on Agricultural Education [1] go much further in the direction of industrial autonomy, for they propose the setting up of :

> . . . a central statutory authority (which we call the National Council for Agricultural Education) charged with the positive duty of providing, at the cost of the National Exchequer, for the different branches of agricultural education and with the necessary powers to enable it to perform this duty. This council should be so constituted that it is outside the Ministry of Agriculture but is under the control of the Minister, who should be answerable for it to Parliament.

This council is clearly intended to have executive powers, and is provided in the report with machinery reaching right down from the centre to the smallest districts.

In both the building and the agricultural reports it is obvious that it is the efficiency of the industry and not the well-being of the worker that is the main consideration. Properly, of course, the two interests ought to be identical, but it is more than doubtful that this dual aim has always been kept in mind. Somewhat perturbing claims are made by some industries concerning the use of the time to be made available in working hours for the education of the young worker. While the Council of the Institution of Electrical Engineers, for example, agrees that there should be part-time day release for apprentices for " general education and vocational instruction " (though, like the majority of educationists, it appears to think that one day a week will be adequate for both purposes), other industries are clearly thinking in terms of day release for technical instruction only, and would scout the idea that there should be time off for general education. Some educationists are unfortunately being equally intransigent ; they are demanding that the part-time release shall be for purposes of general or " cultural " education only. Happily, the Government have on this issue a defined policy : basic education first, occupational training if time permits.

Ideally, there ought to be no antagonism between " general " and technical education. As the Royal Commission on Technical Instruction said more than 50 years ago, " there can be no general education which is not technical, and no technical education which is not general ". But we have to deal with the

---

[1] Report of the Committee on Post-War Agricultural Education in England and Wales. Cmd. 6433. H.M.S.O., 1943.

situation as it is, and the unhappy fact obtrudes that there is in
many minds a very real divorce between " technical " and
" cultural " education. Unless strenuous efforts are made to
prevent it, there are going to develop in the near future two
struggles, for control of the administration of continued education
and for domination of its curriculum. It does not appear to
me to matter greatly who is in immediate control of any particular
part of the scheme, but there must be one ultimate co-ordinating
authority responsible for the scheme as a whole, and I reiterate
my conviction that this should be the Board of Education.
Only thus can it be ensured that the transition from the world
of school to that of adult labour and citizenship shall be wholly
an educative process.

Meanwhile, a number of enterprising firms, not content with
merely planning schemes of education and training, are actually
putting them into operation. In 1942, for example, the old
established firm of W. T. Henley's Telegraph Company initiated
what promises to be a most successful school for their juvenile
employees. The De Havilland Company have set up a works
school which provides for the training of students, apprentices,
and personnel brought into the industry in war-time. Sigmund
Pumps, Ltd., have an apprentice training scheme which aims to
educate boys to become craftsmen, to train young technical
staff to enter the drawing office, and to train craftsmen for
administrative or managerial duties. In 1943 Messrs. Newton
Chambers & Company opened a works college for their juvenile
employees. At present, in view of war-time depletion of staff,
the instruction given is strictly vocational, but it is intended
that as soon as conditions permit the scheme shall broaden out
to embrace also the more cultural aspects of education.

There were, as is well known, a number of firms running
works schools of various kinds before the war, but they were
all too few, and the movement could hardly be said to be making
rapid progress. It is encouraging to find other firms convinced
that it is worth while to go to the trouble and expense, even
in the middle of a world war, of setting up schools. It is equally
encouraging to learn that the firms mentioned above are all
working in close co-operation with the local education authorities.
It may well prove that, in our typically English way, we shall
work out high policy in this matter of education in and for

industry, not by *a priori* decisions taken at the centre, but as a result of what happens in many individual experiments.

PUBLIC OPINION

It would be giving a wholly wrong impression to suggest that anything like a full picture of the movement for educational reform can be gathered from a study of the reports and memoranda prepared by the executives of interested bodies. In fact, the real movement, the genuinely popular movement, has taken place very largely outside the closed doors behind which these executives have formulated their proposals and drafted their programmes. It has not been " led " by anyone. It has been spontaneous and universal. It has found expression in countless public meetings and conferences, organized for the most part by teachers and others engaged in educational work, and in even more numerous private and semi-private discussions, organized or accidental. These have taken place all over the country, but the tragedy is that there has been no effective cross-fertilization of the ideas they have generated. Here, there and everywhere I have found groups grappling with the same problems and arriving painfully at the same conclusions, totally unaware of the fact that in a hundred—it might well be a thousand—other places there were at the same time similar groups similarly struggling. I believe that there exists today a far greater unanimity of opinion of a much more radical nature than is to be found in the official published programmes. But the units which make up that opinion exist in isolation, or very nearly so, and there is no medium which can make them articulate. I hoped that when in the Spring of 1943 the B.B.C. produced, under the title of " Living and Learning ", a series of twelve discussions covering the field of education, there might result a genuine articulation of public opinion. But though the series attracted a very large number of listeners (two millions was the average number, with a peak of four millions), it did not succeed in capturing the public imagination sufficiently to compel any very marked expression of public opinion.

One attempt only on a large scale has been made definitely to link up these units of opinion. In November 1942 the Trades Union Congress, the Co-operative Union Education Committee, the National Union of Teachers, and the Workers' Educational

Association jointly established a Council for Educational Advance under the chairmanship of Professor R. H. Tawney. The aim was to enable the four organizations, which together represent the bulk of the working-class population, to campaign together for " immediate legislation to provide equality of educational opportunity for all children, and thus to ensure that they should be equipped for a full life and democratic citizenship ". The method of working adopted was the organization of public meetings, at each of which a resolution approving the Council's programme was to be moved, the resolution being then forwarded to the President of the Board of Education. In addition, the Council proposed to send deputations at appropriate times to the Board.

The Council's programme is :

1. The raising of the school-leaving age to 15 without exemption by the end of the war, and to 16 not more than three years later.
2. Free education under a single secondary code for all children after the primary stage.
3. Common standards of staffing, equipment, and amenities in all schools.
4. Adequate provision of nursery schools and classes.
5. Free medical services and school meals.
6. Maintenance allowances for children in all post-primary schools.
7. Day continued education for all between 16 and 18.
8. Prohibition of employment below the school-leaving age and its control by the education authorities up to the age of 18.
9. The licensing and inspection of any school outside the national system.
10. A unified system of administration to replace the dual control of schools.
11. Free access to universities and higher technical colleges for all who can benefit thereby.
12. Ample provision for adult education.

The campaign organized by the Council has had so far a limited success. It has held many successful meetings at which considerable enthusiasm has been shown, but it has not yet succeeded in fanning to a mighty blaze the enthusiasm I know to be everywhere smouldering. Why not ? First, the organizations, being all specifically representative of the " working classes ", have not attracted much support from those in the higher income ranges—that is, in positions from which effective influence could be radiated. (It has to be remembered that in England " influence ", that impalpable but very real power, is restricted to a very small proportion of the population—a sign of how far we are from being a genuine democracy.) Second, I believe it was a mistake to start out with a fixed programme, to be swallowed whole or not at all. The Council's programme should have been based on a nucleus, and built up from the opinion of the meetings it held. Third, the programme is too strictly " educational ". It is not a " popular " programme, and as set out it has no drama in it. It does not and I think cannot excite the popular imagination ; only a programme which put educational reform in its proper setting as an integral part of general social reform, and which was written in words of fire, could do that.

Fourth, the inveterate and organized opposition to Point 10 by members of the religious denominations, and in particular the Roman Catholics. I have been present at meetings organized by the Council when almost the whole of the time allotted for open discussion has been taken up with the pros and cons of dual control ; I have been at others where the rival groups almost came to blows. Educational *advance* was never mentioned, much less discussed. Nevertheless, the Council for Educational Advance has done valuable work ; and I must add a note of personal gratitude to them for their generous and ready agreement to my request that, whenever invited to speak on one of their platforms, I should not be bound by their programme.

The Government's Policy

On Friday, July 16, 1943, after more than two years of consultation and negotiation with the many interests concerned, the Government made known their policy for the post-war reform of the public service of education in England and Wales. Contrary to expectations, the President of the Board of Education did not straightway introduce a Bill ; instead, he presented to Parliament a White Paper [1] setting forth the proposals he intended to incorporate in his Bill, which he said would follow in the autumn. He took this course, he said, because " It is the desire

[1] Educational Reconstruction. Presented by the President of the Board of Education to Parliament by Command of His Majesty, July 1943. (Cmd. 6458.) His Majesty's Stationery Office.

of the Government that ample opportunity should be given for consideration of the plan as set out in the White Paper, before the stage of legislation is reached."

The procedure was a wise and a democratic one. The issues involved were too grave to be settled above the head of the nation. That the Government realized this was evident from the quotation from Disraeli—" Upon the education of the people of this country the fate of this country depends "—which was set at the head of the White Paper, and from Mr. Butler's words in commending the Paper to the House of Commons. " It is desirable," he said, " that matters which affect the future well-being of the younger generation should be considered by the House and by the country as questions for which the whole nation must accept responsibility." He might well have added that it was not merely desirable, but imperative that they should be so considered. In a democracy, what touches all must be the concern of all.

The plan exceeded almost everyone's anticipations. Not because there was anything novel about the proposals, nor because these went further in the direction of change than had been generally urged ; but because they were built round a central and fundamental proposal which involved a complete re-casting of the entire educational set-up, gave unity to the educational system and an enhanced value to all the other proposals.

The Government proposed :

. . . that the statutory system of public education shall cease to be severally administered for the purposes of elementary and higher education respectively, and be organized in three progressive stages to be known as primary education, secondary education, and further education.[1]

In place of the heterogeneous collection of powers and duties previously possessed by local authorities :

. . . a duty will be placed on each local education authority to contribute towards the mental, moral and physical development of the community by securing the provision of efficient education throughout those stages for all persons in the area capable of profiting thereby.[2]

In making this proposal the Government justified their claim to have recognized the principle that " education is a continuous process conducted in successive stages ".[3] With this principle

---

[1] Educational Reconstruction, p. 7.   [2] Ibid., p. 7.   [3] Ibid., p. 3.

they accepted two others : that there must be equality of educational opportunity, and diversity of provision without impairment of the social unity.

The following are the main proposals by which they hoped to give effect to these principles. Those under A demanded legislative change, those under B could be effected by administrative action.[1]

(A)

1. Improvement of the facilities for the training of children below compulsory school age by the provision of nursery schools wherever they are needed. *The duty to be laid upon local education authorities of making such provision as the Board of Education judge necessary.*

2. Completion of the reorganization of the present public elementary schools, so that well-designed and well-equipped primary schools are available for all children up to the age of 11, and secondary schools with varied facilities for advanced work for all children over that age. *Local education authorities to be required to make a comprehensive survey of the existing provision and of the present and prospective needs of their areas, and to prepare and submit to the Board of Education development plans which will give a complete picture of the proposed layout of primary and secondary schools. When the plans are approved by the Board, the authorities will be required to carry them out, keeping to a time schedule given them.*

3. The raising of the school-leaving age to 15, *without any exemptions for " beneficial " employment,* as soon as possible after the end of the war, with provision in the Act for a further raising of the age to 16 as soon as practicable.

4. Introduction of a system of compulsory part-time education, within the hours of employment as regulated by existing law, *or by any subsequent industrial legislation.* Attendance at first for one day a week, but, say the Government, *this is clearly a minimum.* Residential courses in rural areas if found desirable.

5. Provision of adequate and properly co-ordinated facilities for technical and adult education. *Local education authorities to be required to submit schemes for the provision of such facilities, and to put them into effect, again on a time schedule.*

6. Extension of the existing facilities for securing the health and physical well-being of children and young persons. *Until such time as a comprehensive national health service is set up, it will be the duty of local education authorities to provide, free of charge, medical inspection* and *treatment* (except domiciliary treatment) *for all children in publicly maintained or grant-aided schools, including the Young People's Colleges for continued education. The provision of school milk and meals to be made a duty of the local education authorities.*

---

[1] Quoted from " Educational Reconstruction ", but with some abbreviations and amplifications of phrasing.

7. Introduction of a system of inspection and registration of all independent schools which cater for children of compulsory school age. *Schools considered by the Board of Education to be open to objection because the premises are unsuitable, the accommodation inadequate, the instruction inefficient or the proprietor or a member of the staff not a fit person to have the charge of children, will not be allowed to continue unless the defects complained of are remedied within a specified period. Right of appeal allowed.*

8. Amendment of the existing law so as :

(*a*) To emphasize the position of religious instruction as an essential element of education. *The school day in all primary and secondary schools to begin with a corporate act of worship ; religious instruction to be given in all schools, without limitations upon the times at which it may be given ; the subject to be included among the subjects in which a student can obtain a pass in the teachers' certificate examination ; and (agreed syllabus) instruction to be inspected by His Majesty's Inspectors.*

(*b*) To enable the schools provided by voluntary bodies to play their part in the proposed developments. *Authorities which made agreements for rebuilding or reconditioning schools under the 1936 Education Act can revive those agreements, revising them where circumstances demand, and to receive 50 to 75 per cent grant in aid. All other voluntary schools,* primary or secondary, *whose managers are able and willing to meet half the cost of necessary alterations, improvements and external repairs, to get the remaining half by direct grant from the Exchequer, and carry on as before. All voluntary schools whose managers are unable or unwilling to meet half the cost to become wholly the financial responsibility of the authority which, subject to certain restrictions, will assume the power of appointing and dismissing teachers.* No transfer of the property or ownership of the schools of any of the three types.

9. Adjustment of the present system of local educational administration to the new educational layout. *Authorities responsible for elementary education only (Part III Authorities) to be abolished. County and county borough councils to be the sole local authorities for education, but to be required to set up district education committees in their areas, and to delegate some powers to these, so that local interest in educational affairs shall be maintained.*

(B)

1. Progressive decrease in the size of classes in primary schools.

2. Abolition of the Special Place examination and adoption of other arrangements for the classification of children when they pass from primary to secondary schools.

3. Introduction of a common code of Regulations applicable to secondary schools of all types, so framed as to secure that standards of accommodation and amenities generally are raised to the level of those of grammar schools.

4. Remodelling of the curriculum of secondary schools.

5. Expansion of the Youth Service.

6. Improvement of the facilities for enabling poor students to proceed to the universities.

7. Reform of the present methods of recruiting and training teachers.

The publication of this White Paper set up a landmark in English education. In it was offered a framework within which it is possible to create an enlightened and genuinely democratic national system of education. There are gaps in the framework, some of which cannot yet be filled in. The " master key which will open the whole building " [1]—an adequate supply of teachers of the right quality—is not supplied ; that waits on the report of the McNair Committee. The problems of the relationship of the public schools and the grant-aided secondary schools are also left over until such time as the Fleming Committee has reported. The sections in the Paper on adult education and the Service of Youth are brief and vague ; there is no mention of reform at the Board of Education, and the implicit suggestion that when the country has a comprehensive national medical service the School Medical Service as such will cease to exist is thoroughly unsatisfactory. Worst of all, the timetable proposed (in a financial appendix) for putting the Act when passed into operation is far too leisurely. But these are defects which can be remedied during the time allowed for public and Parliamentary consideration of the proposals. The crucial fact is that in the White Paper a new layout is proposed for English education—a genuinely democratic and educationally sound layout. To have achieved this is an outstanding triumph.

How we shall fill that framework depends largely upon ourselves. This is, of course, the vital task. The framework provided by legislation is, after all, no more than the skeleton ; it is our part to clothe it with flesh and endow it with life. In three directions we may look for substantial assistance from the centre. In 1941–2 the President of the Board of Education set up three departmental committees of inquiry, one to examine the secondary school curriculum, and the related question of external examinations, one the recruitment and training of teachers, and one on the relationship between the public schools and the publicly provided system of education, under the respective chairmanships of Sir Cyril Norwood, Mr. (now Sir Arnold) McNair, Vice-Chancellor of the University of Liverpool, and Lord Fleming.

[1] Educational Reconstruction, p. 4.

THE NORWOOD REPORT [1]

Ten days after the publication of the White Paper came the report of the committee set up by the President of the Board of Education " to consider suggested changes in the secondary school curriculum and the question of school examinations in relation thereto ".[2]

The committee, which was under the chairmanship of Sir Cyril Norwood, President of St. John's College, Oxford, recommended radical changes in secondary school organization, in the examination system, the award of scholarships to the universities, and the Inspectorate. Following the " Spens " Report of 1939, and in line with the Government's White Paper, the committee envisaged three broad types of secondary education, and consequently three types of secondary schools—Grammar, Technical and Modern—to meet the needs of three main groupings of pupils : those " interested in learning for its own sake " ; those " whose interests and abilities lie markedly in the field of applied science or applied art " ; and those " who deal more easily with concrete things than with ideas ". In suitable circumstances, they suggested, these schools could be combined— though the technical school would generally stand alone. In any case, there must be easy transfer between them, and each type should provide a variety of courses.

Every child would enter one of these three types of secondary school at about the age of 11, the allocation being made by the primary school head teacher on the basis of the pupil's school record, supplemented where necessary by intelligence and other tests. As special interests and abilities are often not clearly discernible at 11, the first two years would be spent in a " Lower School " presided over by a teacher charged with the responsibility of discovering which type of secondary education each child is fitted for.

During this period transfer to the Lower School of another type of secondary school should at any time be possible. To ensure this, the curriculum of all the Lower Schools should be

[1] The substance of this section was originally written as an article for the Ministry of Information, for publication overseas.
[2] Curriculum and Examinations. Report of the Committee of the Secondary School Examinations Council appointed by the President of the Board of Education in 1941. His Majesty's Stationery Office, 1s. 6d.

approximately the same : it should consist of physical education, religious instruction, English, history, geography, mathematics, natural science, art, handicrafts, music, and one or two foreign languages. Final allocation to the appropriate type of secondary school would be made at 13+.

The report does not deal with the curricula of technical and modern schools. In the grammar school, special provision should be made throughout for physical education, religious instruction, and the teaching of English. Foreign languages, mathematics, and natural science are regarded as of fundamental importance, and with history and geography should be part of the curriculum for all pupils. Opportunity should be available for one or more of the subjects art, music, and handicraft, with special facilities for pupils showing marked ability in these subjects.

The committee held that no new subjects were required in the grammar school curriculum, and that generally speaking the traditional subjects should be handled in the way they had been during recent years. They rejected the idea that " life in its many aspects can be anticipated, at least to the extent that many people suggest, by children at school through specific training to meet contingencies and situations ". Such subjects and topics as were suggested to the committee as claiming special attention— e.g. economics, social studies, ethics, clear thinking—they said depended for their study and appreciation upon the traditional subjects of the grammar school curriculum, which would be largely displaced if all the topics for which a place was claimed became the subject-matter of direct instruction. The report gave separate chapters to the teaching and learning of each of the curricular subjects, special attention being given to training in habits of clear thought and clear expression of thought in the English language, to physical education, and to religious education. A chapter was devoted to Wales and the Welsh language.

Of the School Certificate Examination—taken at about the age of 16—the committee said that for twenty years, thanks to the skilful and devoted labours of the University Examining Bodies, it had rendered useful and valuable service in exerting a steadying influence on the work of the schools, giving them direction and defining levels of achievement. But the time had come when teachers no longer needed such guidance and direction as could best be given by means of an external examination ; and there was no doubt that the School Certificate to-day unduly dominated the mind of the pupil. Accordingly, it was recommended that steps be taken towards making this examination an internal one, set by the teachers as part of their general assessment of their pupils. A transitional period of seven years was proposed during which the university examining bodies and the teachers in co-operation would conduct an examination along freer lines than at present, and would grant to all pupils—there would be no pass or failure, but only a grade mark—a certificate showing examination performance and an appraisement of the pupil's character and daily work.

This new school certificate examination was not to carry exemption from University matriculation. To meet the requirements of university entrance, of entry to professions, and similar needs, a School Leaving examination, it was proposed, should be conducted twice yearly for pupils of 18+. This examination would replace the present Higher School Certificate Examination, which was regarded as too specialized, and which had come to be used for two purposes—to test Sixth Form work and to select pupils for State scholarships—to the detriment of many students.

For the award of State scholarships and local education authority scholarships it was proposed that an examination, for which no detailed syllabuses should be prescribed, should be held once a year, in March, by the university examining bodies. On the results these bodies would make recommendations to awarding committees. The final award should be made by the State, which should bear the cost of the scholarships ; and these should be of sufficient value to enable holders to take full part in the life of the university. Universities should be able to continue to offer scholarships, and the winning of a college scholarship at Oxford or Cambridge, or a university scholarship at one of the other universities, should constitute a claim upon public funds for assistance towards the cost of living at the university. Local education authorities should have the right to make awards to scholars to assist them at universities, and the State should pay half the cost of such awards—this proportion being in line with the general proportion of grant aid to local authorities from the central exchequer.

One of the most interesting recommendations of the committee was that there should be an interval between the end of school life and entrance upon university studies. Six months (April–October) was proposed, and it was suggested that some form of public service might be undertaken.

Another interesting and valuable proposal was that the Inspectorate should be renamed His Majesty's Educational Advisory Service, and considerably increased in numbers. The committee regarded the maintenance of the present spirit and professional competence of H.M. Inspectors as essential to the success of the proposals made in their report. The Inspectorate should continue to be a branch of the education service having an independent status (as had always been implied by their title of *His*—or *Her*—*Majesty's* Inspectors), and their numbers should be sufficiently increased to make it possible for them to conduct a full inspection of every school at least once in five years and to maintain a real contact during the intervening periods.

The general trend of all the committee's proposals was to throw increased responsibility upon the teachers, in the belief that only on the basis of a wider freedom and a greater share of responsibility for an education centred on the interests of the child could the profession acquire the higher status in the community it should undoubtedly enjoy. Much stress was laid upon the importance of the school record from the primary stage onwards ; and to assist teachers in this respect the committee recommended that the technique of school records be made the subject of immediate investigation and research. They further recommended that the Board of Education should establish machinery for encouraging research into educational problems, and collate and publish the results.

These proposals are enlightened, and it is to be hoped that, with some modifications in detail, they will be adopted. But by far the most interesting and significant feature of the report was the fact that all the recommendations were based upon and derived from a reasoned philosophy of education. The committee went right back to the ultimate question of purpose, and defined clearly their position in respect of education as a whole and secondary education in particular.

" Education," they said, " from its very nature must be ultimately concerned with values which are independent of time or particular environment, though realizable under changing forms in both . . . no programmes of education which concern themselves only with relative ends and the immediate adaptation of the individual to existing circumstances can be acceptable."

By formulating this and other definitions of purpose and deriving logically from them a system the Norwood Committee have rendered a great service to English education. That the validity of these definitions was quickly queried by more than one able thinker does not greatly detract from the essential value of this service, which is that a genuine attempt was made to explore the fundamental question of purpose in education.

FEES IN SECONDARY SCHOOLS

The White Paper proposed that fees should be abolished in schools maintained by the local education authorities. On August 27, 1943, a special report [1] by the Fleming Committee recommended that tuition fees should be abolished also in all schools aided by grants from public funds. The report was signed by 11 only of the 18 members of the committee, and a minority report was submitted by the dissentients.

The majority held that if the time had come when all children should receive a secondary education, the arguments which led to the decision to abolish fees in public elementary schools now applied with equal force to the secondary schools. The minority contended that if sufficient free places were provided to satisfy the requirements of the local education authority, there was no reason why fees should not be charged for the other places. Both groups agreed that any proposal involving a possible extension of public control over the schools must be accompanied by provisions safeguarding the reasonable independence for the school, and proposals were made to this effect.

[1] Abolition of Tuition Fees in Grant-aided Secondary Schools. His Majesty's Stationery Office.

CHAPTER V

CLIMAX

THE EDUCATION BILL

The Government's White Paper, *Educational Reconstruction* received an almost overwhelmingly cordial reception from practically every shade of professional and public opinion. This is not to say that all its proposals were regarded as uncontroversial; in particular, the Part III Authorities hated the idea of being replaced by district education committees, and they said so loudly and at length. But the White Paper as a whole received an unprecedentedly unanimous welcome ; everyone acclaimed it as truly heralding a new era in English education, an era in which as the Paper claimed, it would be possible :

. . . to secure for children a happier childhood and a better start in life ; to ensure a fuller measure of education and opportunity for young people, and to provide means for all of developing the various talents with which they are endowed and so enriching the inheritance of the country whose citizens they are.

The Education Bill which Mr. R. A. Butler introduced into the House of Commons on December 15, 1943, more than lived up to the promise of the White Paper. All the legislative changes which this had proposed were included, and one or two important modifications showed that the President of the Board of Education and his advisers had listened to, and endeavoured to meet, the criticisms excited by the Paper's more controversial proposals. In particular, while the county councils and the county borough councils were still named as the only local authorities for education, the Part IIIs disappearing, the proposal for district education committees was dropped. In its place an idea which was new to English local government was included.

For the purpose of securing that the functions of local education authorities will be exercised with due regard to the circumstances affecting different parts of their areas and with the co-operation of persons having special knowledge of such circumstances, provision shall be made by schemes (hereinafter referred to as " schemes of divisional administration ") for partitioning the areas of authorities into such divisions as may be conducive to efficient and convenient administration and for constituting bodies of persons (hereinafter referred to as " divisional executives ") for the purpose of exercising on behalf of the authorities, in such of the divisions as may be specified in the schemes, such functions relating to primary and secondary education as may be so specified.[1]

This proposal was to affect the areas of the counties only, and the proviso was added that no scheme need be made in respect of any particular area if the Minister judged it unnecessary. The schemes were to be made by the authorities, and the only powers they were forbidden to delegate to their divisional executives were the powers to borrow money and to raise a rate.

By way of further concession to the Part III Authorities it was proposed that any municipal borough or urban district council could, before October 1, 1944, lodge with the Minister " a claim that the borough or district be excepted from any scheme of divisional administration to be made by a local education authority." If the borough or district had had at the last census (1931) a population of not less than 60,000, or at March 31, 1939, not fewer than 7,000 " pupils on the rolls of the public elementary schools," then the Minister had to admit the claim. Other boroughs or districts could become " excepted " only if the Minister, " after consultation with the local education authority and such other councils as appear to him to be concerned " was satisfied that there were special circumstances to justify it.

The privilege attaching to an " excepted district" was to be that it could make, after consultation with the local education authority, its own scheme of divisional administration " which shall provide for the exercise by the council of that borough or district of the functions thereby delegated as the divisional executive." A very real privilege ; but the Part IIIs were not satisfied. They wanted autonomous powers, and their spokesmen in Parliament put up a long and resolute—but completely unsuccessful—fight to retain them.

Another important concession was made by the President of the Board of Education to the religious denominations. The 50 per cent Treasury grant offered to the voluntary school managers[2] would not be limited to alterations to existing premises. If it were judged necessary to move a school to a new site because (i) the existing premises could not be so altered as to conform to the new, and much more exacting, building regulations which the President proposed to make when the Act was passed, or (ii) a

[1] First Schedule, Part III (i).   [2] See page 225.

shift in population, a slum clearance scheme, or other action by a housing or planning authority made it necessary, the President was to be empowered to pay half the cost of erecting the new school building. This concession did not, of course, please the opponents of the Dual System.

In its original form the Education Bill was in five Parts containing 111 Sections, with nine Schedules attached. Part I (Sections 1–5) dealt with the Central Administration, Part II (Sections 6–65) with the Statutory System of Education, Part III (Sections 66–71) with Independent Schools, Part IV (Sections 72–98) with a variety of administrative and financial matters, and Part V (Sections 99–111) with the application, commencement and interpretation of the Act, and the amendment or repeal of previous enactments. It was proposed that Parts I and V should come into operation on the passing of the Act, Parts II and IV on April 1, 1945, and Part III on a date, after April 1, 1945, to be appointed by Order in Council.

As promised in the White Paper, the Bill provided for :

(i) The reorganisation of the statutory system of public education, and of its administration ;

(ii) The laying of a comprehensive obligation upon the local education authorities to secure efficient educational facilities for all people in their areas ;

(iii) The raising of compulsory school age ;

(iv) Secondary education for all children ;

(v) Compulsory part-time education between the end of compulsory full-time education and the age of 18 ;

(vi) Medical treatment for all children and young people in maintained and grant-aided schools between the ages of 2 and 18 ;

(vii) Registration and inspection of all private schools for children of compulsory school age ;

(viii) The making of religious instruction and worship compulsory in maintained and grant-aided primary and secondary schools.

The foregoing are only the most important points in this revolutionary measure. The fundamental reform was contained in Section 7 which read :

The statutory system of public education shall be organised in three progressive stages to be known as primary education, secondary education, and further education ; and it shall be the duty of the local education authority for every area, so far as their powers extend, to contribute towards the[1] moral, mental and physical development

[1] During the passage of the Bill through Parliament the word " spiritual " was inserted at this point.

of the community by securing that efficient education throughout those stages shall be available to meet the needs of the population of their area.

In respect of primary and secondary education it was to be the duty of the local education authority to secure that there should be available for their area sufficient schools for the provision of both ; and it was laid down that :

the schools available for an area shall not be deemed to be sufficient unless they are sufficient in number, character, and equipment to afford for all pupils opportunities for education offering such variety of instruction and training as may be desirable in view of their different ages, abilities, and aptitudes, and of the different periods for which they may be expected to remain at school, including practical instruction and training appropriate to their respective needs. (*Sec. 8 (1)*).

In fulfilling their duties under this Section, the local authority were also to have regard to the need (i) for securing that primary and secondary education were provided in separate schools, (ii) for making provision for children below compulsory school age, (iii) for making provision for children handicapped in body or mind, and (iv) to the expediency of providing boarding accommodation for children " for whom education as boarders is considered by their parents and by the authority to be desirable." (*Sec. 8 (2)*).

In respect of further education it was to be the duty of the authority to secure :

(*a*) full-time and part-time education for persons over compulsory school age ; and

(*b*) leisure-time occupation, in such organised cultural training and recreative activities as are suited to their requirements, for any persons over compulsory school age who are able and willing to profit by the facilities provided for that purpose. (*Sec. 40.*)

In respect of compulsory part-time education the authority was, not later than three years after Part II of the Act came into operation :

to establish and maintain county colleges, that is to say, centres approved by the Minister for providing for young persons who are not in full-time attendance at any school or other educational institution such further education, including physical, practical and vocational training, as will enable them to develop their various aptitudes and capacities and will prepare them for the responsibilities of citizenship. (*Sec. 42 (1)*).

An important change was to be made in the powers accorded to the President of the Board of Education.[1] Hitherto, his duty had been defined as " the superintendence of matters relating to education in England and Wales." Now it was to be :

to promote the education of the people of England and Wales and the progressive development of institutions devoted to that purpose, and to secure the effective execution by local authorities, under his control and direction, of the national policy for providing a varied and comprehensive educational service in every area. (*Sec. 1 (i)*).

An equally important change (provided it was taken seriously) was proposed in the statutory duty proposed to be laid upon the parent of a child of compulsory school age. Hitherto this had been (since 1876, when it was first imposed), " to cause his child, between the ages of 5 and 14, to receive efficient elementary instruction in reading, writing and arithmetic." Now it was to be :

to cause him to receive efficient full-time education suitable to his age, ability and aptitude, either by regular attendance at school or otherwise. (*Sec. 34*).

Among the most daring proposals in the Bill was that the compulsory school age should be raised to 15 on April 1, 1945. To insert such a provision in a Bill laid before Parliament at the height of a total war, with victory by no means in sight, betokened either complete irresponsibility or a serene confidence in the country's powers of recuperation. No one who knew him would accuse Mr. R. A. Butler of irresponsibility, and it is fitting, therefore, that tribute be paid to his courage and confidence. I had it from his own lips, on more than one occasion, that he believed, given favourable circumstances, the school age could be raised on that date, and that he intended, if it were at all possible, to do so. Alas ! circumstances did not prove favourable, and his first pronouncement after the Bill became an Act had to include the postponement of the raising of school age. He had prudently inserted in the Bill a clause allowing for a postponement of not more than two years.

The Passage of the Bill

The Education Bill was given a second reading in the House of Commons on January 19 and 20, 1944. The debate ended without a division ; indeed, everyone applauded the Bill as a

---

[1] During the passage of the Bill this title was changed to that of Minister of Education, and the Board of Education became the Ministry.

whole. But it made clear where the main points of controversy were going to lie. The spokesmen of the Part III Authorities proclaimed their antagonism to the proposed administrative set-up. The opponents of the Dual System declared their distaste for the proposed compromise with the religious denominations, while the Roman Catholics argued the case for a 100 per cent grant for their schools forcefully and cogently. Opposition speakers protested against the retention of tuition fees in grant-aided schools, and pleaded for a date for the raising of the compulsory school age to 16. Another body of speakers, chiefly on the Government side, argued for advisory councils on adult, technical and agricultural education in addition to the two Central Advisory Councils the Bill proposed (one each for England and Wales) " to advise the Minister upon such matters connected with educational theory and practice as they think fit, and upon any questions referred to them by him." (*Sec. 4 (i)*).

The succeeding debates occupied nineteen days only in the House of Commons, as opposed to fifty-nine for the Education Act, 1902, and they were much less stormy ; in fact, for the most part they were exceedingly tranquil. The spokesmen for the Part III Authorities, notably Mr. Lipson (Cheltenham) and Mr. Hutchinson (Ilford), fought their case so resolutely that the progress in Committee was at first snail-like, and later occasional small storms blew up over Dual Control ; but the only real " crisis " occurred when Mrs. Cazalet Keir carried against the Government an amendment incorporating acceptance of the principle of equal pay for men and women into the Section authorising the Minister of Education to approve salary scales for teachers. This brought the Prime Minister, Mr. Winston Churchill, into the debate with a demand for the annulment of the amendment. By making the issue one of confidence in the Government, Mr. Churchill had his way. Thereafter the debates proceeded even more quietly, and progress was more rapid than before. By the end of July the Bill had passed through both the House of Commons and the House of Lords, and on August 3 it received the Royal Assent and passed into law as the Education Act, 1944.

Numerous tributes were paid to the Bill and its main authors, Mr. R. A. Butler and his Parliamentary Secretary, Mr. J. Chuter

Ede. One must suffice here ; it was typical. Mr. Colegate (Wrekin) said that :

> This measure, the first and greatest, in my opinion, of the recon-struction measures, fulfils, I think, the legitimate hope of everybody who has the interests of education at heart and who has had a realistic understanding of what is happening in the world to-day.

THE McNAIR REPORT

Exactly two months before the Education Bill became law, on May 3, 1944, the long-awaited McNair Report on the recruit-ment and training of teachers and youth leaders was published. It is a measure of the quality of this Report that it was applauded as cordially and as unanimously as the White Paper and the Education Bill.

The virtue of the McNair Report was that it recognized that reform could not be achieved by mere readjustment of existing training facilities and training college curricula. Fundamental changes were required ; " the standing of education " must be raised, and the teaching profession made more attractive to men and women of first-rate intellectual quality and character ; the field of recruitment must be widened, and the employment of married women as teachers no longer forbidden. Above all, the distinction between education and training must be abandoned ; what was wanted was better educated teachers, and the nation must spare no efforts to secure them.

It was a pity that the McNair Committee could not agree on one fundamental issue : who was to accept the responsibility for the training of teachers. Half the Committee wanted the uni-versities to do this by setting up Schools of Education, organic federations of approved training institutions working in co-operation under the aegis of the university, through which all candidates for teaching must pass. The other half wished to retain the Joint Examing Boards, representative of the universities and the training colleges, which had been operating since 1930. But on all other points the Report was unanimous.

Thus, with the Education Act and the proposals from the McNair Committee, the scene was set for reconstruction on the grand scale. But " legislation can do little more than prepare the way for reform," as the authors of the White Paper wisely said. The long and difficult process of putting the Education Act, 1944, into operation will take many years. By the time it is accomplished it is to be hoped that the country will be ready for another advance as significant as that chronicled in these pages.

INDEX

Administration, Units of : see *Educational administration*
Adult education, 144–55, 177–8, 211, 224
Adult education, Residential, 150–1, 177
Agricultural education, 136, 218
Agricultural work for schoolchildren, 158–9
Agriculture Executive Committees, County War, 117, 118, 119
Air Defence Cadet Corps, 111
Air-raid protection for schools, 48, 54, 55, 61, 67–8, 75
Air Training Corps, 110–13, 121, 135, 141
Animal biology, 157
Apprentices—control by school, 209 ; part-time release for education, 218
Archbishops' proposals on Christian education (" Five points "), 189–95
Army Bureau of Current Affairs (A.B.C.A.), 153–4
Army cadets, 113, 121, 135
Army education, 151–5, 234
Army Educational Corps, 151–2, 153
Army trainees in technical institutions, 131, 133–5
" Art for the People " exhibitions, 149
Arts courses at universities, 143
Ashmolean Museum—lectures for children, 59
Attendance at school, Compulsory—considered in abeyance, 29 ; to be enforced, 32 ; difficulties of enforcing, 47, 50–7 ; position in April 1940, 60 ; effect of Blitz, 69 ; L.C.C. to enforce, 75

Barnsley, 45
Beal Central School, Ilford, 57, 95
Bermondsey evening institutes, 148
Bernhard Baron Settlement, 71
Beveridge report, 233–4
Bevin, Mr. E., 121, 200

Birkenhead, 57
Birmingham, 45
Blitz, Schooling in the, 66–78
Board of Education :
    Evacuation—lack of co-operation with Ministry of Health, 17 ; suggested taking over by Board, 52
    Juvenile welfare branch set up, 46, 98
    Pre-school child, responsibility for the, 86
    Reform—attitude to, 201–2 ; Confidential memorandum containing proposals : see *Green Book*
    War-time nurseries division set up, 87
Boy scouts, 108–9
Boys, Registration of : see *Registration of youth*
Boys' Clubs, National Association of, 109
Braddock, Mr. T., 126
Braley, Canon E. F., 192
British Institution for Adult Education, 149
Broadcast discussions on education, 220
Broadcasting, School, 43
Building industry, Training for the, 209, 217
Butler, Mr. R. A., 86, 92, 93, 121, 194, 205, 223, 235

Camp boarding schools, 57, 95–7
Camps Act, 1939, 95
Camps Corporation, National, 95
Chalk, Mr. W. T., 198
China—youth service, 104
Christian education, 165, 189–95
Christian Education Movement, 193
Christian News-Letter, x, 169, 174
Christian Science Monitor, x, 95
Church schools, 189, 190, 191, 192, 195, 196–7, 213, 225
Churchill, Mr. W., 33, 62, 120–1, 232–3

239